Global Perspectives on Multilingualism

Global Perspectives on Multilingualism

Unity in Diversity

EDITED BY

María E. Torres-Guzmán

Joel Gómez

Teachers College
Columbia University
New York and London

Published by Teachers College Press, 1234 Amsterdam Avenue, New York, NY 10027

Library of Congress Cataloging-in-Publication Data

Global perspectives on multilingualism : unity in diversity / edited by Maria E. Torres-Guzman, Joel Gómez.
p. cm.
Includes bibliographical references and index.
ISBN 978-0-8077-4972-2 (pbk. : alk. paper)
1. Education, Bilingual—Cross-cultural studies. 2. Multilingualism—Cross-cultural studies. 3. Multicultural education—Cross-cultural studies. I. Torres-Guzman, Maria E. II. Gómez, Joel R.
LC3715.G56 2009
370.117'5—dc22

2009009856

ISBN: 978-0-8077-4972-2 (paperback)

Printed on acid-free paper
Manufactured in the United States of America

16 15 14 13 12 11 10 09 8 7 6 5 4 3 2 1

Contents

Acknowledgments

When a project comes to full completion there are always mounds of people to thank. We have lots for which to be grateful. As Vygotsky proposes, thinking is social. We, individually, push to make our own that which we jointly think and create with others. From the initial thought about the possibilities of this book to its completion, we have many who have joined us in the journey. Our gratitude goes out to Ofelia Garcia for encouraging us to pursue what we, at one point, thought of as a second volume that would reflect the work of many authors we heard speaking about imagined multilingual schooling at the 2004 Language Symposium at Teachers College, Columbia University, in New York City. The book project, however, took on a path of its own. Thus, we want to express gratitude to the contributors of this volume for the multiple transformations of their texts and for their patience.

We, the editors, are responsible for the shape the book has taken, but we especially want to acknowledge Eric Larsen for carefully wading through each chapter at the editing phase. Yesenia Moreno, Dhyana Kuhl, Kami Lambert, and Wendy Swartz were extremely helpful at the final stages of formatting and provided invaluable feedback; Dhyana, thank you for your watchful eye. We want to acknowledge our editor, Brian Ellerbeck at TC Press, for believing in this project. Finally, for their unwavering support, Maria thanks Juan, her husband; and Joel, his children—Rebecca and Benjamin. They were always there to hear the daily stories in the process. Gracias.

Caminante, no hay camino
se hace el camino al andar.
Al andar se hace camino
y al volver hacia atrás
se ve la senda que nunca
se ha de volver a pisar.

Voyager, there is no road.
Only by walking
you make a path.
A path is made
and when looking back
we see the road
never to be walked again.

—Antonio Machado,
Proverbios y Cantares XXIX
in *Campos de Castilla,*
translated by María E. Torres-Guzmán

1

Introduction

Multilingualism for Understanding

María E. Torres-Guzmán and Joel Gómez

Bi/multilingualism, as a world phenomenon, increasingly has come into prominence as more population groups come into contact through the globalization of the different forms of communication, transportation, and the market economy. For example, it is not uncommon now to see automatic teller machines providing language options for completing transactions. Multilingual and multicultural mass media commercials are also more common now than in the past. This is in sharp contrast to earlier periods when nation-states were created and consolidated, and when minoritized and less prestigious language groups were balkanized within the dominant society.

In the nation-states of the past, the languages of the disenfranchised linguistically diverse groups mainly remained marginalized, in their communities, and were not incorporated into mainstream business, legal, or entertainment activities. In the 1960s, many culturally and linguistically diverse groups, as well as mainstream groups, began to recognize this balkanization as an evil element in society and sought empowerment of the historically dominated groups in a variety of forms. For example, *Brown v. Board of Education* legally ended historically segregated schools and paved the way for efforts to improve social and educational opportunities within society.

Concurrently, organizations such as UNESCO created policies that promoted the economic, health, linguistic, and social well-being of all cultural and linguistic communities. For example, in 1953, UNESCO published its landmark report, "The Use of Vernacular Languages in Education," which established the rights of multilingual societies to establish education through their home language.

In the latter part of the 20th century, the discourse for language and education rights contributed to the creation of policies such as the 1968

Title VII of the Elementary and Secondary Education Act of the United States, known as the Bilingual Education Act.

Within the past decade, the world population not only has grown dramatically, but also has experienced dramatic immigration flows as groups from resource-poor regions move toward those that are resource-rich. Newly formed multination configurations, such as the European Union, also have come into existence, while previous confederations such as the USSR have become fragmented. The convergence of these situations and the growth of the significance of the markets—and of the language, English, in which much of their business occurs—have created a world in which issues of multilingualism have become more prominent.

Within this book, we explore multiple situations of bi/multilingualism within and across nations—from the claims of indigenous populations and the exigencies of multilingual, multination states to the expansion of English as a world language. We examine how countries around the world conceptualized multilingualism within their unique sociocultural and political circumstances and how within this set of situations we can explore what they have in common. We asked the contributors not only to describe the circumstances of multilingualism in their country but also to create the narratives they wanted others to hear as their reality. Furthermore, we asked them to project multilingualism into desired, albeit imagined, futures.

We invite the reader to examine, as we have, the authors' contributions as applications and interpretations that give meaning to their work as educators within their multilingual context. Each communicates his or her imagined futures as an educator within a multilingual society based on his or her legacies, experiences, and dreams. Taken together, however, these multiple ways of conceptualizing multilingualism provided us, the editors, and will provide you, the reader, with a rich context for informing the emerging concept of *bi/multilingualism for understanding*. We believe this concept can assist future debates about language diversity within our country as well as in other parts of the world.

We, the editors, offer you in this introduction our interpretation of what each of the authors contributes toward the development of the concept of bi/multilingualism for understanding by first examining the concept of understanding itself, as discussed by Wiggins & McTighe (2006), and by applying it within the context of the linguistic arguments proposed by Dascal (1999). This will be followed by a discussion of two distinct beliefs about language and their tendencies to bring together and/or separate groups. We call for a shift in metaphors about multilingualism and its use within education in the language debates within the United States. It is in this context that we will present a brief intellectual map of the chapters. (It should be noted that each chapter has an abstract. While this is unusual for an edited book, we felt it appropriate to honor the variety of languages emphasized by the articles. While no more than a token, it ensures the possibility of access to the general content for non-English language speakers.) In the Afterword, we will provide an analysis of our new understandings and how they challenge concepts within the field.

MULTILINGUALISM FOR UNDERSTANDING

Sociocultural theory takes to heart what Machado (2006) proposes—that each situation is unique. Furthermore, it proposes that languages are socially constructed. Multilingualism, within this theory, is a phenomenon arising from situations in which different language groups come into contact. We, then, ought to be able to trace bi/multilingualism from the moment that humans with different languages first encountered one another. Nonetheless, it was not until the 1950s that we began to study it as a phenomenon with the work of Einar Haugen (1953) and Uriel Weinreich (1953).

Three ideas form the conceptual framework for this volume. The first is the distinction that Wiggins and McTighe (2006) make between knowledge and understanding. The second focuses on the distinctions that Dascal (1999) makes of arguments for linguistic diversity. The third focuses on Quintero's (2006) call for a shift to new metaphors in education based on an educational system that is dynamic and transformational.

Concept of Understanding

In Wiggins and McTighe (2006), knowledge is defined as what is known and can be transmitted. Understanding, however, goes beyond what is known and refers to how knowledge is used to create empathy, to explain, to create a perspective, to gain a deeper understanding of self, and so forth. We purport to use this definition in *Global Perspectives on Multilingualism* to emphasize going beyond what is known about multilingualism. We purport to use this definition to encourage readers to recreate and regenerate their views of multilingualism through their disruption of past conceptualizations as well as through imagining what could be.

The concept of bi/multilingualism for understanding within this volume will embody and address a variety of linguistic needs of people in contact within diverse sociocultural and political contexts in a nation or a region. Furthermore, it is a call for understanding as empathy, as we deliberately

> Try to find what is plausible, sensible, or meaningful in the ideas and actions of others, even if those ideas and actions are puzzling or off-putting . . . to rethink a situation . . . [and] a change of heart as we come to understand what formerly seemed off or alien. (Wiggins & McTighe, 2006, p. 99)

In *Global Perspectives on Multilingualism,* we utilize the above definition of understanding to explain, interpret, apply, and expand our own perspective of the phenomenon of bi/multilingualism and to cull from the contributions to this volume a new way of seeing, listening, thinking, and projecting into our imagined futures. *Multilingualism for understanding,* thus, is a concept that has emerged in part from Wiggins & McTighe's conceptualization and in part from the contributions on multilingualism by the authors to this volume.

Arguments for Linguistic Diversity

Dascal (1999) proposed five perspectives favoring linguistic multiplicity that provided us with a way of theorizing about the concept of multilingualism for understanding. The perspectives derive from "practical evidence" as well as from ethical, ontological, epistemological, and cognitive foundations. Let us look at each of these in turn.

Human history is the grounds for considering the practical evidence in favor of linguistic diversity. Throughout history in many parts of the world, even as groups developed separate languages, they also developed cross-cultural and linguistic communication for commercial, religious, or cultural purposes. Today, amid globalization of market economy, scientific exchanges, and the pervasive media, we continue to engage in transcultural and multiple-language exchanges. If these international exchanges were seen as Babelian confusion rather than immensely beneficial, we would not pursue them. From this perspective, wherever language differences become a barrier, translations are possible, even though they may be imperfect and prone to blunders. Dascal proposes that cross-cultural understandings gained through observation and translation can be used to support dialogue, exchange, and tolerance not just for the markets but also for human needs, including social justice through education. This is fundamental to the concept of multilingualism for understanding. We want to advocate for cross-cultural understandings that unite rather than divide our world.

What Dascal calls an ontological argument for diversity, or how we come to know about ourselves, is based on the philosophical stance that there is no *I* (individual identity) without a *Thou*. As we individually construct our reality, we necessarily become embedded in a *We*, since we do not exist outside of our social group. The *I* and the *We* (the group identity) are formed mutually by *I–Thou* dialogues; they are complementary. Pushing us to consider the *You* (plural) as opposed to the *We*, Dascal proposes that the *You* is another community, another *We*, that we face. These multiple *We*'s are what make up the linguistically heterogeneous communities that are characteristic of our globalized world. The concept of multilingualism for understanding is based on the *We* that is inclusive of the different populations that find themselves in contact and in need to communicate.

The ethical argument that Dascal constructs is based on what we judge of value in the context of varied understandings of how we can be. Dascal points to the bidirectionality, the embeddedness, and the dynamics of "knowing." When we learn about "other," we implicitly are making a comparison with "self." This can occur in any social interaction, whether in the markets, in the media, or in education.

There is a human tendency to make invidious comparisons between the other and ourselves, particularly when that other speaks a language we do not understand. The process goes something like this: *We* are superior because our knowledge is scientifically based, our outlook is progressive, and our actions are based on reason rather than emotion. *They*, on the other hand, are like the primitives of the Tower of Babel because we do not understand their ways of speaking, thinking, behaving, or judging, nor can they explain themselves intelligently, meaning in our language and with our logic. Thus, *their* ways are less valuable than *ours*.

Dascal proposes that we need to suspend the invidious comparisons if the other is to have more than "museum value," and, from this base, we can strive for unity in differences. Only then can learning occur in a bidirectional way. There is no human being that is "inferior" and no language that is "primitive"; no way of life or culture is "valueless" and, most important, there is no justification for being indifferent to any human suffering (http:/www.tau.ac.il/humanities/philos/dascal/papers/ethical.htm). Thus, we argue that multilingualism for understanding implies that all of us need to embrace tolerance and celebration of one another's languages, to embrace who we are, and to imagine how we want our world to be.

Dascal's epistemological argument (i.e., what we think about our knowing and how we know it) is based on two understandings. The first is that in order to know about language, we have to not only *know* many languages but also *know about* many languages. Otherwise, our theorizing about language and about the role of language in the construction of knowledge will be limited. Thus, we would lose the capability of knowing about different ways of being as we lose languages. The second understanding is that all knowledge stems from social interaction and critique, the positioning of alternative viewpoints that creates the foundation for intellectual development. Based on these two understandings of knowledge, Dascal emphasizes the urgency not only of collecting linguistic data from endangered languages before they disappear but also of learning about the range of worldviews and knowledge contained within and expressed in nondominant languages. It is not just language, but also the capacity for reflection and its expression in language, that is an essential human activity. Even when we think we have the truth, there is the chance, however small, that truth may lie elsewhere. There are those who, like Machado, would argue that to arrive at truth is not possible because truths are multiple, depending on the viewer and his or her sociocultural and temporal circumstances. The point here is that knowledge about and expression of such knowledge in "other" languages exists and such knowledge could be important for furthering human development. Thus, embracing multilingualism for understanding goes beyond empathy; it is at the core of the creation of knowledge.

Dascal's cognitive argument focuses on the mental flexibility and creativity of humans as well as their ability to see things from different perspectives and adapt to different environments in order to survive. Dascal observes that the ability to walk the path of another (not exactly, according to Machado) not only enhances interpersonal understanding but also enriches us cognitively, because we are opened up to new views and ideas as we experience them.

Dascal's framework supports the notion that a positive perspective of the multiplicity of languages is one such alternative view. It is a way to grasp that "ours is not the only way to see and interpret the world" and that we must entertain multiple ways of seeing if we are to increase our understanding of the world. We want to establish multilingualism for understanding as a way of increasing the knowledge that will help us sustain our world and create new ones in the future.

Our lengthy explanation of Dascal's proposed perspectives serves to set up our conversation about how these pragmatic, ethical, ontological, epistemological, and cognitive arguments merge in the concept of multilingualism for understanding. The distinctions Dascal's arguments provide are important for understanding not just the different contexts we explore within this volume, but the variation in discourses within each of the stories and their relationship to the different arguments. The variation in ways of arguing for language diversity also is a context itself. It is a world context with a variety of linguistic responses to diversity within a globalized, albeit partially, world. The point is that individual countries and linguistic responses within educational settings by themselves would not give us the holistic view that the concept of multilingualism for understanding can.

TRANSFORMING RATHER THAN FIXING EDUCATION

Quintero, in her book *Muchas Reformas, Pocos Cambios* [Many Reforms, Few Changes] (2006), calls on her readers to imagine, consider, and create new educational metaphors that capitalize on the many opportunities that educational institutions already provide us. She proposes that when curricula, instruction, and school organizations are responsive to what we know about how knowledge is constructed, not only do we come to understand how traditional fixed notions of knowledge within disciplines have shifted, but we also come to understand the conceptual shifts in learning and how to support learning organizationally and in society. The process of transmission and socialization does not accurately conceptualize the work of teachers and students. She argues that we need to view the work of schools as an always-unfinished negotiation of what is and what ought to be. Each teacher (and school) needs to walk with his or her students toward learning, creating their paths as they go; to quote Machado, "Your footsteps are the road, and nothing more." Quintero's main point is the need for systemic understanding of learning and the creation of an organization that corresponds and supports it.

Quintero's dynamic and holistic view of learning helps us envision the educational linguistic responses as dynamic and transformational, based on the past and future as anchored in the present (Cole, 1996, and Engeström, 1999, cited in Encino, 2007). She argues for a shift in metaphors as she proposes that what we need already exists, although as isolated possibilities (Fullan, 2003). She argues for an imagined world in which the continuous negotiation is supported by a system that promotes transformation rather than reifying canonical knowledge and anticipated outcomes. The system ought to support educational structures that create spaces of freedom to recreate self and knowledge in each locally situated setting, while at the same time drawing on narratives of excellent examples of dynamic models of teaching/learning as inspirations for others to dare to dream alternative futures in their unique settings and to develop a systemic framework for shifts to be perpetual.

From a critical theoretical perspective, we understand that the fate of languages in contact is associated with broader issues of power relationships where some languages have greater status than others and that these language statuses are reflective of their sociocultural histories of participation (Cole, 1996, and Engeström, 1999, cited in Encino, 2007). Thus, our aim is to search for ways in which we can learn from the "other" experiences of bi/multilingualism that can help us go beyond the traditional discourse of divisiveness that positions groups to focus on a litany of scarcity in the field of bi/multilingualism and to risk dreaming in metaphors of unity and abundance.

Even before the study of multilingualism as a phenomenon, we have had metaphors that we historically have called upon as a way of speaking about multiple tongues in contact. The traditional, mainstream metaphor for the "multiplicity of languages" is the biblical account of the Tower of Babel, where the multitude of languages served to separate people from one another. As a consequence of defying God's will, we are condemned to not understanding one another.

There are some alternative stories that have promoted multiple languages as beneficial because they tend to help human beings reduce conflict. We came across a story of the past, from a community we will call Redondo.[1] There was a deity in this community that we will call iZemia. iZemia was the namer of the community. She gave each group different words and, thus, possibilities of thought and expression that would eventually develop into a variety of languages. Her belief was that when humans are in tension and feel some offense has occurred, the first emotion is fear and the first reaction is to counterattack. When there are multiple languages as in this type of social event, fear is usually embodied in the tongue that resonates with the core being of the individual. iZemia believed that when humans move from fear to open their hearts within a potentially conflicting situation, they will move to try to understand and be more diplomatic. Here is a human situation that occurs in everyday life in which unity not only lies within diversity of languages but where diversity promotes unity. The perspective arising from the story of the lands of Redondo are the opposite of the Tower of Babel; it can serve to disrupt our conformist thinking. This is what our subtitle—*Unity in Diversity*—reflects.

The juxtaposition of the Tower of Babel metaphor and iZemia's story of multiple languages as a metaphor gives us choices. Choosing iZemia opens up the possibility of the positive view of bi/multiculturalism for different populations—indigenous/nonindigenous, language minorities/language majorities, immigrants/nonimmigrants, and so forth. This makes embracing the concept of multilingualism for understanding the varied linguistic situations and linguistic responses possible, and it also permits the exploration of our new understandings of teaching/learning relationships in language-learning contexts.

GLOBAL PERSPECTIVES

With a view of linguistic diversity as beneficial, and old metaphors giving way to new ones, we will now present the issues that are examined by the contributors in this volume, with an expectation that their insights can guide us toward a future where multilingualism is valued and seen as a human freedom. Within this volume, our intention is to use the contributions of our authors, representing seven countries, to explore bi/multilingualism as a global phenomenon. What might we garner from each of their contributions to assist us in understanding multilingualism? What can we learn about the global phenomenon of multilingualism and contributing factors from the mosaic of multilingual issues that the authors present?

Bloch (Chapter 2), Wildsmith-Cromarty (Chapter 3), and Omoniyi (Chapter 4) focus on multilingualism in African educational institutions, public and private, from preschool to university levels. The varied and changing geographical, political, and language landscapes of Africa provide a vibrant background for the contributors' discussions about the existing rich multilingual resources. In South Africa alone, 31 languages have been known to coexist. Twenty-four of these are living languages. Unfortunately, seven of the languages of South Africa have not been attended to and are now either languages with no mother tongue speakers or extinct (Ethnologue, n.d.).

In Nigeria, the number of languages is even more varied. Until recently, 521 languages were spoken by its people, of which two do not have mother tongue speakers and nine are currently extinct. We wonder to what extent we may be losing human knowledge with the death of these languages. More important, however, the knowledge of their existence and death educates us about the nature of language. All languages are dynamic; they have a life cycle; and they are responsive to the roles society assigns them at any given moment, situation, and time.

It is in the backdrop of the life and death cycle of languages that our contributors engage and question the future of remaining living languages. They discuss the context of missed opportunities to optimally utilize the multiple languages as resources. They contextualize class and ethnic struggles around the postcolonial possibilities and the nature of the relationship between developing African languages and the social, political, and economic situations in which they exist. Their contributions, focusing on local South African and Nigerian situations, are global in that their analyses are of the viability of the rich oral literacy traditions the children and their communities bring to school and the utility of those traditions within today's schools. They speak to the issues of standardization, the development of a written literature, and the necessity of shifting pedagogies and of cultivating the languages to meet the requirements of globalization. The contributors do not stay rooted in the dualisms of the past; they go beyond to propose that the status of multiple languages has to be viewed in the context of the multilayered and complex realities of postcolonialism. They speak to promoting the development of the different African languages, second-language acquisition, and multilingualism as a way of transforming the social, political, and economic worlds.

Bloch, Chapter 2, describes the persistent presence of the apartheid legacy that equates instruction in the mother tongue to "inferior" education in South Africa. African languages continue to experience constrained lives in comparison to the ample movements of English and other ex-colonial languages in different, usually official, domains. She works with the notion that African languages have "a rich oral *and* a precolonial written tradition" that could be marshalled to support the development of their full capabilities even as they face the exigencies of globalization. By focusing on early childhood literacy, she engages the reader in entertaining different shifts in thinking, behaving, believing, and judging necessary for the African languages to assume center stage as integrative powerful tools of learning. Bloch brings forth the relationship between economic worlds and publishing. She dreams of the eradication of the high levels of illiteracy when she imagines the possibilities of mentoring African writers, the creation of a rich body of children's literature in African languages, and the development of exemplary teacher education programs where graduates can step into programs with an abundance of linguistically appropriate instructional materials.

Wildsmith-Cromarty, Chapter 3, provides a broad picture of the language situations in South Africa and the continuum of uses of African languages and English within schools. She connects the policies and practices of curricular offerings of English and the African languages in the schools to the subtractive linguistic realities the majority of pupils face. Beyond policy, she speaks to the relationship between affluence and affirmation of African cultures and languages. Wildsmith-Cromarty analyzes the role of funding, adequacy of curriculum development, and language of instruction in connection with the difficulty and the harm African native-speaking children experience in schools. She, like Quintero, brings together different experiences that are realities, although in isolated ways, in classrooms throughout South Africa.

In this way, Wildsmith-Cromarty adds to the argument of multilingualism for understanding. She utilizes these identified experiences to build a conglomerate of rich instructional strategies within a cohesive theoretical framework for greater promotion and development of the African languages, second languages, and bi/multilingualism. She makes it possible for the reader to understand that if the African languages are not promoted and developed to meet today's exigencies, there will be even graver problems in schools. Her imagined future includes not only basic research on the languages and their uses and standardization of the languages and reconceptualization of competence according to multilingual norms, but also applied research in schools.

The last chapter about the African continent is Omoniyi's, Chapter 4, which focuses on elite bi/multilingual schooling as a place where the resources of the multiple languages are part of the curricular design of schools in Lagos, Nigeria. He confirms what Wildsmith-Cromarty describes as one of the salient contradictions of multilingual worlds—while linguistic diversity is a reality in people's lives, it is far from a reality within academic environments. Schools are generally monolingual and subtractive.

While specifically focusing on private schools as places reflecting shifts in global structures, Omoniyi proposes that they ground the country's thinking about the possibilities of multilingualism in African schools. He examines the relationship between the global tendencies toward English and the more localized needs of the student populations, be it another European language or an African one. Specifically, he examines the uses of English, other European, and African languages in three private schools as part of the regular curriculum and as cocurricular activity. Despite the difficulty of documentation that Omoniyi describes, he dares to dream about what it might take for the optimal development of multilingualism, where the abundance of African and other languages become viable mediums of instruction, in addition to being taught as subjects within public school settings.

From the African continent, we move to the European Union (EU), which presently has 27 member states with 23 official languages. Its policy of official multilingualism proposes that each of the countries, upon applying to become a member, determine the language it desires and proposes to use in the official business of the EU. It also recognizes that the "unity in diversity" principle applies internally within each of the member countries and thus acknowledges the many more minoritized and regional languages beyond those recognized as official. Furthermore, there is an officially expressed prohibition of discrimination based on language. Nonetheless, the EU does not push for multilingualism for understanding as important for all populations.

Vančo examines the issues of bilingualism in Slovakia, and Neumann and Roth, and Budach examine the issues in Germany. While there are 10 living languages within the Slovakian state (Ethnologue, n.d.), Vanco, Chapter 5, focuses on the over half a million Hungarians who live within the existing boundaries of the state of Slovakia. She focuses on the schooling of the Hungarian and the plight of the Hungarian language.

In Germany, out of the 29 languages rooted in the country, two are presently extinct. Both Neumann and Roth, Chapter 6, and Budach, Chapter 7, specifically focus on the language and education issues of various types of immigrants—guest workers and other immigrant groups associated with the movements of populations with the formation of the EU. Their analyses are not just local but national and transnational as well.

Vančo documents the linguistic diversity and governmental language policies within Slovakia at different points in history. She shows the push for monolingualism, where policies serve to restrict the recognition and development of languages other than Slovak despite the existence of multiple languages within the country. Vančo illustrates through her analysis of the role of the Hungarian language in education an instantiation of how languages are socially and symbolically constructed. She reflects on the relationships of power in a broad economic and political sense, while illustrating what happened historically to the Hungarian language and its speakers. Specifically, she looks at the maintenance and shifts in monolingualism and bilingualism among the Hungarian and the Slovakian populations, explores the differences in educational attainment, and compares the linguistic development of Hungarian in both Slovakia and Hungary.

As Slovakia has only recently become a member of the EU, she imagines the possibility of a multilingual state where the different minoritized and immigrant populations are recognized and promoted, and where the Hungarian language, as spoken within Slovakia, receives recognition. She dares to dream about the documentation of the development of Hungarian within the Slovakian context. In a territory that has citizens who have had up to six "nationalities" in their lifetime, she also dreams of a space where language activists and professional leaders come together to engage in the kind of language planning that may be necessary for the Hungarian language to continue to live and develop.

Neumann and Roth summarize the local German-based studies that explore the relationship between bilingualism and academic achievement for immigrant and German students. They contextualize their study within a policy context. The German citizens currently are discussing their responsibility for funding multiple languages within school settings. Neumann and Roth report on four studies where the evidence consistently shows that bilinguals do well in academic subjects and in the learning of the first and second languages, and where there is an absence of harmful or negative effects on the acquisition of German. Furthermore, they analyze the quality of the schools and the different participating populations, as well as the quality of the instructional personnel. Similar to other studies that have focused on immigrant groups associated with the population movement within the EU, Neumann and Roth move to imagine a world of multilingual schools that systematically extend dual-language enrichment programs to the children of historically and socially created guest workers within the German borders.

Budach focuses on how dual-language education programs bring together different sectors of society in a mutually beneficial arrangement that favors multilingualism. German middle-class parents who want their children to be competitive, and see the knowledge of multiple languages as providing their children an edge, have come together with parents of minoritized-language children who want their children to maintain the heritage language. The programs chosen by parents promote the view that students from diverse language backgrounds can serve as language models and resources for one another. The EU promotion of multilingualism is a backdrop to the convergence of interests locally.

Budach examines the role of the dual-language education programs in relation to the German dominant-language ideology, and to the traditional literacy practices and language curricula, through a microanalysis of two types of instructional activities that occur within a German/Italian dual-language education program context. Through the vignettes, Budach also demonstrates how the students create their social identities around roles that call for valuing the minoritized language; how students who usually are excluded find a space as experts; how the value of the minoritized language is extended beyond the classroom walls into the homes; and how the children begin to cross over to see themselves in the other students' shoes. Budach's imagined multilingual world is one where programs that bridge the different interests are valued, extended, well staffed, and funded at levels that secure their growth.

In the last three chapters, we have combined Asia, Pacifica, and Latin America. In Chapter 8, Li focuses on the exigencies of contemporary societal globalization goals in Taiwan. He connects the movement toward democracy with the acknowledgment of the country's multilingual character. In Taiwan, the 22 out of 26 living languages have been moving into a democratic process since the 1980s.

Li examines the development of laws and regulations, policies, and commissions that focus on the language and educational rights of indigenous populations, the European and Asian languages, the children of international professionals recruited as part of Taiwan's high-technology industry, and the language of the markets. While remaining a bit cautious about how the relative status of the languages will play out—as languages of instruction and as subjects taught—Li dares to imagine a harmonious world within Taiwan. He dreams of a world where there is sufficient funding for the legislated equality of languages and from which the country can secure its place in our globalized world. He bases his dreams on the varied purposes for multilingualism.

In Chapter 9, de Mejía, Tejada, and Colmenares start where Li leaves off. While Colombia still has 80 living languages of the 101 languages documented as spoken as a first language (Ethnologue, n.d.), the focus of this chapter is on the contemporary exigencies many developing countries feel with respect to the role of English in maintaining or improving their status within the market economy. The authors describe the experiences of university faculty with schoolteachers in a private school in Colombia. They explain how English takes on a particularly significant role among the education of the elite in Colombia and how the scarcity of adequately prepared teachers of English calls for new ways of teacher development.

De Mejía, Tejada, and Colmenares propose that while policies can inform practice, on their own they will not transform educational systems, and argue for the need to "blur the divide" of traditional dualisms such as the researcher and the researched, the practitioner and the curriculum designer, or educational theories and classroom practices. They further argue that these dualisms perpetuate educational structures and relationships that in turn inhibit the creation of spaces for transformation.

In lieu of this traditional dualism, the authors propose a partnership between "experts" and "practitioners" in the spirit of empowerment, where it is not the powerful transferring power to the less powerful, but where all participants are engaged in critical reflection of language in educational practices. De Mejía, Tejada, and Colmenares extrapolate from their work with other colleagues and a group of teachers to dream about the possibilities of grass-roots and bottom-up efforts to develop, create, and nurture multilingualism.

Barnard, in Chapter 10, takes us into the linguistic landscape of New Zealand—from the historical linguistic policy changes among the Maori, New Zealand's indigenous population, to the new English as a second language and heritage-language policies affecting the Pacifica and Asian immigrations, and then to the neglected linguistic challenges of the deaf community. Barnard examines the levels of community support, the attention given to language in the curricula of schools, and the attitudes toward the languages among their speakers. He explores the relationships between these factors with the situation of the Maori language within the country's economic and political power relationships.

Barnard imagines a paradigm shift that would assist many New Zealanders to go from the dualism embedded in resentments and marginalizations centered on traditional ethnic conflicts to the idea that diversity is beneficial to all. In other words, Barnard offers that multilingualism is good not just for some, but for all populations. He comes closest to the concept of multilingualism for understanding as he identifies the linguistic landscape and pushes on the need for it to move to cross-cultural understanding. Barnard identifies a series of metaphors stemming from Maori philosophical ways of life that promote cooperation, commitment, connectedness, and quality language teaching that would support multilingualism for all.

Barnard acknowledges, as Wildsmith-Cromarty does within the context of South Africa, that what happens in schools is connected to what the society values. Thus, what he dreams about for schools requires a systemic and coherent set of educational and language policies and curricular practices that aim to develop multilingual proficiencies for all children. Ultimately, he calls on society to make ethical decisions about our future direction in reducing inequities, altering power differentials, and changing the structures of privilege so that all children, and our future on the planet, can embrace iZemia's metaphor and see language diversity as beneficial.

BI/MULTILINGUALISM IN THE UNITED STATES

Our understandings of bi/multilingualism are increasingly important as children from multiple-language backgrounds fill the classrooms in our nation's schools. The United States has 47 million speakers of other home languages, 18% of the total population (MLA Language Map Data Center, n.d.). Within schools, 19% of students are foreign-born and second-generation immigrant populations; 6% of them do not possess sufficient English to engage in English-only learning situations (Capps et al., 2005). The language diversity of our nation, and many other nations in the world, is greater than ever before. Visceral reactions in the public sphere in the form of debates around the role of multiple languages in education seem to be more and more frequent.

The language debates generally are associated with the rights of language minorities and views about immigration. Language minorities refer here to populations that historically are linked to the territories of a nation but that have a language background that is not the dominant national language. Some examples of these populations are indigenous, like the First Nation peoples within Canada or the Maori within New Zealand; some are associated with territorially and politically annexed people such as the Hungarians within Slovakia; some are tribal languages such as Shona in Zimbabwe; and some are nations within nations, as with the Basque Country in Spain and the Navajo in the United States.

Within the United States, nationalistic language debates have created conflict and engendered anti-bilingual education legislation in California, Arizona, and Massachusetts. This form of nationalism has served to restrict rather than expand our cultural and linguistic freedom; it has served to make language choice for learning an imposition rather than an outgrowth of our understanding the cognitive need for language freedom. Yet we would like to argue that the issues raised in the bilingual and English-only debate are, in fact, complementary from an ethical perspective and that multilingualism for understanding might open minds and hearts that up to now have been closed. Perhaps we are naive in our purpose, but we feel an urgent need to ask our readers to engage with us in exploring the possibility of multiple languages within schools and societies.

The anti-bi/multilingual campaigns argue, based on pragmatic/economic concerns expressed in public discourses, that they stand for "do[ing] away with incompetence, waste and abuse" and "roll[ing] back our well-intentioned but failed welfare state" (Unz, 1994, cited in

Crawford, 2000, p. 115). This argument represents an underlying ethical concern within our society about the citizenry's obligations vis-à-vis the welfare and livelihood of both noncitizens (i.e., immigrants) and citizens (i.e., language minorities). Within the current dynamics of neoconservatism and neoliberalism, the pragmatic/economic argument, which is subsumed into the market-based dynamics, has increased in importance and is viewed as having a reality of its own rather than being treated as a social-ethical issue.

At the same time, the pro-bi/multilingual forces have gone from a discourse of minoritized language and immigrant human rights to one that is concerned with the scientific nature of pedagogy, as the burden of proof of effectiveness within policy increasingly has fallen on the shoulders of pro-bilingualism. The focus has been on the linguistic and cognitive development of the young in relation to school achievement (Brisk, 1998; Hakuta, 1986; Thomas & Collier, 2002) and on the relationship between language and thought (Bialystok, 2001; Moll, 1988; Vygotsky, 1986). Matters such as the mental, affective, and social processes that underlie language development; the optimal age of second-language learning; and the relationship between language and educational attainment have been subject to intellectual debates within this framework. While the grounding is in scientific thought, the underlying issues also correspond to the ethical questions of how we want to be as a society. Within the broader scheme of political thought, the pro-bilingual forces have assumed a basic social welfare posture in relation to the role of government within our society. The belief is that people participate in society and their ability to do so is not just a private matter; governments have the responsibility of developing the capabilities (including the multiple languages) of their citizens.

What brings the two sides together are the ethical and ontological arguments that reflect who the public is in relation to who is being served by particular programs, and how the public feels about integrating these populations into the world of the privileged. Crawford (2000) proposes that what underlies the anti-bilingual movement in the United States is what linguistic accommodation symbolizes—"a public recognition that limited-English speakers are part of the community and therefore entitled to services from government, even if that may entail 'special' programs and expenditures" (p. 27). Underscoring this anti-bilingual sentiment is the recognition that linguistic accommodations represent a step toward changing the power, ethnic, and class relationships of our society and privileging language groups, at least temporarily. This feeds the fears that change brings with it and sparks the thought that one day there may be fewer advantages and rights for those who are today's privileged. In other words, this discussion is about the kind of life we—both those in favor of and those who are against bi/multilingualism—want to live: what is desired, what is valued, and what should be put in place now for future generations.

CONCLUSION

Our aim, therefore, is to look into the world of bi/multilingualism, as presented by the contributors, not just individually but collectively, so that we can highlight the aspects that are excellent in the examples provided. We purposefully shift from a metaphor of divisiveness and scarcity of alternatives to propose an image of unity with an abundance of linguistic possibilities. Our guiding question was: What aspects in the world (real and imagined) of multilingual schools can we see as forward looking that can help us construct a sustainable, systemic view and propagate a message of greater inclusion?

Within, we embrace bi/multilingualism as a resource (Ruiz, 1984). As we do this, we ask one another (our readers and ourselves) to step out of our/your fears and into a spirit of generosity and trust. We need to consider one another's world—ways of perceiving, believing, behaving, and judging—and the benefits of using multiple languages to survive as a species. We acknowledge that a requirement for stepping out of our fears is a shift in the traditional concept of bi/multilingualism so that it can be seen as a resource for a diverse set of issues in our increasingly global society. In order to do this, we need to critique the past views of bi/multilingualism in particular, as it was narrowly applied solely in reference to less powerful segments of the population. We want the reader to understand that multilingualism is an issue of the less powerful and the more powerful. It is our issue. We also need to acknowledge the phenomenon as an ever-changing one that will evolve from the conceptualization within as it faces new situations. This ever-changing aspect of the concept of multilingualism for understanding has inspired us because we can visualize how it can be put to use in and for a future that gives way to an ever more inclusive, diverse world. Thus, our call to scholars of bi/multilingualism from around the world—South Africa, Nigeria, Germany, Colombia, Slovakia, New Zealand, and Taiwan—represents an invitation to create these imagined futures.

NOTE

1. All names are fictionalized for the sake of anonymity. The community has a policy of orality, which means that they do not write their stories. The story within, however, comes from historical documents. What we use here as a story is the essence of the role of the deity in relation to language, even though we understand that the community views this character in a more complex way.

REFERENCES

Bialystok, E. (2001). *Bilingualism in development: Language, literacy, and cognition.* New York: Cambridge University Press.

Brisk, M. E. (1998). *Bilingual education: From compensatory to quality schooling.* Mahwah, NJ: Erlbaum.

Capps, R., Fix, M. E., Murray, J., Ost, J., Passel, J. S., & Herwantoro, S. (2005). *The new demography of America's schools: Immigration and the No Child Left Behind Act.* Retrieved February 5, 2008, from http://www.ncela.gwu.edu/stats/2_nation.htm

Crawford, J. (2000). *At war with diversity: US language policy in an age of anxiety.* Clevedon, England: Multilingual Matters.

Dascal, M. (1999). Chapter 8: An alternative view. Retrieved February 1, 2006, from http://www.tau.ac.il/humanities/philos/dascal/papers/8.htm

Encino, P. (2007). Reframing history in sociocultural theories: Toward an expansive vision. In C. Lewis, P. Encino, & E. B. Moje (Eds.), *Reframing sociocultural research on literacy: Identity, agency, and power* (pp. 49–74). Mahwah, NJ: Erlbaum.

Ethnologue. (n.d.). Retrieved April 4, 2008, from http://www.ethnologue.com/web.asp

Fullan, M. (2003). *The moral imperative of school leadership.* Thousand Oaks, CA: Corwin Press.

Hakuta, K. (1986). *Mirror of language: The debate on bilingualism.* New York: Basic Books.

Haugen, E. (1953). *The Norwegian language in America: A study of bilingual behavior.* Philadelphia: University of Pennsylvania Press.

Machado, A. (2006). *Campos de Castilla.* Madrid, España: Editorial Alianza.

MLA Language Map Data Center. (n.d.). Retrieved April 4, 2008, from http://www.mla.org/map_dat&dceindow=same

Moll, L. C. (1988). Some key issues in teaching Latino students. *Language Arts, 65*(5), 465–472.

Quintero, A. H. (2006). *Muchas reformas, pocos cambios: Hacia otras metáforas educativas [Many reforms, few changes: Towards other educational metaphors].* Hato Rey, PR: Publicaciones Puertorriqueñas.

Ruiz, R. (1984). Orientations in language planning. *The Journal for the National Association for Bilingual Education, 8*(2), 15–34.

Thomas, W. P., & Collier, V. P. (2002). *A national study of school effectiveness for language minority students' long-term academic achievement, final report.* Retrieved June 6, 2005, from http://crede.ucsc.edu/research/llaa/1.1_final.html

Vygotsky, L. (1986). *Thought and language* (Rev. ed.). Cambridge, MA: MIT Press.

Weinreich, U. (1953). *Languages in contact: Findings and problems.* New York: Linguistic Circle of New York.

Wiggins, G., & McTighe, J. (2006). *Understanding by design.* Upper Saddle River, NJ: Pearson Education.

2

Enabling Biliteracy Among Young Children in Southern Africa

Realities, Visions, and Strategies

Carole Bloch

Writing from a multilingual education perspective, in this chapter I focus on the challenges facing early literacy and biliteracy learning and teaching in southern Africa, particularly South Africa. I give information about how the language policies and pedagogical approaches in Africa have tended to hinder literacy learning and the development of reading and writing practices in African communities. I provide examples of research and materials development initiatives from my place of work in Cape Town, the Project for the Study of Alternative Education in South Africa (PRAESA). I also discuss ways of addressing the urgent need to stimulate and support reading and writing habits in African societies by deepening the uses of African languages in print, particularly through the development of children's literature.

Kweli phepha, elibhalwe ngombono wemfuno engeelwimi ezininzi, kugqaliselwa ikakhulu kwimingeni ejongene nobugcisa bokufunda nokubhala kubantwana abasebancinci, kwakunye nokufunda nokufundisa ubugcisa bokufunda nokubhala ngeelwimi ezimbini kuMazantsi e-Afrika, ingakumbi eMzantsi Afrika. Ndinika ulwazi malunga nendlela imigaqo-nkqubo yeelwimi neendlela zokufundisa e-Afrika zithi zithintele ngayo ukufundisa ubugcisa bokufunda nokubhala, nokuphuhliswa kokuqeqeshwa kwabantwana ukuba bafunde ukubhala nokufunda ingakumbi kuluntu lwe-Afrika. Ndikwanika nemizekelo yophando neenzame zokuphuhliswa kwezixhobo zokufundisa abantwana ukufunda nokubhala kwindawo endisebenza kuyo eKapa, iProjekti yoPhando ngeMfundo engenye eMzantsi Afrika (iPRAESA). Ndixoxa nangeendlela zokujongana nesidingo esingxamisekileyo sokuba zandiswe ngamandla iinzame zokuvuselela nokuxhasa ukuba iindawo zoluntu e-Afrika ziziqhelanise nokufunda nokubhala ngokuthi kuzikiswe ukusetyenziwa

Global Perspectives on Multilingualism, edited by María E. Torres-Guzmán and Joel Gómez.

kweelwimi zesiNtu kwizinto ezibhaliweyo, ikakhulu ekukhuliseni uncwadi lwabantwana.

THE EDUCATION-LINGUISTIC TERRAIN

All African societies are multilingual. Yet most children do not enjoy the normality of attending school where their mother tongue or a familiar language is the language of learning. When they do, it is not for long as the school quickly pushes them into learning in a language that is new to them. This is a major contributing factor to the enormous problems with literacy learning among children before and since the advent of universal primary education.

In the following pages, I focus on some of the ways South Africa is trying to address this disconnect of languages students experience, from my perspective as coordinator of the Early Literacy Unit at the Project for the Study of Alternative Education in South Africa (PRAESA). A multilingual education institute based at the University of Cape Town, PRAESA has been in existence since 1992. It is one of the few organizations in South Africa that concentrate entirely on language planning, policy, and implementation.

FROM THE COLONIAL TO POSTCOLONIAL STATUS: WHAT IS THE DIFFERENCE?

I now address the statuses of the languages in the South African context and outline what I perceive to be some of the key factors that have shaped early childhood literacy development in southern Africa.

The development of African languages in high-status functions, such as in teaching beyond the first few grades, in publishing scholastic books, in writing legal documents for the courts, and the like, has been held back by the hegemonic status of the postcolonial language, in this case, English, brought about by colonial conquest and postcolonial language policies. African languages have extremely low status, particularly as languages in print. This is evidenced by the kind of print we see used and displayed in both urban and rural settings. For instance, most signs in African languages are those that make sure that negative and prohibitive messages are understood, such as NO JOBS, NO DUMPING, DANGER, TRESPASSERS WILL BE PROSECUTED. Moreover, there is only one African-language daily newspaper in South Africa (in isiZulu), and few food or other commercial packaging uses African-language print.

It is safe to say that the power and status functions of language are marked most clearly in printed form. In *Decolonising the Mind,* Ngugi wa Thiong'o (1993) makes the fundamental point that while the dislocation of children from their mother tongues in school actually does not destroy the vitality of oral language, it has serious negative impacts on literacy development.

> So the written language of a child's upbringing in the school . . . became divorced from his spoken language at home. There was often not the slightest relationship between the child's written world, which was also the language of his schooling, and the world of his immediate environment in the family and the community. (p. 17)

A fundamental principle in education is that appropriate and effective teaching begins with and builds on what children already know and can do. For young children this implies, above all, extending their oral language development, in various ways, including moving them toward insights and understandings about literacy itself. Since this happens so rarely for young African children, the "written world" that Ngugi refers to rarely comes into existence.

The following general scenario would strike a familiar chord for many teachers across the African continent. From Grades 1–3, the language in education policy can vary (and change rapidly, depending on which politician is in power) from 3 years in the mother tongue to "straight for English," or something in between. Furthermore, there are situations (usually urban) that are multilingual in the sense that several languages are spoken by the children but frequently are unknown by the teacher. These children require special consideration, such as an "explanation" why mother tongue education is not feasible. Irrespective of the particular policy, most teachers tend to communicate with children and teach in an indigenous language that they and (most or all of) the children share. The impending switch to English, the ex-colonial and market language in early childhood development (ECD)—which includes nonformal preschooling and the "foundation phase" of formal education, Grades 1–3, referred to as the reception years—depends on the confidence of teachers. Teachers often do not know English well and do not have training in second- or foreign-language pedagogy. Thus, the switch to English is experienced by many teachers as profoundly disempowering in relation to their ability to assist students and to the students' abilities to do the schoolwork. Usually, from Grade 4 onward, the official medium of instruction is English and almost all reading materials (textbooks, etc.) are in English. The children have to write in English, and all assessment (which is almost exclusively written) takes place in English.

A strange, almost conspiratorial social arrangement has evolved in which all participants in the system "play the game" by pretending that learning actually is taking place in English. The true situation is that most learning in English is rote learning, and meaning making is expected or achieved only occasionally. Learning in English thus is reduced largely to exercises to get students through tests and exams. Apart from the few exceptions that prove the rule, children's creative impetus and desire to learn are crushed.

The underlying assumption is that the ex-colonial language is a necessary condition for educational achievement, as knowing such language carries the possibility of entering the world of the markets, which is dominated by the ex-colonial language, that is, English. According to Ngugi wa Thiong'o, the fact that people find it so difficult to imagine that African languages can and should be developed and used to perform functions that English, or for that matter French, can, reflects a "colonized" mind. As Ngugi (1993) states:

> The real aim of colonialism was to control the people's wealth . . . [but] economic and political control can never be complete or effective without mental control. To control a people's culture is to control their tools of self-definition in relationship to others. For colonialism, this involved two aspects of the same process: the destruction or the deliberate undervaluing of a people's culture, their art, dances, religions, history, geography, education, orature and literature, and the conscious elevation of the language of the coloniser. The domination of a people's language by the languages of the colonising nations was crucial to the domination of the mental universe of the colonised. (p. 16)

Similarly, people also find it hard to accept the observation, so often made by my colleague Neville Alexander, that only a small percentage of citizens actually need to know English well and that society, if it is to achieve real democracy and escape mediocrity, has to give people the choice of performing their everyday business in their mother tongue. Alexander calls what is occurring in many African countries a "static maintenance syndrome." By this he means that although African languages are valued and accepted, the uses of the languages are limited to only certain, generally oral, purposes. He points out that

> people begin to accept as "natural" the supposed inferiority of their own languages and adopt an approach that is determined by considerations that are related only to the market and social status value of the set of languages in their multilingual societies. (Alexander, 2002, p. 119)

Understood in this light, one of the urgent tasks in African society in general, and in education more specifically, is to find ways to exploit the creative potential of African languages. To accomplish this, the rift between their oral and written forms must be healed, so that literacy can become widely available and be used as part of people's daily lives. This will give both children and adults the chance to use their language more fully and to experience their worlds as coherent and meaningful.

EARLY LITERACY TEACHING AND LEARNING IN POSTCOLONIAL AFRICA

Various factors have combined to perpetuate the widespread lack of social and cultural practices related to reading and writing in southern Africa, one very powerful one being the pedagogy that is characteristic of early schooling. Views about the nature of literacy that originated in the United States and Europe in the first half of the 20th century continue to have influence today. Reading then was widely understood as a psychological perceptual activity, which led to a focus on the relationships between sounds and symbols. In what many Africans call the North, that is, North America and Europe, this view gave rise to strongly behaviorist skills-based approaches to literacy that included the notion of "reading readiness," which enabled the textbook industry to sell nonprint activities and materials (see Gillen & Hall, 2003, p. 4).

In Africa, where print tends to have little if any significance for social and other exchanges in many communities, educational systems often are staffed by untrained or poorly trained teachers and teacher trainers. All of the developments in African education that were initiated to achieve universal primary education have included as a central tenet the requirement of instilling basic literacy and numeracy. This was, and to a great extent continues to be, executed by these teachers and trainers, most of whom have been educated through the ex-colonial language, which they often have not mastered. Methods based on the view of literacy as autonomous sets of skills that can be broken down, learned, and then later used in learning either a first or a second language have been applied rigidly over many decades, largely without question as to their relevance to meaning making and its role in learning languages.

The significant shifts in understandings about literacy in the United States and Europe that gradually have given rise to new literacy pedagogies during the second half of the 20th century have barely begun to be noticed within the school world in South Africa. I am referring here to (1) the notion that reading and writing are ideological in nature and form part of a society's social and cultural practices and that there are many different literacies that come into existence for various reasons (Heath, 1983; Street, 1984; Taylor, 1983), and (2) research and theoretical insights about children's written language development such as emergent literacy and whole language (Goodman, 1986; Holdaway, 1979).

In print-scarce regions, such as in many parts of South Africa, it has continued to be accepted that conditions of poverty in the "third world" produce children who generally are unable to grasp even the basics. The corollary is that teachers have extremely low levels of faith in children's ability to learn. The fact that so many children grow up in communities where they rarely if ever come into contact with meaningful reading and writing in their home languages has not influenced the design or implementation of curricula in any other way. The South African school world is still gripped by the erroneous belief that reading and writing can be taught in social and cultural vacuums as sets of skills that constitute the "tools" for reading and writing (Bloch, 2002).

This has had devastating consequences for learning and creativity. In classrooms across Africa, children are still forced to begin Grade 1 with readiness activities that include coloring in or tracing over shapes, letters, and numbers, and drill in chanting sounds and forming letters—outside of any interesting context of use that might make sense to them. These activities delay even further the time when they actually will start engaging with print and finding out about reading and writing. Ironically, in the African continent, resonant with oral wisdom and stories, textbooks loaded with decontextualized low-level skills and drills are favored. Such teaching methods have given rise to recent assessment results in the Western Cape Province and nationally in South Africa that are appalling. They suggest that most Grade 3 and Grade 6 children are unable to read at grade level and that numeracy performance is even worse (see media statement issued by the Western Cape MEC for Education, on May 25, 2004). The endemic problems are that children learn to decode, but do not understand what they are reading, and that they learn to copy sentences, but cannot compose their own text.

At best, those who can afford them use "readers" with restricted, unnatural language. Storybooks and other meaningful texts are conceptually viewed as irrelevant for school learning and effectively discarded as supplementary material, a luxury that most African children don't have. Youngsters are denied opportunities to experience the richness of print stories in their own languages.

Yet—as we are reminded in an article in *Le Monde Diplomatique* (Dijan, 2004) about the rediscovery of ancient manuscripts from Timbuktu in Mali—there is a tradition of African literacy going back to the very origins of writing in Pharaonic Egypt and other sites in the Levant. The fact is that Africa has both a rich oral *and* a precolonial written tradition that has not, as yet, been exploited to inspire teachers. Rather, the system produces teachers who act as agents to transmit a mind-numbing and alien literacy curriculum, often in a poorly understood language. They unwittingly collude with the system to negate the need for real reading materials (such as storybooks). What chances do teachers have to be inspiring role models when they have been unable to engage with print in their own languages (and often even in English) either as children or adults? Given these circumstances, it does not appear too harsh to propose that the perpetuation of a system that holds back the development of a written children's literature in African languages has contributed to crippling the development of effective literacy teachers.

The situation is even more complex: Those active in promoting the use of the mother tongue in education in Africa are often linguists and language scholars who are passionate about dissecting and getting teachers to transmit the "correct" form of the language. Perhaps unintentionally, they tend to strengthen the case for narrow skills-based methods. On the other hand, only a few Africans have been trained as early childhood literacy specialists who have knowledge and understandings about how young children learn. The effect on teachers is that they tend to teach literacy in the mother tongue as if it were actually a foreign language.

All of these factors have mingled conceptually to lead even the best-intentioned development work in African contexts to focus much more on textbook production and distribution than on a fundamental transformation and intensification of teacher education. Teacher guides instruct teachers in minute detail as to what they should do in each lesson. However, apart from the fact that the guides are generally in English rather than a language that teachers are likely to know well, if teachers are not given the chance to understand and reflect on why they do what they do, the use of textbooks will have, at best, limited success. Furthermore, it is not in any case sufficient merely to have textbooks, even good ones, in one's own language. Findings from her research in the United States led Purcell-Gates (1995) to observe that

> written language is apparent in the environment only to the extent that it is recognized or noticed. It is recognized or noticed only to the extent that it is used by fellow members of one's sociocultural/sociolinguistic group. (p. 50)

It is important to take note of such cautionary words in print-scarce contexts such as those we find in many parts of Africa. It is all too easy to think that once we have printed materials in appropriate languages, our problems will be over. The challenge is far more complex. We need solutions at different levels of society—political and economic as well as social and cultural—so that people have opportunities to tune into the uses of written language and make these personally meaningful, thereby coming to incorporate reading and writing into their lives.

NOT "EITHER/OR," BUT "BOTH/AND"

At the heart of the work that PRAESA is engaged in lies a simple question to which we feel we have to find the answer: How can we move from the existing situation, in which the languages of the former colonial powers dominate, to one where the indigenous languages of Africa become dominant (Alexander & Bloch, 2004)?

The Early Literacy Unit at PRAESA tries to encourage new ways of thinking and acting in relation to early literacy development and learning. Since 1997, South Africa has had a progressive language in education policy that promotes additive bi/multilingualism. We now refer to what is slowly emerging as its practical manifestation as "mother tongue-based bilingual education" (see for example Western Cape Education Department, 2002), because this term provides a clearer statement of what is required in most African multilingual school systems. However, one of the persistent legacies of apartheid education is a myth that is alive in the minds of many parents across the country—they equate mother tongue-based bilingual education with inferior education. This is one reason why there is still widespread resistance to the use of African languages as languages of teaching in education. English is equated and conflated both with literacy and with "good education." Our organizational stance is clear: It is not a matter of *either* mother tongue *or* English, but *both* mother tongue *and* English are necessary for a quality education within our context.

This message is gaining ground, albeit slowly, since little has been done by the government to provide parents with the information they need to make informed choices about what is best for their children's language development and learning. Thus, the gap between policy and practice is substantial, and there is much advocacy and other persuasive work for language activists to undertake. As Alexander (2004) points out, there is a lack of governmental political will to implement policy.

> The fundamental issue is the failure of government to answer the simple question: Should we base the education system of the new South Africa on the mother tongues (L1s, home languages) of the learners or should we base it, essentially, on the English language, even though the latter is the home language of under 9% of the population of the country and is "understood" by fewer than 50% of the population? The accumulation of evidence confirming that the prevailing English-mainly default language-medium policy, instead of compelling the decision makers to consider seriously going over to the policy of mother tongue-based bilingual education, elicits denialist and compensatory educational responses along the lines of "simply" improving the competence of the learners in English. (p. 12)

In the absence of a committed position by the government on this issue, PRAESA has concentrated on initiating and exploring the dynamics of small-scale research and materials development projects so that when the time comes for significant implementation, we will have some models to consider.

READING FOR ENJOYMENT—THE FREE READING IN SCHOOLS PROJECT

Arising from insights gained between 1998 and 2003 while developing Xhosa–English biliteracy among a group of children in a multilingual school in Cape Town (see Bloch & Alexander, 2003; Bloch & Nkence, 2000), we realized that changes in language medium and teaching approaches could succeed only if they were accompanied by broader changes in teachers' attitudes toward reading. Apart from our own experience, we were inspired by research on Free Voluntary Reading (FVR) cited by Krashen (1993), which suggests that readers who engage in FVR are superior in reading comprehension, writing fluency, writing complexity, attitude toward school, and self-esteem; that people who say they read more, write better; that reading as a leisure activity is the best predictor of comprehension, vocabulary, and reading speed; and that free reading has a dramatic effect on acquiring a second language.

In the following pages, I describe the Free Reading in Schools Project (FRISC) that was conducted in the Western Cape Province to stimulate and support reading for enjoyment.

We ran the FRISC project from 2002 to 2004 to enable teachers and children to experience the enjoyment of reading stories in both their mother tongue and English and to try to deepen our understanding of how story reading can assist with biliteracy development and additional language learning. Krashen (1993) suggests a minimum of 1 year is needed to see results, and it was clear to us that since most African children have had few book-related experiences, they would need more time.

Since none of the schools had sufficient appropriate reading material on site, despite the former Minister of Education Kadel Asmal's 1999 declaration to "break the back of illiteracy," PRAESA donated storybooks. A PRAESA literacy specialist demonstrated reading aloud for teachers (who had already agreed to be in the classroom for the free reading time), with the understanding that the teachers would begin reading aloud to the children so that the literacy specialist could monitor the process and provide support and feedback. Time also was set aside for the children to select their own books to read silently or with a friend, and there was no expectation that they would do any formal or didactic activities related to their reading. Workshops were held periodically to raise and discuss particular issues with teachers, such as strategies for reading aloud, where to get and how to select appropriate reading materials for different age groups, how to meet the reading needs of multilingual groups, and how to ask open-ended questions about stories.

Analyzing and writing up the process proved to be invaluable, mainly because it identified as critical some issues that, on the surface, seemed too obvious to bother about. I use extracts from the notes of Xolisa Guzula, the facilitator of the FRISC project at three different schools, to illustrate some of these.

The first observation is at the beginning of the project when Guzula was getting to know Blesbok Primary (all school names are pseudonyms), a very large school catering to children living in an ever-growing informal settlement on the outskirts of Cape Town that is typical of many communities found at the edges of towns and cities in South Africa. Its inhabitants are mainly Xhosa speakers who have come from the rural areas of the Eastern Cape in search of jobs. People live in shacks and are extremely poor.

> Later on I went to read to the Grade 4s. . . . I found a "coloured" woman who was teaching them about their rights. She had a pipe [to keep "control"] in her hand and the children were very noisy. Fortunately, her period was over and I started with my reading. I asked the class whether they had been read to before or even now at school and at home. They told me that they have never been read to. They are not read to at school. I told them that I go to their school to make sure that stories are read to them and that they have access to storybooks so that they can choose books out of interest and read them. They were happy and as I read the story they gave me all the attention they could give me. The class was dead silent, you could even hear a coin dropping on the floor. Even though I went there having prepared to read only one story, I ended up reading three stories for them because they kept asking me to read the next one. (August 2001)

Consistently and unsurprisingly, the children, whoever they are, love listening to stories. This fundamental and wonderful fact, which we see as the starting point for many further insights—educational and otherwise—is a surprise to many teachers, who do not readily understand the value of stories. One can surmise that this has to do, at least in part, with teachers seeing themselves as the givers of skills and knowledge, and with a corresponding difficulty in viewing the children as meaning makers and constructors of their own knowledge.

The second observation is from Zimbini Primary, located in an established former township of Cape Town, where the teachers and pupils speak only isiXhosa, but the medium of instruction is English after Grade 3. It is known as one of the old primary schools in the area and also is regarded as the best. The notes capture the ongoing challenge Guzula has experienced when trying to encourage teachers to take on the role of reading daily to children.

> Teachers at Zimbini seem very enthusiastic about reading when one speaks to them. However, in practice, it is a different story. Grade 4 children reported at one stage that their teacher last read to them before June (2002). They read on their own. The teacher has witnessed me on many occasions reading to the class but hasn't taken that initiative. Sometimes when I'm there she asks them to read silently but she does other things, like going to the office or attend to another teacher to discuss their things. (November 2002)

The next observation, back at Blesbok, illustrates the frustration Guzula sometimes has felt in situations where the best interests of the children were not considered and she had to deal with the problem that arose when teachers under duress took advantage of the extra support she represented to them.

> The teacher sees me in the staff room and says, "let's go but I'm going to leave the children with you. I am busy." I told her that this period [lesson time] is very important like her other periods. She said that she's very busy because one of the students has passed away. I told her that I understand that but can't she do what she needs to do afterwards. The teacher says she is not sure whether to give children books to read or read to them but she is going to leave them at 11:00. I tell her to give children books so that they can read on their own. She then asks two boys to go and fetch books with her. Meanwhile children are spending most of their time sweeping the classroom. Books don't stay in the classroom. This is depressing and frustrating. There are only two posters with nouns and verbs on the walls. After the literacy half hour I went to the staff room and found the teacher eating fish and chips with another teacher. And it seemed that this is what kept her busy. I sense that the teachers are not taking the literacy half hour seriously. Later on she came to ask me what I did with the children. I told her that we did folktales. The teacher told me that she is tired from being an MC in the memorial service and her body is sore from practicing drum marjorettes with the

> children. That was the excuse she could give me. I was angry and frustrated. (no date)

This extract gives a sense both of the daily hardships that often can make people appear "tough" and of the seeming incapacity of many teachers to value reading enough to promote and support it with their children. Our most fundamental challenge is the large number of teachers who themselves need to be nurtured emotionally and to have their own interest in reading stimulated and nurtured if they are to inspire others.

I don't want to paint a completely gloomy picture—there are some motivated and inspiring teachers as well. The next observation is from Sunshine Primary, a small independent Christian school situated not far from the University of Cape Town. A multilingual (English, Afrikaans, Xhosa) school that is relatively well resourced, it recently had employed a Xhosa teacher specifically to support Xhosa development among first- and additional-language speakers. Most of the teachers are bilingual Afrikaans/English, and most of the children speak an African language (mainly Xhosa) and come from predominantly middle-class backgrounds.

> Reports from the Xhosa teacher (Teacher C) were positive ones as she reported that most parents are helping their children to read isiXhosa at home. Children in Teacher C's classes hadn't had teaching in mother tongue, especially those who were doing Grade 4 last year. The Grade 1's at the moment are the lucky ones because they are starting to learn mother tongue from the very beginning. Teacher C also reported that there was only one exception, in a Grade 1 class where a child's parent threatened to move the child to another school because she hadn't sent the child to the school to learn isiXhosa. The parent was angry because the child was mainly interested in reading Xhosa books at home and that they do not see where the child is going to go with isiXhosa. (June 2002)

This account gives a sense both of the hope that keeps us going and of the enormous challenges we face in addressing parental attitudes about using African languages in school. The sentiment expressed by this parent is a common one and reflects the belief that the use of one language will hinder the development of another—such parents feel that their child already knows the mother tongue and doesn't need to "waste time" on it at school.

The final observation, back at Zimbini Primary, points to the importance of establishing authentic and supportive mentoring relationships, as well as the fact that the shortage of reading materials in African languages is a major constraint in developing reading in African languages.

> Teacher D is much better now. She seems to understand how the project works. [The fact that she is] making time to chat with me and I am trying to build a good relationship with her has provided her with new insights into the project. She reported using different strategies in the classroom, like getting children to touch books and read on their own. For most of this year, she's only been reading aloud to them. She's worried about the level of the books in Grade 5 because the children say the books are boring. It seems like for next year we'll need novel-like books for them to read. It has only been a year and ¾ and we've run out of books in African languages. (November 2002)

TOWARD A CULTURE OF READING

It is difficult for people who have grown up in an English-language environment to imagine a situation in which there is no body of written children's literature and to appreciate the implications of literally running out of books for learning to value one's mother tongue and for literacy learning. Yet for most African-language-speaking children across Africa, getting ahold of storybooks in one's language is a rare gift.

I now discuss a materials development process that we initiated to support the development of a culture of reading. PRAESA secured financial support in 2001 from the Royal Netherlands Embassy for what we see as an essential project to break through the economic argument that "there is no market for African languages, therefore no point in publishing in these languages." While the attitude still dominates, it is being systematically challenged, albeit in small ways, and there are now some publishers who are specializing in multilingual and African-language materials. PRAESA's intention has been to help stimulate the market by developing, distributing, and monitoring the use of stories, both original and translated, for children ranging in age from preschool to teenagers. A translation unit has been established at PRAESA to deal with various issues. In addition to developing a feeling for translating children's literature, they have set out to learn about and deal with a range of complex issues that arise when working with languages that have not been widely used in print. In some cases, PRAESA has published materials. In other cases, we have collaborated with publishers willing to publish in African languages by guaranteeing print runs that make the process worthwhile for them. Working in Afrikaans, Xhosa, and English, PRAESA has developed several books for children, including both originals and translations (Bloch, 2005).

An important consideration has been how to facilitate the mentoring of new African writers and illustrators. For historical reasons, this domain has rested largely in the hands of middle-class English or Afrikaans speakers. Most educational publishers are too busy dancing to the tune of government deadlines for textbook submissions to spend the time necessary to mentor. We recently conducted two workshops for writers and illustrators at PRAESA and collaborated with a local publisher, New Africa Books, to produce six original stories that are now available in 11 languages. Although the stories and illustrations are in some ways "raw," they demonstrate how such opportunities can give creative expression to voices previously unheard, and certainly these stories resonate powerfully for many South African children. We are convinced that we need to increase substantially both original writing and illustration and translations in order to give birth to a substantive body of children's literature. The first publication of Stories Across Africa was completed in 2007—it is a pan-African set of Little Hands books that are already available in 24 languages (see http://littlehands.book.co.za).

TEACHER TRAINING

One way we know that the early literacy situation is so serious across the continent is the anecdotal evidence we have amassed from interacting for over 3 years with teacher trainers, language planners, and African language specialists from several African countries, including Namibia, Swaziland, Botswana, Mozambique, Burkina Faso, Ethiopia, Malawi, Kenya, and Cameroon. They were all participants in a series of five week-long intensive courses, conducted by PRAESA at the University of Cape Town, designed to train trainers for multilingual education. We included components on early language and literacy learning as well as materials development for multilingual classrooms. Our aim was to empower trainers so that they could share effective pedagogical ideas and strategies with teachers. Many countries have undergone curriculum change or are in the midst of it, and the thrust is usually toward learner-centered education. However, it is extremely difficult to get beyond the level of rhetoric when trainers themselves have not had opportunities to experience what they are expected to impart. In Namibia, for example, where learner-centered education has been "implemented" since independence in 1991, and many staff have undergone many workshops, I know from my experience as an early literacy specialist on the Upgrading of African Languages Project of the National Ministry of Education, supported by the GTZ (1999–2007), that few, if any, teachers know how to actually transform the information they receive into practice. In addition, participants have related anecdotes about associated sociocultural issues such as lack of political will to support mother tongue education, the dearth of learning materials, the lack of teacher training, and overcrowded classrooms, not to mention the devastation caused by the HIV/AIDS pandemic and other social and economic factors.

To help address teacher preparedness issues, and to help ensure that participants have access to what they need for training, PRAESA has completed a set of training materials for literacy in multilingual settings, Training for Early Literacy Learning (TELL). These free materials can be downloaded from the Internet (www.tell.praesa.org). This endeavor has been a collaborative effort between PRAESA and the National Centre for Language and Literacy (NCLL) at Reading University in the UK. Viv Edwards, a colleague from NCLL, and I discovered that we deal with many similar language-related pedagogical issues, and rather than reinvent the wheel, we decided to adapt a set of training materials she had already developed for early literacy in the UK. We have considered very carefully how these materials can facilitate the conceptual shifts trainers and teachers need to make. For instance, whereas traditional methods view speaking, listening, reading, and writing as separate subjects, the TELL materials emphasize the integrated nature of language learning, providing information and activities that allow trainers and teachers to explore relevant pedagogical points and engage in reflective exercises. The materials provide a generic structural framework to which trainers in different countries will be able to add their individual and local intricacies.

Assuming that demonstrations of good practice facilitate comprehension, we also have made two videos for trainers and teachers—*Feeling at Home with Literacy* and *Building Story Bridges to Literacy*. The first video, set in Cape Town, follows Zia, a Xhosa-speaking child, from home to school and then back home again, highlighting that literacy can be part of home *and* school practices, that it can be enjoyable, that young children are resourceful when they start making meaning using print, that the mother tongue can be used alongside English for teaching and learning, and that play and imagination are important for early literacy development. The second video is a short animated film and was created with rural, print-scarce African settings in mind. Its intention is both to help parents and community members appreciate the value of telling and reading stories for children's literacy learning and to provide suggestions for how to get involved.

CONCLUSION

The work I have described is in progress. There is no doubt that we must struggle against prevailing global economic conditions. The previously mentioned article in *Le Monde Diplomatique* ends with the following words:

> The cost of saving the Timbuktu manuscripts is estimated at $5.6 million—which is 60 times less than the sum that EuroDisney has just demanded from shareholders to save its Paris theme park. Yet the preservation of this gold mine of African history is still at risk. (Dijan, 2004, pp. 10–11)

Despite the ugliness of this reality, there are many points of light that keep us going. A recent language-focused initiative on the whole-continent level is gaining strength and support. We now have an officially constituted language organization of the African Union, the African Academy of Languages. Under its umbrella, several continent-wide projects that are furthering the intellectualization and development of African languages are in various stages of implementation. These include a joint masters program, a translation project, a terminology project, the Year of African Languages in 2006–2007, and the Stories Across Africa project. StAAF is creating common anthologies of stories found or written in different communities and reworking and illustrating them for children to read in their own language wherever they are (Bloch, 2008). The energy generated by these projects is helping to engender a sense of purpose and a love of reading among future African citizens.

REFERENCES

Alexander, N. (2002). Linguistic rights, language planning and democracy in post-apartheid South Africa. In S. J. Baker (Ed.), *Language policy: Lessons from global models* (pp. 116–129). Monterey, CA: Monterey Institute of International Studies.

Alexander, N. (2004). Language policy: The litmus test of democracy in "post-apartheid" South Africa. *Discourse Journal, 2*(32), 7–12.

Alexander, N., & Bloch, C. (2004, September). *Feeling at home with literacy in the mother tongue*. Keynote presented at the 29th International Board on Books for Young People (IBBY), Cape Town, South Africa.

Bloch, C. (2002, August). *Enabling effective literacy learning in multilingual South African early childhood classrooms*. Keynote presented at the conference on Teaching Reading Materials Development in the Foundation Phase, St. Mary's School, Durban, South Africa.

Bloch, C. (2005). Building bridges between oral and written language: Facilitating reading opportunities for children in Africa. In N. Alexander (Ed.), *Mother tongue based bilingual education in southern Africa: The dynamics of implementation* (pp. 69–80). Frankfurt am Main: Multilingualism Network.

Bloch, C. (2008). Little books for little hands. A Stories Across Africa Project. *The Lion and the Unicorn, 32*(3), 271–287.

Bloch, C., & Alexander, N. (2003). A luta continua: The relevance of the continua of biliteracy to South African multilingual schools. In N. Hornberger (Ed.), *Continua of biliteracy: An ecological framework for educational policy, re-*

search, and practice in multilingual settings (pp. 91–121). Clevedon: Multilingual Matters.

Bloch, C., & Nkence, N. (2000). Glimmers of hope: Emergent writing and reading in a multilingual foundation phase classroom. *Proceedings from the Teachers Inservice Project's Third Annual Colloquium (TIP)* (pp. 125–133). Cape Town, South Africa: University of the Western Cape.

Dijan, J. M. (2004, August). Mali: The fabulous past of Africa. *Le Monde Diplomatique*, pp. 10, 11.

Gillen, J., & Hall, N. (2003). The emergence of early childhood literacy. In N. Hall, J. Larsen, & J. Marsh (Eds.), *Handbook of early childhood literacy* (pp. 3–12). London: Sage.

Goodman, Y. (1986). Children coming to know literacy. In W. H. Teale & E. Sulzby (Eds.), *Emergent literacy: Writing and reading* (pp. 1–14). Norwood, NJ: Ablex.

Heath, S. B. (1983). *Ways with words: Language, life and work in communities and classrooms.* Cambridge: Cambridge University Press.

Holdaway, D. (1979). *The foundations of literacy.* Sydney, Australia: Ashton Scholastic.

Krashen, S. (1993). *The power of reading.* Englewood, CO: Libraries Unlimited.

Ngugi wa Thiong'o. (1993). *Decolonising the mind: The politics of language in African literature.* London: James Currey.

Purcell-Gates, V. (1995). *Other people's words: The cycle of low literacy.* Cambridge, MA: Harvard University Press.

Street, B. V. (1984). *Literacy in theory and practice.* Cambridge: Cambridge University Press.

Taylor, D. (1983). *Family literacy: Young children learning to read and write.* London: Heinemann.

Western Cape Education Department. (2002). Language policy in the primary schools of the Western Cape. Retrieved August 14, 2008, from http://wced.wcape.gov.za/documents/lang_policy/index_exsum.html

Western Cape Education Department. (2004). Media statement. Available online at http://wced.wcapegov.za/comms/press/2004/28_gr6study.html

3

Multilingualism in South African Schools

Where to Now?

Rosemary Wildsmith-Cromarty

This chapter explores multilingualism as a metaphor of abundance with reference to schools in South Africa. It describes the conditions that currently exist in different types of schools in terms of multilingual language use and the major challenges facing language specialists and educators in these schools. These include the use of African languages to facilitate understanding of subject matter where English is the language of formal instruction, the promotion of language awareness in multicultural classrooms, the need to develop the major African languages as languages of instruction, and the learning of African languages by all students in multicultural schools. The chapter draws on selected research projects to illustrate the successful implementation of multilingual practices and considers ways in which current practices might be adjusted to allow for a greater diversity in language use.

Leli phepha licwaninga ngokuthuthukiswa kwezilimuningi (multilingualism) ezikoleni zaseNingizimu Africa. Lichaza izimo njengoba zinjalo ezitholakala ezikoleni mayelana nokusetshenziswa kwezilimuningi ezikoleni, kanye nezinselelo ezibhekene nabasebenzi abangongoti ezilimini ezikhulunywayo kanye nothisha abafundisa kulezi zikole. Lokhu kumbandakanya ukusetshenziswa kwezilimu zomdabu (African languages) ukuze kubelula ukuqonda isifundo leso esifundwayo uma leso sifundo ngokomthetho sifundiswa ngolimu lwesiNgisi; ukuqhakambisa ubukhona bezinye izilimu emakilasini lapho kunabafundi abavela emasikweni ahlukahlukene; isidingo sokuthuthukisa izilimu zomdabu eziqavile ukuze kufundiswe ngazo emakilasini kanye nokufundwa kwezilimu zomdabu yibo bonke abafundi abasezikoleni ezinabafundi abaxubile ngokwamasiko. Leli phepha lide litomula izingxenye ezikhethekile ezitholakala emsebenzini owucwaningo ukuze kukhonjiswe impumelelo esibekhona ekusetshenzisweni kwezilimuningi (multilingualism) bese futhi liveza nezindlela ezingenza ngcono isimo esikhona njengamanje sokugqugquzelwa kokusetshenziswa kwezilimu ezahlukahlukene.

The South African Constitution (1996) enshrines multilingualism as a national resource to be protected and promoted in all spheres of public life, including education. It favors the iZemia metaphor that proposes that multiple languages are of benefit. South Africa's language policy recognizes 11 official languages: four from the *Nguni* group (isiZulu, isiXhosa, Siswati, and isiNdebele); three from the *Sotho* group (Sesotho, Setswana, and Sesotho sa Leboa—Northern Sotho); two from other groups (Tshivenda and Xitsonga); Afrikaans; and English. In a recent document on language policy in higher education, the government proclaimed the right of individuals to receive education in the language of their choice where reasonably practicable (South Africa, 2002, p. 4). It further described the challenge facing higher education as "the simultaneous development of a multilingual environment in which all our languages are developed as academic/scientific languages" (p. 5). In order to promote multilingualism in education, the previously marginalized indigenous languages need to be developed and promoted. However, conflict does arise around language. Specifically, the desire for English and its increasing use as an almost exclusive medium of instruction are in direct conflict with this ideal. The question facing language educators in South Africa is how to reconcile government ideology with the realities of language use in South African classrooms. This chapter explores the meaning of *multilingualism* with reference to the tension between English and African languages in various types of state schools.

To date, the official business of the country is carried out mainly on a monolingual basis, that is, in English (Wildsmith-Cromarty & Young, 2006). This includes the legislature, where minutes of parliamentary debates are translated into English; the political sphere, where speeches are in only one language; the private sector; and education. Most schools use an African language as the medium of instruction for the first 3 years only, after which English becomes the official language of instruction from grades 2–12. The functions of the African languages in the educational domain thus remain subsidiary, even though many learners struggle with English. A further complicating factor is the presence of more than one African language as a primary language in the schools in major urban areas such as Johannesburg. English, in such case, serves as a *lingua franca.*

In terms of development, substantial work had already been carried out in the areas of terminology and orthography on the African languages prior to the period of Bantu education under the apartheid era (1955–1975) (Mahlalela & Heugh, 2002). This development was necessary as the African languages were used as languages of instruction for the first 6 years of school. However, many of the textbooks and word lists developed during this period fell into disuse with the advent of the Bantu Education Act in 1953, which relegated mother tongue instruction to 4 years only. The importance of the African languages for learning and as tools of communication for official purposes therefore was gradually diminished. Even the speech communities themselves did not perceive the African languages as adequate for learning academic subjects, so there seemed to be no need for further technical, academic, or scientific development of these languages.

After the advent of democracy in South Africa in 1994, various government bodies were tasked with the further development of the African languages. This is a continuing process and, to date, various terminology lists for different subject areas in the school curriculum, including mathematics and science, have been developed. As knowledge in these subjects in particular has advanced since the pre-Bantu education era, there is a need to update existing terminology and orthography in the African languages before they can be used as languages of instruction. Recent research has revealed that a number of newly created terms are unfamiliar to both teachers and learners, as there has been a lack of consultation with the local speech communities in the development of these terms (Wildsmith & Gordon, 2006). The result is that the current situation with regard to the use of African languages in the schools remains a form of code-switching, where teachers use English for instructional purposes, that is, to introduce new concepts to their learners, but code-switch to the African languages for explanatory purposes. Nevertheless, there are various projects that attempt to promote the use of the African languages in the educational domain, and these will be described later in this chapter.

For the purposes of this chapter, the term *multilingual* may refer to either the composition of school populations or the language use of these populations in the everyday school context. For example, a given school population may manifest rich linguistic and cultural diversity, but language use in the classroom may remain monolingual, that is, English. The *context* here is potentially multilingual, but this does not mean that the school engages in multilingual practices, in the sense of using more than one instructional language. If we differentiate between language use for building cognitive academic language proficiency (CALP) (Cummins, 2000) and that for developing basic interpersonal communication skills (BICS), then we may be able to distinguish *multilingual practices* as far as BICS are concerned (i.e., for social purposes during recess and after school) but not for the facilitation of academic learning. This is an area that currently is being addressed in South African education in terms of various language policies, but implementation is slow.

With respect to the individual, we also need to consider what the term *multilingual* means in relation to the degree of competence in a speaker. For example, we need to consider what an individual's dominant language may be and/or what the heritage language, or mother tongue, means for a bi/multilingual person, especially if we are advocating the use of the mother tongue as a medium of instruction (MOI) (Skutnabb-Kangas, 1988). Furthermore, what does "communicative competence" mean in relation to each of the languages in a person's repertoire (Cook, 1992)?

Multilingualism has been defined as the "capacity to use several languages appropriately and effectively for communication in oral and written language" (Cenoz & Genesee, 1998; Cook, 1995). In South Africa, the process of acquiring several languages (or *parts* of several languages) simultaneously has not been widely researched (Slabbert & Finlayson, 2002). The acquisition and use of multiple languages is complex because of the interactions that are possible among the languages being learned and the processes involved in learning them. This may include drawing on multiple languages simultaneously in order to communicate effectively in a given context (a form of code-switching)—a phenomenon that also can be related to the unequal linguistic balance of each language in a learner's repertoire (Cook, 1992, 1995; McCormick, 2002). Issues such as these have a direct influence on the ultimate success of a multilingual language policy.

In terms of language use in South African schools, practices range from predominantly monolingual to bilingual to multilingual and, at the extreme end of the continuum, mixed (Slabbert & Finlayson, 2002). These practices tend to depend on the regional context and whether it is urban or rural. The descriptions that follow of the various school profiles are necessarily impressionistic, as systematic, regional descriptions of language use, inside and outside of educational institutions, have yet to be developed (Mesthrie, 2002). However, for the purposes of this chapter, three state school types will be considered—rural, urban township, and urban suburban.

LANGUAGE IN EDUCATION IN SOUTH AFRICAN SCHOOLS

State schools are generally of three main types in South Africa: (1) rural, (2) urban township, and (3) urban suburban (Jordaan & Suzman, 2002). Pupils in the different types of schools experience varying degrees of exposure to the different languages, including the medium of instruction, which, in most schools across the country (except for certain Afrikaans-medium schools, where Afrikaans is the language of instruction), is English. This situation has evolved historically and continues for both social and economic reasons. Many parents want their children to learn English and to be educated through the medium of English (Bosch & de Klerk, 1996). This leads to a situation of subtractive bilingualism (Skutnabb-Kangas, 1988), wherein the indigenous home languages of the pupils become marginalized.

In rural schools, the majority of (if not all) pupils and teachers share an African language as their home language. In these schools, English is used for formal instruction only, with the home language used for classroom management and for explanation or clarification when necessary (Murray, 2002). The multilingualism that ensues is thus a form of code-switching involving only one African language spoken in the region in which the rural school is located. Generally, there is very little exposure to English in rural areas, so it is almost like a foreign language in this setting. This creates difficulties in learning English, which are compounded by difficulties in learning subject matter, since teachers cannot always translate the content accurately into the home language (Wildsmith & Gordon, 2006). Since the form of a home language spoken in rural areas is regarded as the "deep" variety, it has been adopted as the "standard" variety in language development work and in education. The move toward standardizing rural varieties has led to vigorous debates concerning the viability and status of other, more urban varieties of these languages (Anthonissen & Gough, 1998; Lafon, 2005).

In urban township schools, various African languages are the home languages of pupils and teachers, depending on the region. These schools are thus *multilingual* in terms of the number of background languages represented in the school. However, they are not necessarily multilingual in their use of various languages for instructional purposes. In urban townships, there is greater exposure to English, and teachers are often more proficient in it than their rural counterparts (Waner, 2002). In the various subject classes, however, there tends to be code-switching for clarification purposes between English and one of the African languages (Adendorff, 1993; Moodley, 2003). In these schools, as in the wider urban township environment, the phenomenon of "mixed" codes, or "multiple code-switching," has become a sign of group identity (McCormick, 2002; Slabbert & Finlayson, 2002). There are also accounts of teachers switching to an urban mixed code such as Iscamtho in order to clarify concepts presented in isiZulu (Ntshangase, 2002). Since a mixed code, and not a particular home language, is used in the classroom setting, many urban African children have little exposure to the standard variety of their home language.

In urban suburban schools, pupils come from linguistically diverse backgrounds, including European, Asian, and African languages. These schools are becoming increasingly multilingual and multicultural in terms of both teacher and pupil profiles. In these schools, teachers and pupils do not necessarily share a home language. Very often, teachers are either English or Afrikaans speakers with no (or little) knowledge of an African language. English is the main language of instruction, and if code-switching occurs, it is normally among pupils who "translate" course content for one another in the absence of either bi- or multilingual competence on the part of teachers. In some classes, teachers allow the use of the home language during groupwork in order to introduce an affective element i.e., to allow learners to express their knowledge and their feelings, which they find difficult to do through an ex-colonial language (Chick & McKay, 2001).

In these schools, there is adequate exposure to English, but students from languages other than English do not necessarily receive adequate exposure to the African languages. Often African languages taught as subjects in these schools are inadequately resourced and not highly valued. The result has been the loss of proficiency in the home language by African-language-speaking pupils (Waner, 2002). Moreover, other pupils fail to learn an African language effectively. However, it is in these schools that most of the initiatives toward promoting multilingual learning in the classroom have taken place. Although only state-run schools are described in this chapter, private schools in South Africa tend to resemble urban suburban state schools. English is the language of instruction and the majority of pupils are from higher-income socioeconomic groups, with scholarships being given to deserving pupils who are mainly African-language speakers.

From the school contexts outlined above, various challenges can be identified that face language educators attempting to create multilingual climates in schools and classrooms.

1. The major role that English plays as the primary medium of instruction in all schools in South Africa is one of the greatest challenges, since it has officially relegated the African languages to a secondary role. In rural and urban township contexts in particular, this situation has led to various strategies that use African languages in de facto ways to optimize learning. Three of these will be discussed below: strategic code-switching, preview–review, and translation.
2. The increasing presence of African-language speakers in the pupil population in urban suburban schools points to the need for affirming these students' cultural knowledge and building their self-confidence. This is achieved through intervention strategies that promote multilingual language awareness in multicultural classrooms. A number of ways of doing this are described below.
3. The difficulties that non-English-speaking children have in learning subject matter through the medium of English suggest that the major African languages need to be developed as languages of instruction and academic learning in order to provide a firm cognitive foundation for learning, rather than including them in ad hoc ways.
4. If the goal is to move previously marginalized African languages toward center stage in order to develop them as instructional

languages and promote language awareness, then it follows that adequate resources and time should be provided for the learning of African languages by speakers of both African and non-African languages in multicultural schools.

MULTILINGUAL INITIATIVES

In this section, a number of projects will be described that go some of the way toward achieving multilingual goals. Although they represent only a small sample of the many projects that currently are under way in South Africa, they have been selected, first, because they address the challenges outlined above in creative and effective ways, and, second, because not all of them have been widely reported elsewhere. All of these projects have one thing in common: the promotion of multilingualism in South African educational institutions.

Use of African Languages to Facilitate Learning

To optimize the learning experiences of pupils who have difficulty learning through English, teachers traditionally have used African languages to facilitate understanding. In contexts where the majority of pupils and teachers are African-language speakers, strategic code-switching is common (Moodley, 2003). In both rural and urban township schools, various studies have focused on the functions of code-switching between home languages and the medium of instruction (Adendorff, 1993; Murray, 2002). These include clarification, instruction, explanation, and asserting solidarity and in-group identity. Developing functional categories helps teachers appreciate the value of using a multilingual approach, thereby increasing tolerance for other languages in the classroom. It also serves to disabuse teachers and principals of deficit notions of codes and code-switching (Adendorff, 1993).

The preview–review method provides a more systematic approach that is suitable for fairly homogenous classes. The home language is used to introduce key concepts and subject matter in order to give learners a preview of the content of the lesson. Similarly, a review in the home language is provided at the end of the lesson to consolidate learning. An alternative form of this is the "home language into English" method, wherein the lesson begins in the home language in order to establish understanding of key concepts and subject matter, with a gradual transition to English (Smallbones, 2001). This approach systematizes code-switching, by maximizing the use of African languages to both facilitate understanding and promote multilingualism.

One project in a multicultural school used translations of African folk tales and other stories into the African language to achieve similar objectives at the foundation level. Taking maximum advantage of their abilities in oral storytelling, for example, the teacher asked the African-language speakers to tell the stories in isiZulu to the *whole* class, supported by dramatic performance, before introducing the children to the stories in English (Gounden, 2003). This approach served to increase the self-confidence of the African-language speakers while at the same time allowing the other learners to experience what it is like to only partially understand a lesson. The African learners also were able to gauge the success of their storytelling and dramatic efforts by the amount of story content other pupils understood. In this way, they were able to bring their prior knowledge to the task of new learning while at the same time exposing the other children to the African language in a natural, enjoyable way (Wildsmith-Cromarty & Gounden, 2006).

A second effort to encourage multilingual learning at the foundation level is a biliteracy program run by the Project for the Study of Alternative Education in South Africa (PRAESA) in a multilingual school in Cape Town. Children are in their second year of learning to read and write in English and isiXhosa simultaneously (Bloch, 2000). The focus is on the natural and creative use of the home language for meaningful expression. This type of program provides a foundation for using the home language as a vehicle for academic learning later on.

Language Awareness Activities

Yet another type of intervention for promoting multilingualism takes place in the multicultural schools, where various "language awareness" approaches are used. These approaches aim to develop understanding of the life experiences and diverse perspectives of other cultures and languages of the learners in a multilingual, multicultural classroom. At the dawn of the new democracy in South Africa, teachers in the urban suburban schools experienced increased anxiety with the sudden influx of children from diverse cultural and linguistic backgrounds. Many of these teachers, however, responded to it as a challenge and devised innovative and creative ways in which to reach *all* the pupils in these classrooms (Smallbones & Clarence-Fincham, 1997).

These language awareness activities include multilingual games, poems, songs, plays, and the use of colloquial expressions that draw on the pupils' multilingual backgrounds, thereby affirming their knowledge and building self-confidence. Activities range from the use of translation as a technique to pool the knowledge of learners from different language backgrounds when discussing colloquial expressions to describe everyday events or phenomena (Versveld, 1995), to exploring the reasons why various languages express the same phenomena or events differently. Through these techniques, learners begin to understand the close relationship between language and identity, and the fact that multilingualism is actually an expression of multiple identities (Agnihotri, 1995). Another technique is the use of specific cultural genres, such as a Xhosa praise poem to an Arum lily, as a bridge toward the understanding of more scientific genres, for example, plants in a biology lesson (Kenyon & Kenyon, 1996).

The use of drama further encourages an open exploration of various sociocultural issues surrounding language. This includes a critical language awareness perspective, which aims to uncover the hidden norms operating in the classroom and make explicit the competing discourses in the classroom and how they either advantage or disadvantage certain students (Smallbones & Clarence-Fincham, 1997). In multicultural classrooms, there are diverse subject positions, identities, and frames of reference, which may lead to conflicts and tensions. Activities involving writing stories, songs, and plays that deal with such issues, and in which the discourses of *all* students may be accommodated, such as songs and colloquial expressions, help promote the view of language as a resource rather than as a problem (Smallbones & Clarence-Fincham, 1997).

Development of African Languages in Education

Research at the University of the Witwatersrand, Johannesburg, on the effects of using English as the medium of instruction on the home language (Jordaan & Suzman, 2002; Waner, 2002) revealed that absolute proficiency levels (Bialystok, 2001) of Zulu learners in both their home language and English, across regions and school types, were not as high as they should have been for academic learning, thereby highlighting the need for the development of CALP in both English and the home language.

isiZulu was selected as the home language in this study, since its use as an additional language of neighborhood communication, particularly in metropolitan areas, appears to be strengthening across all educational levels (Pan South African Language Board, 2001). The study investigated Zulu pupils' understanding, at the end of the primary level, of key concepts drawn from materials in the Language, Literacy, and Communication; and Mathematical Literacy, Mathematics, and Mathematical Sciences learning areas of the new curriculum. The concepts that occurred most frequently in these two areas were used to construct a test that would reveal learners' proficiency levels in the two languages. The concepts were first built into test items in English and then translated into isiZulu, with a further back-translation into English in order to ensure greater validity (Brislin, 1970). The tests were administered to Zulu mother tongue learners in three types of schools: urban multicultural schools in Johannesburg, urban township schools in Soweto, and rural schools in KwaZulu-Natal. These schools represented varying degrees of exposure to the two languages in their educational contexts. The results were not unexpected. Relative proficiency was found to be dependent on the degree of exposure to a language and on whether it was used as a language of learning (Jordaan & Suzman, 2002; Waner, 2002). However, the low levels recorded for absolute proficiency in both languages is a cause for concern.

The challenge for both researchers and educators is to find ways to encourage the development of cognitive academic language proficiency in classrooms where the medium of instruction is not the home language, and where the home language is not sufficiently developed to carry the academic content. Two projects that have attempted to address this problem are the Home Language Project (HLP) (Owen-Smith, 2005; Rodseth & Rodseth, 2004) and the Concept Literacy Project (CLP) (Young, Van der Vlugt, & Qanya, 2004), both of which have supported the development of African languages for instruction by providing learning materials at the secondary level.

The HLP addresses the issue of mother tongue loss in urban multilingual schools by promoting the learning of more than one African language alongside the official language of learning and teaching (English), and by encouraging African pupils to use their home language as a "cognitive and linguistic frame of reference" (Rodseth & Rodseth, 2004). Teachers are shared among school clusters, and pupils are grouped according to language clusters (Nguni, Sotho) so that they may withdraw from mainstream classes once a day for an hour to learn their home languages as first languages. This project challenges the current practice in the Gauteng region of selecting only one of the nine official African languages as an additional language of study, especially in schools with a wide range of local languages as mother tongues. Although the selected language is taught as a "first" language, not all African children use the selected language as a home language, and often both first- and second-language speakers are grouped together in these classes, thereby lowering the level of achievement expected of the first-language speakers, and increasing the level of difficulty for the second-language speakers. The HLP counters the negative effects of this practice by encouraging multilevel teaching and using the African-language speakers as assistants in the language study classes. In addition, the project encourages teachers of other subjects in the schools to make use of the home language in their classes wherever possible. It also provides literature and other reading material in the African languages for extensive reading purposes and encourages home support.

For teachers in schools that are not well resourced, this project offers a template for inservice educator training that will help them to provide home language development for their learners. It also has demonstrated the positive effects that learning in the home language can have on the self-image of the learners and their attitude toward their language (Owen-Smith, 2005).

The CLP (Young et al., 2004) is based at the University of Cape Town and collaborates with applied linguists and academics involved in science and mathematics education at the Universities of KwaZulu-Natal and Rhodes. It focuses on providing home language annotations in teacher-support materials for core scientific and mathematical concepts in three languages: Afrikaans, isiXhosa, and isiZulu. Mathematical and scientific content is checked for accuracy before it is translated into the various home languages. Although the focus is on providing support for learning mathematics and science through English as the main MOI, it also develops academic concepts in the African languages through translations, which are then presented to teachers in workshops for feedback. Some of the findings to date have been in the isiZulu project, where the mixed feelings that teachers initially had with respect to the use of isiZulu as an instructional language stemmed from their own difficulty in switching to isiZulu, as their professional language was English; in addition, they did not perceive isiZulu as a resource for learning and teaching. Thus, the teachers had to learn how to apply isiZulu to knowledge construction (Vygotsky, 1930/1978), and this, in turn, encouraged them to start thinking in their own home language about the concepts they were teaching. Another finding related to the issue of a standard variety of isiZulu as opposed to non-standard varieties. Many teachers did not recognize some of the translated terminology in isiZulu (Wildsmith & Gordon, 2006). The terminology had been newly coined by the various language boards constituted for the very purpose of standardizing the language. Thus, when teachers encountered the unknown vocabulary, they resorted to English as a *lingua franca* to teach the terms and then used isiZulu to explain the meaning of the terms to the learners. The results of this process eventually feed into the work of the National Lexicography Units and Language Development Research Centres established by the government to develop these languages for instructional purposes.

Finally, there are two initiatives designed to develop academic content in an African language at the tertiary level that are worthy of mention here because of the "backwash" effect they could have on the schools. The first is the establishment of the first bilingual degree at the University of Limpopo, with English and an African language (Sesotho sa Leboa–Northern Sotho) as languages of instruction (Joseph & Ramani, 2004; Ramani & Joseph, 2002; Ramani, Kekana, Modiba, & Joseph, 2007). This degree offers two parallel majors: Multilingual Studies, offered in Northern Sotho, which aims to develop CALP in the African language as well as create specialists in multilingual issues, and Contemporary English Studies, offered through English, which aims to develop students' proficiency in English to a high level. The researchers responsible for the establishment of this degree have sought to transfer resources from English-language pedagogy, learning materials, and academic readings to Sesotho sa Leboa through the training of African-language-speaking teaching assistants and the translation of key texts. Furthermore, Ramani and colleagues (2007) argued for developing discipline-specific terminology through the pedagogical process. This project has had an empowering effect on both teachers and students, as students have researched the cultural and communicative resources in their own communities and critically reflected on their own multilingual repertoires (Ramani et al., 2007).

The second initiative at the tertiary level stems from the work of PRAESA at the University of Cape Town, where a bilingual Xhosa–English approach has been used in the Advanced Certificate in Multilingual Education (Heugh, 2002).

Learning African Languages

One way to develop and promote a language and increase its status in a society is to teach it as an additional language in educational institutions. However, the learning and teaching of African languages as subjects in state schools has hitherto been poorly resourced and understaffed. In some regions, multicultural schools have made little provision for teaching African languages, as either a first or an additional language (Chick & McKay, 2001). Where they are offered, both L1 and L2 pupils are grouped together in the same class. Native-speaking teachers often are drawn from other subject areas, so they are not professionally trained to teach language. On the other hand, non-native-speaking teachers who are trained language teachers may not necessarily be very proficient in the African language (Wildsmith & Godlonton, 1997). Often these teachers use the L1 children in the class to provide peer support for the L2 learners. Either way, neither group is receiving the type of instruction required for optimal language learning. In addition, the pedagogy used for teaching African languages has tended to focus on language structure, and consequently learning the language becomes an intellectual exercise rather than the development of a tool for meaningful communication. Research has shown, however, that L2 learners generally feel positive about learning African languages and genuinely wish to speak them in order to be able to communicate with their peers (Wildsmith-Cromarty, 2003a).

To address the pedagogical problems surrounding the teaching of African languages, a study was mounted at the University of KwaZulu-Natal that was aimed at revising the first-year isiZulu curriculum (for L2 speakers) and transforming pedagogical practices from the bottom up—that is, from the learner's point of view (Wildsmith-Cromarty, 2003b). One of the researchers joined the course as a learner and, with the collaboration of her co-learners and the teachers, embarked on a qualitative, longitudinal study of the experiences of the learners with regard to the course content, the way it was presented, the choice of learning materials, and the classroom pedagogy. Findings from diary studies of observations and reflections, questionnaires on specific issues arising in lessons and materials, and interviews with both teachers and students revealed ways in which more communicative approaches might be implemented. In response to the findings, the teachers revised their practices and materials as the course progressed, until a far more communicatively oriented course had been developed (Wildsmith-Cromarty, Gordon, & Godlonton, 2007).

This was an organic process, involving various role reversals for teachers and learners, but the experience afforded valuable insights into both the nature of effective language teaching and the nature of multilingualism. A backwash effect of this research was that the results were fed into another course for mother tongue speakers who were learning how to teach isiZulu as a subject at the secondary school level.

FUTURE DIRECTIONS

This chapter has described some of the abundant multilingual contexts and practices that are found in South African state schools. Clearly, more must be done to promote multilingual competence for all learners, thereby increasing exposure to the country's indigenous and exogenous languages as a societal resource, while at the same time addressing the language rights of all speakers. Future research should focus on the nature of multilingualism, both individual and collective; language development; language awareness; and language teaching.

Nature of Multilingualism

More research is needed into multilingual speakers' use of their respective languages according to topic, context, and function, and how this is affected by their level of competence in each language in their repertoire. We need to ascertain whether we are dealing with variable competence (a measure of competence according to a monolingual norm) or *multiple competencies* (a measure of competence according to a multilingual norm) (Cook, 1992, 1995). If we recognize multilinguals as fully proficient speakers who happen to draw on more than one language in order to fulfill various communicative purposes, and who have specific configurations of linguistic competencies that reflect unique interactions among the languages they know (Cenoz & Genesee, 1998), then we need to take this into account when specifying languages of instruction. This also has implications for the development and use of a standard variety of each language, particularly in multilingual contexts where learners use a mixed code for everyday interaction.

Indigenous Language Development

There needs to be a serious move toward using African languages for learning, particularly in situations where teachers and pupils share the same language. At a recent workshop on the standardization of African languages in South Africa, a distinction was made by Deumert (2005) between "standard languages" and "language standards." Standard languages tend to be derived prescriptively from language boards and lexicography units, whose job it is to monitor and prescribe "acceptable and appropriate" language use in terms of grammar and to create terminology for academic purposes. This often leads to alienation from the language on the part of urban learners who speak a mixed variety. However, mixed varieties of the indigenous languages are seldom used by choice for writing (Lafon, 2005), which has implications for the development of CALP in these languages.

Language standards, on the other hand, imply a bottom-up approach to standardization in which regularity is based on how people actually use a language in everyday communication. This implies the use of variable standards, which might be more accessible to learners in the short to medium term. In the long term, however, "the development of fully-fledged standard languages is an imperative in linguistic communities which are internally diverse . . . particularly . . . for the production of educational material" (Deumert & Webb, 2005, p. 7). This is important for CALP development, since pupils typically have had very little experience writing in their mother tongues and often find it difficult. A multilingual approach to early literacy development, such as Bloch's (2000) biliteracy approach, is one way of addressing this problem. Developing standard varieties is also important for teaching the indigenous languages as additional languages.

Language Awareness

Language awareness activities in multicultural classrooms need to be increased. South African educators in multicultural schools need to encourage respect for all languages rather than be threatened by them. Ideally, teachers should be at least bilingual (one of the languages being an African language) or multilingual. Subject teachers must be helped to use other languages when necessary, or work in collaboration with teachers of an African language. More activities that draw on all languages equally, such as drama, poetry, dance, and games, need to be fostered in multicultural classrooms.

Language Teaching

Finally, since teaching a language as a second or an additional language improves its status, a major effort needs to be made to encourage others to learn African languages. A more radical move would be to use African languages as languages of instruction for certain subjects, which really translates into the content-learning approach to language acquisition. A condition for effective language teaching is, of course, the availability of literature in the language. This is something that needs far more attention in South Africa—the development of a critical mass of creative writers in the various languages.

Progress in the above areas will ensure that South Africa moves toward a multilingual climate within a metaphor of abundance beyond policy and into multiple practices in all its educational institutions.

REFERENCES

Adendorff, R. (1993). Teacher education: Code-switching amongst Zulu-speaking pupils and their teachers. *South African Journal of Applied Language Studies, 2,* 13–26.

Agnihotri, R. (1995). Multilingualism as a classroom resource. In K. Heugh, A. Siegruhn, & P. Pluddemann (Eds.), *Multilingual education for South Africa* (pp. 3–7). Johannesburg: Heinemann.

Anthonissen, C., & Gough, D. (1998). A pragmatic or purist approach to language standards: Implications for outcomes-based education. *Per Linguam, 14,* 39–53.

Bialystok, E. (2001). *Bilingualism in development: Language, literacy, and cognition.* New York: Cambridge University Press.

Bloch, C. (2000). Don't expect a story: Young children's literacy learning in South Africa. *Early Years: An International Journal of Research and Development, 20,* 57–67.

Bosch, B., & de Klerk, V. (1996). Language attitudes and their implications for the teaching of English in the Eastern Cape. In V. de Klerk (Ed.), *Focus on South Africa* (pp. 231–250). Amsterdam: John Benjamins.

Brislin, R. W. (1970). Back-translation for cross-cultural research. *Journal of Cross-Cultural Psychology, 1,* 185–216.

Cenoz, J., & Genesee, F. (1998). Psycholinguistic perspectives on multilingualism and multilingual education. In J. Cenoz & F. Genesee (Eds.), *Beyond bilingualism: Multilingualism and multilingual education* (pp. 16–32). Clevedon: Multilingual Matters.

Chick, K., & McKay, S. (2001). Teaching English in multi-ethnic schools in the Durban area: The promotion of multilingualism or monolingualism? *Southern African Linguistics and Applied Language Studies, 19*, 163–178.

Constitution, SA. Act No.108 of 1996. Pretoria: Government Printer.

Cook, V. (1992). Evidence for multi-competence. *Language Learning, 42*(4), 557–591.

Cook, V. (1995). Multi-competence and the learning of many languages. *Language, Culture & Curriculum, 8*, 93–98.

Cummins, J. (2000). *Language, power and pedagogy: Bilingual children in the crossfire*. Clevedon: Multilingual Matters.

Deumert, A. (2005). The notion of a "fully-fledged standard language." In *The Standardisation of African Languages in South Africa*, report on a workshop held at the University of Pretoria, South Africa, pp. 17–34.

Deumert, A., & Webb, V. (2005). Framework for an investigation into the status of the standard forms/varieties of South Africa's African languages. In *The Standardisation of African Languages in South Africa*, report on a workshop held at the University of Pretoria, South Africa, pp. 7–13.

Gounden, J. (2003). *A balanced reading approach for grade one and two English L1 and EAL learners*. Unpublished masters dissertation, University of KwaZulu–Natal, Pietermaritzburg, South Africa.

Heugh, K. (2002). Editorial. *Perspectives in Education, 20*(1), vii–x.

Jordaan, H., & Suzman, S. (2002). The effects of English education on home language competence. *Proceedings from University of Natal's Annual SAALA Conference*, Pietermaritzburg, South Africa.

Joseph, M., & Ramani, E. (2004). Academic excellence through language equity: A new bilingual BA degree (in English and Sesotho sa Leboa). In *Curriculum responsiveness: Case studies in higher education* (pp. 237–262). Pretoria: South African Universities Vice-Chancellors' Association.

Kenyon, A., & Kenyon, V. (1996). Evolving shared discourse with teachers to promote literacies for learners in South Africa. In D. Baker, J. Clay, & C. Fox (Eds.), *Challenging ways of knowing: In English, mathematics and science* (pp. 19–28). London: Falmer Press.

Lafon, M. (2005). IsiZulu and isiSoweto in Gauteng schools. *Proceedings from University of Pretoria's Workshop on the Standardization of African Languages of South Africa*, pp. 133–136.

Mahlalela, B., & Heugh, K. (2002). *Terminology and schoolbooks in Southern African languages: Aren't there any?* (Occasional Papers No. 10). Cape Town: PRAESA.

McCormick, K. (2002). Code-switching, mixing and convergence in Cape Town. In R. Mesthrie (Ed.), *Language in South Africa* (pp. 216–234). Cambridge: Cambridge University Press.

Mesthrie, R. (Ed.). (2002). *Language in South Africa*. Cambridge: Cambridge University Press.

Moodley, V. (2003). *Language attitudes and code-switching behaviour of facilitators and learners in language, literacy and communication senior phase outcomes-based education classrooms*. Unpublished doctoral dissertation, University of Natal, Durban, South Africa.

Murray, S. (2002). Language issues in South African education: An overview. In

R. Mesthrie (Ed.), *Language in South Africa* (pp. 434–448). Cambridge: Cambridge University Press.

Ntshangase, D. (2002). Language and language practices in Soweto. In R. Mesthrie (Ed.), *Language in South Africa* (pp. 407–418). Cambridge: Cambridge University Press.

Owen-Smith, M. (2005, May 6). Maths and science education: It's the language mix that counts. *Business Day*, pp. 10–11.

Pan South African Language Board. (2001). *Language use and language interaction in South Africa: Final report on a National Sociolinguistic Survey* (PanSALB Occasional Papers No. 6). Pretoria: Author.

Ramani, E., & Joseph, M. (2002). Breaking new ground: Introducing an African language as medium of instruction at the University of the North. *Perspectives in Education, 20*(1), 233–240.

Ramani, E., Kekana, T., Modiba, M., & Joseph, M. (2007). Terminology development vs. concept development through discourse: Insights from a dual-medium BA degree (in Sesotho sa Leboa and English). *Southern African Linguistics and Applied Language Studies, 25*(2), 207–221.

Rodseth, W., & Rodseth, V. (2004). Developments in the Home Language Project (HLP) since SAALA 2002. *Proceedings from the International SAALA 2004 Conference on Multilingualism*, University of the North, South Africa.

Skutnabb-Kangas, T. (1988). Multilingualism and the education of minority children. In T. Skutnabb-Kangas & J. Cummins (Eds.), *Minority education: From shame to struggle* (pp. 9–44). Clevedon: Multilingual Matters.

Slabbert, S., & Finlayson, R. (2002). Code-switching in South African townships. In R. Mesthrie (Ed.), *Language in South Africa* (pp. 235–257). Cambridge: Cambridge University Press.

Smallbones, M. (2001). When teachers can't speak their learners' mother tongues: Are language aides the solution? *Proceedings from the International Literacy Conference*, Cape Town, South Africa.

Smallbones, M., & Clarence-Fincham, J. (1997). I'm not so sure about all this rainbow nation stuff: Developing critical awareness in a multilingual classroom. *Proceedings from the 17th Annual Conference of the Southern African Applied Linguistics Association*, Johannesburg, South Africa.

South Africa. (2002). *Language policy for higher education*. Pretoria: Government Printer.

Versveld, R. (1995). Language is lekker: A language activity classroom. In K. Heugh, A. Siegruhn, & P. Pluddemann (Eds.), *Multilingual education for South Africa* (pp. 23–27). Johannesburg: Heinemann.

Vygotsky, L. S. (1978). *Mind in society: The development of higher psychological processes* (M. Cole, Trans.). Cambridge, MA: Harvard University Press. (Original work published 1930)

Waner, N. (2002). *The understanding of key words in the grade seven curriculum by ESL learners in English and their home language*. Unpublished masters dissertation, University of the Witwatersrand, Johannesburg, South Africa.

Wildsmith-Cromarty, R. (2003a). Do learners learn Zulu the way children do? A response to Suzman. *South African Journal of African Languages, 23*, 175–188.

Wildsmith-Cromarty, R. (2003b). Mutual apprenticeship in the learning and teaching of an additional language. *Language and Education, 17,* 138–154.

Wildsmith-Cromarty, R., Gordon, M., & Godlonton, M. (2007). African language curriculum reform at tertiary level from both learners' and teachers' perspectives. *Proceedings from the 38th Annual Conference on African Linguistics and the 11th Annual Conference of the African Language Teachers' Association,* University of Florida, Gainesville.

Wildsmith-Cromarty, R., & Gounden, J. (2006). A balanced reading programme for grade one and two learners of English as a first and as additional language. *Per Linguam, 22*(1), 1–22.

Wildsmith-Cromarty, R., & Young D. N. (2006). Applied linguistics in Africa. *Encyclopedia of Language & Linguistics* (2nd ed., Vol. 1, pp. 336–342). Amsterdam: Elsevier.

Wildsmith, R., & Godlonton, M. (1997). Teaching and learning Zulu as a second language. *Proceedings from the 25th South African Association for Language Teaching (SAALT) 1997 Annual Conference,* University of Natal, Pietermaritzburg, South Africa.

Wildsmith, R., & Gordon, M (2006). The role of the home language in learning mathematics and science. *Proceedings from the Joint Annual SAALA/LSSA Conference,* University of KwaZulu-Natal, South Africa.

Young, D., Van der Vlugt, J., & Qanya, I. (2004). Concept literacy and language use in maths and science in teaching the national curriculum. *Proceedings from the International SAALA Conference on Multilingualism,* University of the North, South Africa.

4

African Cityscapes and Schools

Imagining Multilingual Education

Tope Omoniyi

In this chapter, I analyze the multilingual complex constituted by three "international schools" in relation to language policy within the Lagos City school system and the postschool social worlds for which the pupils are being prepared. I attempt to identify the global and local sociolinguistic forces at play and the roles that elite schools might play in working out the tensions between them, with particular reference to Lagos as an African urban setting. I argue that although private international schools are located on the margins of urban multilingual education, they are adequately resourced to serve as laboratories for multilingual education programs.

Ohun ti o je mi logun ninu ori yii ni pe mo satupale ilaa eto eko olopo ede ninu awon ile-iwe meta kan ti awon akekoo ibe je orisiirisii eya ati omo oniruru orileede. Mo se agbekale itupale mi naa ni ibamu pelu ilana ajemo-ede ti ijoba ipinle Eko n samulo re lowolowo ninu awon ile-iwe won gbogbo. Bee, afojusun ise iwadii mi yii ni lati mo iru igbesi-aye ati awujo ti awon akeko wonyi yoo dara po mo leyin ola nigbati won ba pari eko won tan. Mo saapon lati toka irisi at isoro ajemo ede to n doju ko omo eniyan lode agbaye lapapo ati ni ese-kuku. Bakan naa, mo sagbekale ipa ti ile-iwe awon omo otonkulu awujo n ko ki n le baa raye se igbelewon irisi imo-ede awon ile-iwe bee ati ogunlogo ile-iwe miiran to wa yi won ka ni igboro ilu Eko kan naa. A oo si kiyesi pe ilu Eko je okan pataki ninu awon ilu nla-nla ti o wa ni ile Afirika. Mo wa fi ero mi han wi pe bi o tile je wi pe igboro awujo ibi ti ogunlogo ede ti n ba ara won se akolukogba ni awon ile-iwe adani wonyi tedo si, iwulo iwa papo won ni lati baa je ki awon ile-iwe naa da bi osuwon ati dingi ti a le lo lati wo ilana eto-eko awon akekoo olopo-ede laarin awujo ni.

Discussions of multilingualism and multilingual education with reference to postcolonial African cities and nations often are framed within a discourse of resistance to cultural assimilation or domination by former colonial languages. In other words, researchers focus on the promotion of local languages in education and other domains, thus putting them on the same pedestal as English and French. This is in addition to patriotism, the sole agenda of which is to assert the capacity of indigenous languages to support cognitive development and knowledge production (Omoniyi, 1994, 2003b). The resistance perspective assumes a binary opposition between former colonial languages and African languages, but it ignores the fact that there is an equally problematic hegemonic relationship between major and minoritized African languages. Yet, speakers of languages in the latter group, taken together, may constitute a majority percentage of a nation's total population. Furthermore, it often is assumed that African cities are racially and culturally homogeneous and that "African" connotes Blackness. In reality, in the era of globalization, racial and cultural homogeneity increasingly has given way to diversity and hybridity in African cities. The human flows responsible for this may be the consequence of relocation or dislocation; the former is a matter of choice (e.g., pursuit of a better life), while the latter is compelled by circumstances over which people have no control (e.g., war). In this chapter, I will examine the intricate connections between globalization and multilingual education in sub-Saharan Africa, investigate the tensions between the provisions of language policy and the multilingual urban reality, and explore demographic data on the racial and ethnolinguistic composition of three private schools in Lagos, Nigeria, as a basis for imagining multilingual education in the city.

There is still a dearth of critical literature on the multilingual situation in sub-Saharan Africa, and consequently the futurism implicit in "imagining" multilingual schooling can be an arduous task. Before I set out, I need to provide a context.

BACKGROUND

In postcolonial African nations where African and European languages coexist in a state of diglossia, with all the ideological implications of such a relationship, schools have become a platform for global and local sociolinguistic forces to play out the tensions between them. Heller (1996), following Bourdieu (1977), describes education as "a key site for the construction of legitimate language" (p. 139), thus establishing schools as a microcontext in which the politics of multilingualism is made manifest.

The Expatriate Community as Minority

In differentiating between bilingual communities, Edwards (1998), based on Ogbu's (1991) research, identifies two kinds of minorities: voluntary and involuntary. In her view, the contrast in the United States between children from China and Japan, who "tend to enjoy far greater academic success" (Edwards, p. 1), and African-American and African-Caribbean children, who often underperform in school, is a result of differences in their historical trajectories. I will evoke a slightly different sense of minority to characterize the expatriate community and the elites in a "multilingual and complex urban mosaic" (Williams & Van der Merwe, 1996, p. 50) like Lagos City. They often are excluded from discussions of multilingualism and multilingual education in the postcolonial city, but are significant in relation to globalization as an externally driven social process. Members of this Type 1 minority send their children to elite private schools and provide a more global perspective on the language dimensions of national and international migration. The expatriate community is made up of members of the diplomatic corps and their families and foreign employees of either multinational companies or smaller-scale private transnational businesses.

Within this Type 1 minority is a sizeable community of Western Europeans and Americans and local elites for whom the point of reference from a social and cultural point of view is the West rather than the local multilingual African context. They reflect the tensions articulated by Coupland (2003) as follows:

> Globalization is proving to be the salient context for an increasing number of sociolinguistic experiences. The qualities of linguistically mediated social experience that define "local"—inhabitation of social networks, social identities, senses of intimacy and community, differentials of power and control—all potentially carry an imprint from shifting global structures and relationships. (p. 466)

Members of minority ethnolinguistic groups form Type 2 minorities, for whom the frame of reference is the sociocultural, economic, and political milieu presented by their respective African nations. So, for instance, Setswana is ascribed its status and functions in relation to the other languages of the polity called Botswana (Nyati-Ramahobo, 1999). Similar relationships exist between Hausa, Igbo, and Yoruba, and the 400 other languages of Nigeria (Bamgbose, 1991) and between Akan, Ewe, and Twi, and the 250 other languages of Ghana (Dakubu, 1988). Social and cultural ties between Type 1 and Type 2 minorities are often weak or nonexistent. Together they form a broader local sphere, but understandably they respond differently to globalization.

In Lagos, the Type 1 minority exists as a satellite community located on Victoria Island and in Ikoyi in the southeastern corner of the sprawling state of Lagos, which has an estimated population of 12 million. Metropolitan Lagos has an average population density of 20,000 per square kilometer (Lagos State Government, 2004). The density is much lower on Victoria Island and in Ikoyi. In colonial times, these locations constituted the "European Quarters." During post-independence, they were known as the Government Reservation Area, which was inhabited by top government functionaries, company executives, and expatriates. In terms of resources and sociocultural characteristics, the community represents the global perched on the edge of the local. The difference is often clear from architecture to food, and entertainment to education. In other words, the two worlds are not integrated, or only superficially so. Members of the type 1 minority feel minimal pressure to assimilate into the less affluent national mainstream, preferring instead to orient themselves toward the global mainstream.

Lagos City is a "mini-Nigeria" in that its population includes most if not all of the ethnolinguistic groups that make up the nation. While these groups are largely mixed in distribution, there are cluster communities of nonindigenous ethnic groups (i.e., non-Yoruba) in parts of the city. For instance, the Agege and Ajegunle districts have large Hausa and Igbo settlements, respectively. This pattern has direct relevance to the expected language of instruction (LoI) and language of communication (LoC) in schools for particular areas in relation to the language in education policy.

Multilingual Schools

There are two ways of conceptualizing multilingual schools. One way is to regard them as schools whose pupils come from different ethnolinguistic and cultural backgrounds. This is the situation in most urban schools around the world. There were, for instance, by the late 1980s, children from about 170 language groups enrolled in London schools (Edwards, 1996). This increased to over 300 by the turn of the century (Baker & Eversley, 2000). Unfortunately, there are no readily available and accurate data on the demographic distribution of pupils in Lagos schools. However, it is generally believed that many of Nigeria's 250 ethnic groups are represented in Lagos, which gives an indication of the multiethnic composition of the city's schools.

The second way of conceptualizing multilingual schools is a more pedagogical view defined by a focus on the presence of multiple languages in the school curriculum as well as, in some cases, more than one language of instruction to cater to the diversity of the school population. Trilingual schools in the Grand Duchy of Luxembourg exemplify these (Lebrun &

Beardsmore, 1993). By their composition and charter, international schools may be regarded as a nursery for cultivating global citizenship, as articulated by Lynch (1992), when they are not mere national schools on foreign soil (de Mejía, 2002).

Ruth Hill Useem coined the phrase *third culture kids* to describe the intercultural children of international schools, a major field of research (Pollock & Van Reken, 2001) that includes multilingualism and multiculturalism as core interests. The schools affiliated with the diplomatic missions of European states in Lagos are "national schools" in de Mejía's (2002) sense. They are mainly monolingual in the official language of the state, but may teach other European languages as subjects. They do not offer Nigerian languages, or do so only nominally. While socioeconomic class may unite expatriate children and the children of local elites in the private schools, their wider community networks are differently constituted. In other words, the third culture of the school they participate in may be anchored to different root cultures, evidence of which may surface in communicative exchanges.

Since these schools subscribe to exogenous standards of Western European languages, such as Standard British or American English, Française Parisienne, and Berliner Deutsch, their type 1 minority students may never know or meet the broad range of native speakers in their respective home nations. Besides, since their contexts of socialization are so different, it is doubtful that they share similar norms with their compatriots and nurse similar expectations from life.

GLOBALIZATION AND MULTILINGUAL EDUCATION

Multilingual education is a complex concept. Colin Baker (1996) echoes Cazden and Snow's (1990) sentiments in pointing out the imprecision of "bilingual education" as an umbrella label for "education that uses and promotes two languages" and "education for language-minority children" (p. 172). The degree of complexity is conveyed by the different objectives associated with transitional and maintenance bilingual education and the inclusion of language majority children in enrichment bilingual education programs (Ferguson, Houghton, & Wells, 1977; Otheguy & Otto, 1980). These variations suggest that peculiarities of contexts and objectives are bound to determine what perspective on multilingual education is most suitable. In other words, models may vary from one place to another, especially in urban settings. Certainly there are lessons to be learned from looking at other bilingual education policies and programs, such as those of the New York State Education Department (1989). However, the notion is arguably more complex in a context like urban Lagos, where there are not only multiple frames of reference arising out of the colonial historical trajectory, but also varied definitions of majority and minority groups, as I suggested in differentiating between Type 1 and Type 2 minorities. When globalization is factored into this complex equation, the result is a greater, but not insurmountable, challenge for policymakers and educational planners.

Shifts in global structures now alter and shape local sociolinguistic realities. Notions such as the World Bank's Millennium Development Goals and Education for All operate on global principles, but their social consequences are understood only when localized to specific geocultural and political contexts (UNDP, 2005).

In more specific terms, the impact of globalization on multilingual education may be manifested in a number of ways. The global flow of goods and services as it applies to the education sector includes the movement of teachers and educational managers, curriculum content, theories and methodologies of teaching and learning, literature, and so on. The involvement of agencies such as the World Bank and UNESCO in funding education in the developing world serves as a direct link to the globalization network and all the rhetoric associated with these institutions (Ilon, 2002; Klees, 2002). With particular reference to multilingual education and multilingual schools in sub-Saharan Africa generally and Nigeria in particular, I will identify five categories of languages.

Major languages of instruction such as English and French have global capital linked to them and occupy the top of the hierarchy of languages within a multilingual city. These languages serve as mediums of instruction in addition to being offered as curriculum subjects. Other European languages of instruction, like Italian and German, serve the "national schools on foreign soil" (House, 2003, p. 557) and derive additional clout from their status as native languages of member states of the European Union suprastate. These languages are used as mediums of instruction as well as being offered as curriculum subjects in a few schools. Other expatriate languages, like Turkish, Chinese, and Arabic (Lebanese), serve established immigrant community schools. Local African languages in the curriculum are restricted by the National Policy on Education to the first 4 years of primary schooling. Some are offered as subjects on the margins of international school programs. Competence in these languages generally is not considered a measure of educational achievement.

There are many African languages that are neither a medium of instruction nor a subject in the curriculum. They occupy the lowest rung of the hierarchy of languages and have no capital attached to them with respect to the educational system. They are of interest, however, since the language policy specifies that the languages of the immediate community should be used in the early years of schooling (Federal Republic of Nigeria, 1991).

GLOBAL/LOCAL TENSIONS

Globalization impacts elite international schools through transnational curricula, the recruitment of foreign staff, and the pupils' anticipation of nonlocal futures. Let us turn briefly to the tensions created by these forces.

Educational Standards and Attitudes

Private-sector involvement in the provision of education may be rationalized in two ways.

- The burden is too heavy for government alone to bear. This argument represents local investors in the education sector as patriotic, sympathetic, and liberal, and downplays the fact that they service a privileged clientele while placing such institutions beyond the reach of the average local wage earner. In other words, they sustain an elite class in much the same way as public schools in Britain and private schools in the United States do.
- The private sector provides a desirable alternative to a defective system of public education. This viewpoint represents private investors as radical, revolutionary, and critical of an incompetent establishment.

Private education providers sometimes cite both of these rationales as motivation. For instance, the proprietors of the British International School in Lagos claim in their promotional video that

> for some time now in our dear country Nigeria, solid and qualitative education for our fast-growing leaders of tomorrow has been so hard to come by until BIS came to the fore in 2001, September 17th to be precise. . . . The task of providing solid, standard, qualitative education should not be left to the government alone to handle, hence the establishment of the British International School. (Paramole-Shabi, n.d.)

Implicitly, *international* is synonymous with *foreign*, which in postcolonial Africa is preferred to the local, an attitude that permeates other areas of social life as well. From an ideological point of view, this attitude sustains the philosophy on which private education rests; more important for our purposes here, it has an impact on bilingual education policies that include local languages and partially accounts for their occasional failure. The UNESCO-funded Ife Six Year Primary Mother-Tongue Education Project in the 1960s in Nigeria is a case in point. Even though the project proved beyond doubt that the children who went through it not only caught up with their peers in the control group, but actually surpassed them in English-language proficiency by the time they were in higher education (Afolayan, 1976), the recommendations did not translate wholesale into policy.

Language, School, and Community

Schools serve as preparatory ground for entry into a larger postschool world. Thus the LoI and LoC become immensely relevant in characterizing that larger community. Generally, English serves as a *lingua franca* (ELF) among staff and students in Lagos schools outside of the formal classroom. This is understandable, considering that English is the common denominator for the bilingual school-going population of urban Lagos. House (2003) separates these two language functions in arguing that English as a *lingua franca* does not constitute a threat to national languages, as has been widely reported in the literature. His argument that "the ELF speaker cannot be measured in his/her competence vis-à-vis 'the native speaker'" (p. 557) directly opposes what Blommaert (2003), in the same volume of the *Journal of Sociolinguistics*, observes to be the practice in evaluating African immigrants in Western urban contexts.

> The English acquired by urban Africans may offer them considerable prestige and access to middle-class identities in African towns. It may be an "expensive" resource to them. But the same variety of English, when spoken in London by the same Africans, may be a crucial object of stigmatization and may qualify them as members of the lower strata of society. What is "expensive" in Lusaka or Nairobi may be very "cheap" in London or New York. (p. 616)

For our present purposes, the latter claim must be understood within a language ideological framework. It suggests an asymmetrical relationship both between the languages available (or not) in schools and between urban communities in Africa on the one hand and European urban communities of native speakers of the LoI in African schools on the other. It is an acknowledged mission of these schools to prepare children for life in the West, what sometimes is described as anticipatory socialization (cf. Henslin, 2004), and includes all aspects of culture—morals, social practices, tastes in entertainment, sports, and so on. Pitched within the existing framework of globalization, English and French as the LoI and LoC in African schools undermine not only language rights, but all other rights that the liberal world supposedly puts in place to ensure egalitarianism. The linguistic market is tilted against the indigenous languages so that multilingual education and multilingualism that include these languages prepare pupils only for what Blommaert described as the "lower strata" in a global society.

A number of other issues arise. Those third culture children who are native speakers of Western European languages are shortchanged from the perspective of not having access to the multilingual curriculum that their peers in the school system in Europe are exposed to routinely through schools that have a growing supranational vision. On the other hand, while non-European children (African, for instance) enrolled in the schools may acquire bilingual skills in English plus an African language, they do not fit the bilingual mold considered efficient for the New Europe, that is, possession of functional competence in two or three European languages (mother tongue + 1; mother tongue + 2). When the third culture cultivated in these schools becomes globalized through dispersion on graduation, it is debatable whether these two categories suffer the same repercussions or gain the same advantages. The inequalities within existing social structures are not erased locally or translocally. I will now attempt to illustrate the issues I have raised in the discussion so far, by looking at three private schools in urban Lagos as contexts of multilingual education.

A TALE OF THREE SCHOOLS

The data collection for this study was carried out in three international schools in Lagos, Nigeria: the British International School and the sister schools Saint Savior's School, Ikoyi, and Saint Savior's School, Ebute-Metta. These were chosen because their international status indicated that they served a multinational clientele. There are several such schools in Lagos, but in the end I went with these three because my social network guaranteed relatively unencumbered access to the administrators. The data consist of interviews with the heads or their representatives, enrollment data, and an examination of the curriculum.

None of the three schools has a formal bilingual education program in place despite the diversity of the students. Notwithstanding the relatively high standard of education that they offer, these schools do not explore the potential for multilingual education that they represent. This corroborates the usual suspicion that official monolingualism is the rule rather than the exception in elite schools (Carder, 1995).

St. Savior's School, Ebute-Metta, and St. Savior's School, Ikoyi

The two St. Savior's schools were established within months of each other in 1951 to serve the needs of an expatriate community by providing initial education to their children. The first of these schools was located inside the Railway Compound, Ebute-Metta, the headquarters of the Nigeria

Railway Corporation, a major employer of foreign personnel at the time. Thus the site was the hub of expatriate society in Lagos in the period leading up to independence in 1960. However, the city's social geography has changed dramatically since then, and Ebute-Metta has developed into a high-density, relatively lower-income suburb. The pupils were mostly Nigerian, with a few from neighboring West African countries like Cameroon. There was not a single European child on the school register.

The second school was located to the southeast of the city, where Ikoyi and Victoria Island have emerged as new bourgeois districts through federal government and corporate investments. Currently, this area has the largest settlements of expatriates in Lagos. The international character of the school at Ikoyi is used for marketing purposes as if it were an indication of quality education. The 300 pupils represented 12 nationalities, of which four were African: Nigerian (241), Ghanaian (4), South African (3), and Cameroonian (2). Other nationalities represented were Indian (9), British (7), Canadian (3), Lebanese (2), Italian (1), Chinese (1), Russian (1), and Bangladeshi (1). The observed shortfall of 25 between the distribution of pupils by nationality and the claimed total pupil registration gives an idea of the difficulty of eliciting reliable statistical information in this context.

In its 1998/99 annual report, the Board of Management at Saint Savior's School, Ikoyi, notes the following:

> The school will adhere to, but not be limited by, the requirements of the National Curriculum for England, whilst recognizing the importance of the culture of the host country.

The model curriculum includes English as a core subject and modern foreign languages as noncore foundation subjects. Interestingly, according to the administrative manager at the Ikoyi school, both French and Spanish were offered as optional subjects, with 3 half-hour periods a week. In following the National Curriculum for England, international school pupils become participants in a British as well as a European supranational cultural network.

St. Savior's School, Ikoyi, recruits a native speaker of English as head tutor, while its sister school in Ebute-Metta has a Nigerian in that role, a reflection of the fact that they serve different clienteles. Although not explicitly stated, it was implied during fieldwork inquiries that the head tutor was a major factor in expatriate and elite parents' decisions on where they enrolled their children. In a sense, a postcolonial hangover in attitudes means that in the public psyche, a White expatriate head tutor is still seen as an indication of a school's high educational standards. It is difficult to determine what specific factor motivates parents most to enroll their children in these elite schools. Nevertheless, there are ideological issues associated with enrollment in these schools from the point of view of imagining the future of multilingual education and multilingualism. For one thing, citizenship education in this context is more complicated because of the overseas frames of reference.

British International School, Lagos

The British International School (BIS), founded in 2001, was

> conceived, nurtured and specially designed by a group of Nigerian Private Promoters, without any financial contributions whatsoever, from any Government, foreign or local. BIS remains wholly and solely a purely "Private Initiative" of patriotic Nigerians. (Paramole-Shabi, n.d.)

Thus what is essentially a commercial enterprise has been packaged as a public service. BIS is set on a 30-acre site on Victoria Island, which is described as "the choicest part of one of Africa's most popular commercial cities, Lagos in Nigeria." About 75% of the staff received part or all of their educational training in British institutions.

BIS may be described as a multilingual school following the models presented earlier under "Multilingual Schools." The school community includes nationals from 38 countries, the majority of whom have more than one language in their communicative repertoires. Out of a total of 54 students in Year 8, 22 are monolingual speakers of English, but it is not clear whether they are native or non-native speakers. Table 4.1 shows the language distribution for the rest: 31 bilinguals (English + *X*) and one trilingual (English + *X* + *X*). It is obvious from this distribution that English is fundamental to the bilingual model in this community. Since the data were elicited from teachers rather than from the students themselves, it is not clear whether some of these bilinguals have any competence in other local languages, which would make them "unbalanced" trilinguals or even quadrilinguals.

Although English is the predominant LoI at BIS, French, German, and Spanish are taught as subjects and used as mediums of instruction for teaching these language classes, in line with the pedagogical norm in language classrooms in the UK. In contrast, Yoruba is offered as an optional "cocurricular activity" in the same slot as such nonacademic activities as sports, drama, and debating. A communicative language-teaching approach is adopted, and pupils are supervised in actual interactional contexts where they are expected to demonstrate their proficiency in spoken Yoruba (e.g., haggling and buying items in the nearby market). Community members

Table 4.1. BIS multilingual index for Year 8 (2004)

Locals		Foreigners	
English and Second Language	*Number*	*English and Second Language*	*Number*
Yoruba	5	Spanish	5
Hausa	3	Afrikaans	3
Igbo	2	Hindi	3
Ijaw	2	Dutch	2
Isoko	1	Bangla	1
Ibibio	1	Arabic	1
		Danish	1
		Korean	1
		Portuguese and Norwegian	1

are aware of these exercises and enjoy facilitating the process. A not unusual problem is that trained Yoruba teachers are not always available on the staff, so native speakers of Yoruba in other programs are coopted as auxiliary teachers. This scarcity of teachers is similar to that reported for French in Nigerian schools (Omoniyi, 2003a), a reflection of the lameness of claims about the functions and status of languages in the National Policy for Education.

Languages in the Curriculum

One way in which majority or minority status is ascribed to a language is through inclusion in or exclusion from the school curriculum. The private schools in my study follow the National Curriculum for England on behalf of their targeted clientele—children of expatriates or the local Nigerian elite. As a result, English has a privileged slot. A few schools operate on an American system, with the same results. The objective is that upon graduating, children should be able to go on to complete their education in Europe or the United States. The pupils take Cambridge syndicated examinations and/or the SAT Reasoning Test, a college entrance examination in the United States. Slots for languages in the school schedule also corroborate the implicit inequality of status between the languages in most cases. With regard to the various scales of reference at the community, national, supranational, and global levels (see Blommaert, 2003), combinations of languages in the curriculum have varying implications and values attached to them.

In the weekly schedule for Primary 1 at St. Savior's, Ebute-Metta (see Table 4.2), Yoruba has only one slot, whereas English is taught in several slots—grammar, spelling, composition, comprehension, and word building. This is in addition to the fact that it is also the LoI in all subjects except Yoruba. A fairly similar pattern was observed in the schedule at the British International School, where English was allocated 6 hours a week, French had 4 hours, and 1 hour was devoted to "others," which included indigenous languages like Yoruba.

Since private schools are not obligated to follow the National Policy for Education, the imbalance observed in the language distribution is understandable. Public and private education provisions are driven by different missions and visions, and if they differ sufficiently, especially

Table 4.2. Weekly schedule for Primary 1 at St. Savior's, Ebute-Metta

<table>
<tr><th>Time</th><th>Monday</th><th>Tuesday</th><th>Wednesday</th><th>Thursday</th><th>Friday</th></tr>
<tr><td>8:00–8:15</td><td colspan="5">Assembly</td></tr>
<tr><td>8:15–8:45</td><td rowspan="2">Math</td><td>Math</td><td>Workbook</td><td rowspan="2">Arts</td><td rowspan="2">Games</td></tr>
<tr><td>8:45–9:15</td><td>Grammar</td><td>Math</td></tr>
<tr><td>9:15–9:45</td><td>Grammar</td><td>Grammar</td><td>French</td><td>Math</td><td>Yoruba</td></tr>
<tr><td>9:45–10:15</td><td>Reading</td><td>Music</td><td>Quantitative</td><td>Reading</td><td>Math</td></tr>
<tr><td>10:15–10:45</td><td colspan="5">Break</td></tr>
<tr><td>10:50–11:20</td><td rowspan="2">Comprehension</td><td rowspan="2">Nature education</td><td rowspan="2">Social studies</td><td>Word building</td><td>Composition</td></tr>
<tr><td>11:20–11:50</td><td>Handwriting</td><td>Moral instruction</td></tr>
<tr><td>11:50–12:20</td><td>Poetry</td><td>Handwriting</td><td>News</td><td rowspan="2">Computer</td><td>Library</td></tr>
<tr><td>12:20–12:50</td><td>Music</td><td>French</td><td>Health</td><td>Spelling</td></tr>
<tr><td>12:50–1:20</td><td>Scripture</td><td>Spelling</td><td>Gardening</td><td>Verbal</td><td>Word building</td></tr>
<tr><td>1:20–1:30</td><td colspan="5">Rounding off</td></tr>
</table>

ideologically, their coexistence has a potential to impede the national development that initially may have motivated the national policy. Conflict, suspicion, and distrust accompany the hegemonic structure that unequal access to resources puts in place in a polity. Consequently, elite private schools may work at cross-purposes with the state in spite of their stated objective of contributing to its development. Their microlanguage planning and policy focus (Kaplan & Baldauf, 1997) potentially can conflict with the goal of nation building that the Nigerian educational philosophy pursues through its promotion of indigenous languages alongside the official languages—English and French—at least according to the letter if not as yet the spirit. Omoniyi (2003a, 2004) provides a detailed discussion of the language politics at play in the region.

IMAGINING MULTILINGUAL EDUCATION

Compared with the local state schools, BIS and other international schools of its kind have a broader-based curriculum, and a greater potential in terms of resources and a suitable context for offering an elaborate multilingual education program that includes Nigerian languages and thus serves citizenship education more usefully. The "multilingual education" currently offered is characterized by a focus on European rather than Nigerian socialization. The fact that these schools operate under the National Curriculum for England may be taken as indicative of their Nigerian/African clients' attitudes toward membership in imagined Anglocentric global and local community networks.

On the other hand, children who are native speakers of the nine European languages represented in these international schools anticipate complete integration into the European system upon their return home. However, in reality they may not be sufficiently equipped to integrate successfully as a result of the growing dynamism of school curricula in Europe in response to its ethnolinguistic diversity. Another missing element in this replica "offshore" curriculum that may impede subsequent integration is the minority languages of immigrants that define the politics of the UK and European language-in-education contexts.

These international schools are likely to experience the pressures of globalization differently from the Nigerian public schools and the foreign national schools. Their tuition fees often are quoted in US dollars, which ties them to a global financial system, unlike the state schools. At BIS, the annual fees are $10,000 for day students and $17,000 for boarders. It is worth noting here that the estimated average annual wage in the Nigerian civil service until recently was estimated to be about $3,000.

The schools, which include the American International School, set Victoria Island and Ikoyi apart from Mainland Lagos in terms of characterizing Lagos City's multilingual landscape. Public schools supposedly follow the National Policy on Education, which requires the use of indigenous languages as languages of instruction in the first 4 years of primary schooling. In principle, the dominant ethnic group in a particular location determines the choice of LoI. This leaves room for variation in bilingual models in operation in the city based on population distribution and the concentration of ethnic groups in particular districts.

CONCLUSION

In this chapter I have revisited the concept of minority and, in relation to language groups, differentiated between Type 1 and Type 2 minorities, thus identifying a group that often is invisible in the literature on multilingualism, that is, the group of Europeans who have migrated to African cities. The social architecture of postcolonial cities reflects a socioeconomic segregation in which different sections have different language ecologies, that is, languages come together in everyday environments in different ways. These different ecologies form Lagos's multilingual mosaic. It is within this mosaic that the international schools, which were the context of my investigation, use their curriculum to socialize pupils for a future in Western locations.

The issue that arises for the international schools is whether their language curricula are able to accomplish multilingual socialization without support from the sociocultural environment that the same curriculum enjoys in the UK. If these international schools lack the dedicated administrative structures equivalent to those of Brussels for the EU schools, the question I ask is, How can the African city multilingual mosaic, as found in Lagos, assist the international schools in accomplishing a multilingual socialization?

African cityscapes, from the point of view of multilingualism, constitute a complex terrain. It is impossible to talk of a unified school system, considering the differences between the objectives of public and private stakeholders. Different visions and objectives among administrators are bound to impact differently on individuals and groups. Nevertheless, this diversity is a positive attribute that can be developed further (May, 2001; Skutnabb-Kangas, 2000) as proposed through the iZemia perspective of language in this volume.

The issue, then, is to work out ways of harmonizing diversity in order to create models that focus on creating a more egalitarian and just world. The private education sector, and especially elite schools such as the international schools that informed this study, have the resources and potential to push for multilingualism. What is immediately necessary, however, is the introduction of purposeful and research-based model multilingual programs that are broad enough to serve both as a space for socializing expatriate students for the Western world and, at the same time, as a means of integrating them into the worlds in which they live by creating at least awareness of, if not proficiency in, indigenous languages. Only then can these dual-purpose education programs serve the cause of burgeoning liberal democracy in the sub-Saharan region.

NOTE

I am grateful to Roehampton University for funding fieldwork in Nigeria. I wish to thank Mr. Ken Baines and his staff at BIS, and Mrs. Ronke Bajowa and Mrs. E. U. Otah of St. Savior's School, in Ikoyi and Ebute-Metta, respectively, for their kind assistance during data collection. I thank the editors of this volume and Professors Viv Edwards (Reading University) and Nkonko Kamwangamalu (Howard University) for their useful comments on an earlier draft. Finally, I am grateful to Dr. Abiodun Ogunwale, Department of African Languages, Obafemi Awolowo University, Ile-Ife, for providing the Yoruba translation of my abstract.

REFERENCES

Afolayan, A. (1976). The six-year primary project in Nigeria. In A. Bamgbose (Ed.), *Mother tongue education: The West African experience* (pp. 113–134). London/Paris: Hodder & Stoughton/UNESCO.

Baker, C. (1996). *Foundations of bilingual education and bilingualism* (2nd ed.). Clevedon: Multilingual Matters.

Baker, P., & Eversley, J. (Eds.). (2000). *Multilingual capital: The languages of London's school children and their relevance to economic, social and educational policies*. London: Battlebridge.

Bamgbose, A. (1991). *Language and the nation: The language question in Saharan Africa*. Edinburgh: Edinburgh University Press.

Blommaert, J. (2003). Commentary: A sociolinguistics of globalization. *Journal of Sociolinguistics, 7*(4), 607–623.

Bourdieu, P. (1977). The economics of linguistic exchanges. *Social Science Information, 16*, 645–668.

Carder, M. (1995). Language(s) in international education: A review of language issues in international schools. In T. Skutnabb-Kangas (Ed.), *Multilingualism for all* (pp. 113–157). Lisse: Swets & Zeitlinger.

Cazden, C., & Snow, C. E. (1990). English plus: Issues in bilingual education. *Annals of the American Academy of Political and Social Science, 508*, 9–11.

Coupland, N. (2003). Introduction: Sociolinguistics and globalization. *Journal of Sociolinguistics, 7*(4), 465–472.

Dakubu, E. (1988). *The languages of Ghana*. New York: Kegan Paul.

de Mejía, A. M. (2002). *Power, prestige and bilingualism: International perspectives on elite bilingual education*. Clevedon: Multilingual Matters.

Edwards, V. (1996). *The other languages: A guide to multilingual classrooms*. Reading, England: Reading Language and Information Center.

Edwards, V. (1998). *The power of Babel: Teaching and learning in multilingual classrooms*. Stoke-on-Trent: Trentham Books.

Federal Republic of Nigeria. (1991). *National policy on education* (Rev. ed.). Yaba, Lagos: NERDC Press.

Ferguson, C. A., Houghton, C., & Wells, M. H. (1977). Bilingual education: An international perspective. In B. Spolsky & R. Cooper (Eds.), *Frontiers of bilingual education* (pp. 159–194). Rowley, MA: Newbury House.

Heller, M. (1996). Legitimate language in a multilingual school. *Linguistics and Education, 8*, 139–157.

Henslin, J. (2004). *Essentials of sociology: A down-to-earth approach* (5th ed.). Boston: Allyn & Bacon.

House, J. (2003). English as a lingua franca: A threat to multilingualism? *Journal of Sociolinguistics, 7*(4), 556–578.

Ilon, L. (2002). Agent of global markets or agent of the poor? The World Bank's education sector strategy paper. *International Journal of Educational Development, 22*, 475–482.

Kaplan, R. B., & Baldauf, R. B., Jr. (1997). Specific purpose language planning. In R. B. Kaplan & R. B. Baldauf, Jr. (Eds.), *Language planning from practice to theory* (pp. 240–265). Clevedon: Multilingual Matters.

Klees, S. J. (2002). World Bank education policy: New rhetoric, old ideology. *International Journal of Educational Development, 22*, 451–474.

Lagos State Government. (2004). Retrieved September 20, 2004, from http://www.lagosstate.gov.ng/directory/list.php

Lebrun, N., & Beardsmore, H. B. (1993). Trilingual education in the Grand Duchy of Luxembourg. In H. B. Beardsmore (Ed.), *European models of bilingual education* (pp. 101–120). Clevedon: Multilingual Matters.

Lynch, J. (1992). *Education for citizenship in a multicultural society*. London: Cassell.

May, S. (2001). *Language and minority rights: Ethnicity, nationalism and the politics of language*. London: Longman.

New York State Education Department. (1989). *Regents policy paper and proposed action plan for bilingual education*. Albany: Author.

Nyati-Ramahobo, L. (1999). *The national language: A resource or a problem: The implementation of the language policy of Botswana*. Gaborone, Botswana: Pula Press.

Ogbu, J. U. (1991). Minority coping responses and school experience. *Journal of Psychohistory, 18*(4), 433–456.

Omoniyi, T. (1994). *Price-tagging child bilingualism: An evaluation of policy and the socio-economic and political implications of commercialisation of nursery education in Nigeria*. (ERIC Document Reproduction Service No. ED 365 160)

Omoniyi, T. (2003a). Language ideology and politics: A critical appraisal of French as second official language in Nigeria. In S. Makoni & U. H. Meinhof (Eds.), *Africa and applied linguistics* (pp. 13–25). Amsterdam: John Benjamins.

Omoniyi, T. (2003b). Language policies and global forces: Multiliteracy and Africa's indigenous languages. *Language Policy, 2,* 133–152.

Omoniyi, T. (2004). *The sociolinguistics of borderlands: Two nations, one community.* Trenton, NJ: Africa World Press.

Otheguy, R., & Otto, R. (1980). The myth of static maintenance in bilingual education. *Modern Language Journal, 64*(3), 350–356.

Paramole-Shabi, Y. (Producer & Director). (n.d.). *The giant leap for education in Nigeria: The British International School* [Publicity DVD]. (Available from YPCE Communications, Lapal House, Lagos, Nigeria).

Pollock, D. C., & Van Reken, R. E. (2001). *Third culture kids: The experience of growing up among worlds.* Yarmouth, ME: Nicolas Brealey and Intercultural Press.

Skutnabb-Kangas, T. (2000). *Linguistic genocide in education—or worldwide diversity and human rights?* Mahwah, NJ: Erlbaum.

Williams, C., & Van der Merwe, I. (1996). Mapping the multilingual city: A research agenda for urban geolinguistics. *Journal of Multilingual and Multicultural Development, 17*(1), 49–66.

5

Toward Bilingualism in Multiethnic Slovakia

The Formal Education of Ethnic Hungarians

Ildikó Vančo

This chapter presents a brief overview of the history of the Hungarian ethnic minority and of its formal education in Slovakia from 1918 to the present. The Slovak educational system will be described, with special emphasis on the Hungarian minority schools functioning in Slovakia. I argue that in bilingual situations, the minoritized language suffers a decrease in linguistic registers as it constantly encounters the majority language. The significant factors in terms of language maintenance and a range of registers are family, school, and the ethnic makeup of a given settlement. The question is how the minoritized schools can achieve a high level of bilingualism while expanding the social spaces for minoritized language use and thus the expansion of as many registers as possible.

Tanulmányom rövid áttekintést nyújt a szlovákiai magyar kisebbség történetéről és oktatásáról 1918–tól napjainkig. A szlovákiai oktatási rendszert a magyar kisebbség iskolahálózatának szempontjából mutatom be. Foglalkozom a nyelvmegtartás szempontjából meghatározó tényezőkkel, mint a család, iskola és a települések etnikai megoszlása. A kérdés az, hogy a kisebbségi iskolarendszer segítségével hogyan érhető el magas szintű kétnyelvűség oly módon, hogy ugyanakkor a kisebbségi nyelv használata minél több regiszterben valósulhasson meg.

In this chapter, I argue that the Hungarian language situation in Slovakia raises questions about how a minoritized language's efforts to support and strengthen its language can play a role in moving the nation toward acknowledging its multilingual reality. I begin with a brief historical overview of the contact between the Hungarian and Slovakian ethnic groups within the Slovakian state, followed by a close look at formal education in Slovakia and how the nation's language policies affect the Hungarian population. I argue that in bilingual situations, minoritized languages, such as Hungarian within Slovakia, suffer a decrease in linguistic registers as they constantly encounter the majority language. The acceptance of this situation is critical to moving with confidence toward building new social spaces for language use within the reality of bilingualism.

BRIEF HISTORY OF THE HUNGARIAN MINORITY IN SLOVAKIA

The Hungarian nation settled in the Carpathian basin in the 11th century. What began as the Kingdom of Hungary became, in 1867, part of the Austro-Hungarian monarchy. When the monarchy collapsed at the end of World War I, independent Czechoslovak and Hungarian states were created. Due to political considerations, the border between the two countries was drawn much further south than the traditional Slovak–Hungarian linguistic borderline, leaving significant numbers of Hungarian speakers in Czechoslovakian territory.

The interwar period was characterized by a certain ambiguity. On the one hand, there was the destruction of the former Hungarian institutional system (e.g., closing down universities, schools); on the other hand, there were opportunities for creating cultural and political organizations. After World War II, the Hungarian language was severely restricted. Under the Beneš Decrees, all people of German and Hungarian nationality, except those with an active antifascist past, were deprived of their Czechoslovakian citizenship (www.cla.sk/projects/The Beneš Decrees). Between 1945 and 1948, 44,129 Hungarians were deported to Bohemia as forced labor, of whom only 24,000 returned after 1949 (Vadkerty, 2001). In addition, the Hungarian language was forbidden in public.

After the Communist takeover in 1948, the Hungarian minority regained its rights of citizenship, and in accordance with the "doctrine of proletarian internationalism," direct antiminority steps were not taken; however, there were many hidden efforts to assimilate and homogenize. The year 1989, when the Communist regime fell, has come to be known as the year of the change, as it was then that the development of a democratic institutional system began within Czechoslovakia. The present-day Slovak Republic was established in 1993, after the collapse of the former Czechoslovak Republic. As a result, in some regions, some of the older citizens of Slovakia have been members of six different states between the fall of the Austro-Hungarian monarchy (1918) and the present.

Despite the changes in government and the political ambivalence that arose from the fluidity of citizenship and the resulting loyalties, the linguistic and cultural situation has remained fairly stable in the sense that Hungarian is still spoken in Hungarian settlements, although, as we will see below, there is a threat of language shift.

Demographic Characteristics and the Fluidity of Identity Among Hungarians in Slovakia

Table 5.1 shows the distribution of nationalities in the population of Slovakia, based on census data from 1910 to 2001. The 1910 data come from the last census within Austria-Hungary, when minorities were identified on the basis of mother tongue. Later figures are based on self-report of nationality status. During this 90-year period, the Hungarian population has dropped from about one-third to a little less than one-tenth of the total population.

The total number of Hungarians in Slovakia is decreasing as well. In 1991, 567,296 reported that they were of Hungarian nationality, while in 2001 only 520,528 did so. This significant drop was caused not just by a 33% decrease in the natural birth rate among Hungarians be-

Table 5.1. Nationalities of Slovakia, 1910–2001 (in percentages)

Year	Total Population	Slovak	Hungarian	German	Ukrainian	Czech	Other
1910	2,919,794	57.82	30.29	6.79	3.33	0.26	1.52
1921	3,000,870	65.06	21.68	4.86	2.96	2.42	3.02
1930	3,329,793	67.61	17.79	4.65	2.86	3.65	3.43
1950	3,442,317	86.64	10.30	0.15	1.40	1.17	0.33
1961	4,174,046	85.29	12.43	0.15	0.85	1.10	0.18
1970	4,537,290	85.49	12.17	1.10	0.93	1.04	0.26
1980	4,991,168	86.49	11.21	0.06	0.79	1.15	0.31
1991	5,274,335	85.69	10.76	0.10	0.58	1.00	1.88
2001	5,379,455	85.79	9.68	0.10	0.65	0.83	2.96

Note: From Gyurgyík, 1994, and www.statistics.sk/webdata/english/census2001/. In 2001, the Other category included Polish, Romani, Croatian and Serbian, Jewish, Russian, and Vietnamese.

tween 1991 and 2001, but also by a large assimilation of Hungarians (Gyurgyík, 2006).

In the 1991 and 2001 censuses, people were asked to specify their native language as well as their nationality. In 1991, there were 40,925 more people reporting that their first language was Hungarian than reporting a Hungarian identity. In 2001, this difference was 52,401. These differences have a special significance for settlements where the number of minorities does not reach 20% according to nationality status but would reach 20% if the first language were used in calculating whether the minoritized language must be recognized officially.

The Hungarian Language in Slovakia

Hungarian belongs to the Finno-Ugric language family (for typological aspects of Hungarian, see Thomason, 2005). About one-third of speakers of Hungarian live outside Hungary as national minorities in neighboring countries. The Hungarian minority living in Slovakia is the second-largest after the one in Romania.

Certain phenomena of the Slovak Hungarian language variety differ from standard Hungarian, since variations in social and political situations have led to differences in language use (for the grammar of Hungarian outside Hungary, see De Groot, 2005). As a result of the bilingual environment in which the Hungarians in Slovakia live, language contact phenomena can be observed at all linguistic levels, mainly as borrowing at the lexical level. Examples of lexical borrowing are items of clearly Slovak origin; for example, Hungarian Slovak *horcsica* (mustard) from Slovak Slovak *horčica*, HS *nanuk* (ice cream bar) from SS *nanuk*, and so on. Some elements of the Slovakian variety of Standard Hungarian are now being codified (Lanstyák, 2000).

Colloquial and dialect elements appear to a greater extent in Standard Slovak Hungarian than in Standard Hungarian. Since the Slovak variety of Hungarian is not present in all arenas of language use, certain registers, especially language varieties for specific purposes, are missing. The Hungarian used in Slovakia may seem more archaic, since neologisms created in the home country enter more slowly into the Slovak variety, if they arrive there at all. It should be stressed, though, that in spite of these differences, most of the language uses and registers, that is, the language used in different social situations, of Slovak Hungarian are identical to the language varieties used in Hungary and are very well understood by speakers of Hungarian in Hungary and abroad. The colloquial variety of Slovak Hungarian is ranked between the first and second levels on the five-level borrowing scale elaborated by Thomason and Kaufman (1991), whereas there is minimal borrowing in the written variety (Lanstyák & Szabómihály, 2005).

Hungarian-language varieties of Hungary, especially Standard Hungarian, have high cultural prestige. Within this context, the Hungarian-language variety of Slovakia has low prestige, which most probably is related to the vernacular of the speakers and the contact-induced features characterizing their speech (Lanstyák, 2000). The Hungarians of Slovakia (especially teachers and other professionals) usually have a negative evaluation of the contact-induced features of Slovakian origin, the most stigmatized features being the loan words proper. However, most of the more "hidden" types of borrowing, such as semantic loans, are not even noticed by speakers (Lanstyák & Szabómihály, 2005).

Most Slovak Hungarian parents bring their children up with Hungarian as the language of the family, whereas the acquisition of the majority language takes place mostly in schools in an instructed form. Almost all members of the Hungarian minority speak Slovak at a very good level, and only an insignificant minority claim that they do not speak it. However, the expectations of the Slovaks that the Hungarians be able to speak the majority language at a perfect level create a power dynamic in their relationships.

LANGUAGE POLICIES AND PRACTICES IN SLOVAKIA

While there are other national minorities in Slovakia, I will focus on the Hungarian minority, as it is the largest and was once the group wielding the power of government. When Slovakia recently became a member of the European Union, the status of language minorities and language maintenance came into the limelight. In this sense, the treatment of the Hungarian language may be indicative of what is occurring in other minoritized-language groups with respect to language maintenance presently and what may be in store for them in the future.

Even though Slovakia is a multinational state, the Constitution officially declares that it is the state of the Slovak nation, thus implying a monolingual and monocultural country (Simon, 2002). Slovak is the only officially recognized language, and the state considers the use of a minoritized language as strictly an individual right. Therefore, people belonging to national minorities are expected to acquire the language of the majority in order to function successfully in the society they live in. Requests from minority communities that certain governmental positions require proficiency in a given minority language are regarded as discriminating against speakers of Slovak.

Laws broadening the possibilities for minoritized languages have been adopted by the Slovak government in response to conditions set by the Council of Europe and when it became a member of the European Union.

The legal status of minorities and their languages is determined at the highest level by the constitution law (www.concourt.sk) and by the international documents concerning minoritized language use accepted by Slovakia, including the 1990 Document of the Second Meeting of the Conference on the Human Dimension of the CSCE; Recommendation No. 1201 of the Parliamentary Assembly of the European Council of 1993; the European Charter for Regional or Minority Languages, signed in 1995 and operational since 2002 (http://www.coe.int/minlang); the Slovak-Hungarian Basic Treaty, operational since 1997 (www.htmh.hu); and the 1995 Framework Convention for the Protection of National Minorities (www.coe .int/T/E/human_rights/minorities). National minorities and ethnic groups have the right to maintain their cultural institutions and to disseminate information in their first language.

The Law on the State Language, passed in 1995, and the Law on Minority Language Use, in force since September 1, 1999 (www.culture .gov.sk/english), regulate language use in Slovakia. The Law on the State Language mandated the use of only Slovak in official circumstances and restricted the use of minoritized languages in other fields, with serious fines for breaches. This law generated international protests (Simon & Kontra, 2000). In 1999, the Constitutional Court and the Law on Minority Language Use repealed some of the measures, but most of them are still operational. It is possible to register names (first names and family names) in minoritized language form (under the 1993 Law on Names and Surnames and the 1994 Registers Act). The name of a settlement can be indicated in the minoritized language form on road signs only where the minority constitutes at least 20% of the population.

According to these laws, a minoritized language can be used while contacting the local government and state administrative units if the minority population is above 20%. However, those who established the current administrative units made it impossible for the 20% threshold to be exceeded in more than a few places. Here is where the way the census counts the mother tongue becomes significant. Based on the 2001 census, only 501 settlements meet this 20% Hungarian population requirement. Thus, there is enough evidence to say that while there has been progress on the legal front, implementation has not received sufficient attention.

THE EDUCATIONAL SYSTEM

Slovak Hungarians have a developed educational system because the Hungarian minority was allowed to maintain some of its previous elementary and higher elementary schools in Czechoslovakia after 1918. The minority educational system in Slovakia is an organic part of the Slovak educational system, and as such is characterized by the same organizational and curricular features as the majority Slovak system.

Education in Slovakia is compulsory until age 16. Elementary school is for 9 years (from age 6 through 15), followed by secondary education, which currently takes place in three kinds of schools: academic grammar schools, technical secondary schools, and vocational secondary schools. Academic grammar schools offer general education and prepare students mainly for higher education. The mission of technical secondary schools is to provide students with vocational secondary education leading to a school-leaving certificate. The mission of vocational secondary schools is to prepare students for skilled performance in workers' trades and professional activities.

There are state schools, private schools, and church schools at the secondary level. After passing final exams, students have a chance, if they pass entrance exams, to get a bachelor's and master's degree from an institution of higher education. Universities provide doctoral programs for students who have obtained a master's degree.

A joint Slovak–Hungarian management runs the school system—from nursery to secondary education. Certificates and all school documents are bilingual in elementary and secondary schools. The Ministry of Education regulates the content and form of the documents. Curricula and subject requirements are worked out by the National Institute for Education and approved by the Ministry of Education. They are identical in majority and minority schools. In certain cases (e.g., different views of the Versailles Treaty and its consequences, the evacuation of Hungarian nationalities after World War II, etc.), this leads to tensions as the language of contact is exclusively Slovak in both speech and writing.

Hungarian is the language of instruction within Hungarian schools. The biggest problems for the development of Hungarian to its fullest are a lack of materials and the scarcity of Hungarian-speaking specialists. The scarcity of Hungarian-speaking specialists also affects the possibility of teaching Hungarian in schools with Slovak as the medium of instruction. Thus, the teaching of Hungarian, even in Hungarian-language schools, is limited by the availability of human and material resources.

With respect to higher education, the only Hungarian education has been at the University in Nitra, where it was possible in some teacher training branches to study in Hungarian. The situation has been changing, however. As a result of intense political debates, a minority faculty for teacher training programs was established at the University in Nitra in 2004, and a university in Komárno for teacher training and economics majors opened its doors in 2004 (for the education of Hungarians, see Vančo, 2005).

The education indicators of the ethnic Hungarian population differ considerably from the national average and generally can be called unsatisfactory. As shown in Table 5.2, elementary school is the highest level completed for 30.5% of Hungarians compared with 21.1% for Slovaks. In contrast, 7.9% of Slovaks have college or university degrees compared with 4.5% of Hungarians.

Differences and inequities in the educational conditions of the minority and majority communities exist despite the democratic ideal of providing education for every citizen without discrimination. In Slovakia, the Hungarian community has been disproportionately undereducated since at least 1957 (Bauer & Bauer, 1997).

One reason for the lower rates of educational participation and attainment may be the lack of sufficient secondary-level schools and institutions of higher education in the Hungarian language. Another reason may be the low social status of the subjugated Hungarian minority. Presently most of the Hungarian population lives in rural settlements; all settlements that are more than 90% Hungarian have fewer than 5,000 inhabitants. As a result of the economic policies of preceding decades, Hungarian-populated areas have the worst demographic, economic, and social indices in Slovakia and are defined as underdeveloped regions where unemployment rates have been very high for many years.

Let us take a look at language policies and practices as a way of understanding the role of the Hungarian language in the educational conditions of the Hungarian population. As stated above, the status of the Hungarian language underwent many shifts, which are reflected in the degree of bilingualism among the Hungarian population. There are numerous definitions of bilingualism, depending on the criterion used, that is, language of origin, self- or external identification, competence, and/or function. Bilingualism may refer to individuals who are exposed to more than one

Table 5.2. Highest level of schooling completed, 2001

Type of School	Slovaks (%)	Hungarians (%)
Elementary school	21.1	30.5
Secondary vocational school	19.7	23.2
Secondary grammar and technical school with GSCE	29.4	24.8
College and university	7.9	4.5
Without qualification and unknown	1.9	1.2

Note: Data do not include children younger than 16.

language as a result of being born into a family that has a heritage language other than the dominant language (Skutnabb-Kangas, 1997). Another approach is to define bilingualism as the regular use of two (or more) languages, and bilinguals as people who need and use both of their languages in their everyday life (Grosjean, 1992). Most of the more than 90% of Hungarians in Slovakia who speak Hungarian as well as Slovak (Csepeli, Örkény, & Székely, 2000; Zel'ová, 1992) are bilinguals according to the latter definition.

The high levels of bilingualism among the Hungarians are directly related to the area of settlement. Children living in the mostly contiguous area of Hungarian settlements generally start the acquisition of the majority language when they enroll in elementary school. Those living in more scattered settlements normally start becoming bilinguals at kindergarten age (from 2 to 6).

Children going to schools where Hungarian is the language of instruction—with the exception of a few who come from mixed marriages—learn Slovak as a second language in school. In Hungarian elementary and secondary schools, there is one lesson a day. In kindergarten, for example, there are 30-minute Slovak "lessons" every day in which children learn the most common expressions of the Slovak language in a playful fashion. Until Grade 4 this lesson deals with the Slovak language; in higher grades, Slovak literature and grammar are taught as well. In secondary schools, the jargon of specific topics also is taught, enabling students to acquire specific registers that they might need in their future jobs or professions. Students must take a final exam in Slovak language and literature at the end of their secondary education.

About 20% of the school-age population end up attending elementary and secondary schools where Slovak is the medium of instruction, and approximately 50% of those attending technical secondary schools are in Slovak-medium schools (Lanstyák & Szabómihály, 2005).

The emphasis on Hungarian-language schools results in additive bilingualism. The first language is maintained and the second language (i.e., the language of the majority) is developed (Skutnabb-Kangas, 1984). However, this is not the case with Hungarian children going to school with Slovak as the language of instruction. They have no lessons at all in their first language. The classes are heterogeneous from a linguistic point of view—from monolingual Slovak to monolingual Hungarian with varying degrees of bilingualism. The objective is not the establishment and maintenance of bilingualism, but rather the establishment of Slovak monolingualism. In several reported cases, teachers have demanded the use of Slovak during breaks (Sándor, 2000). Thus, Hungarians in Slovak-only schools experience subtractive bilingualism.

In Slovak-only schools, the ties Hungarian students generate toward their first language and culture are looser than they would be in Hungarian-language schools. Students also are likely to accept uncritically the values of the majority, and thus more likely to experience language shift or assimilation. Their bilingualism slowly fades away because in certain registers they will lack the ability to use their first language. This shift impacts the language use in the family, since the child brings the language of the school into the family, and thus Slovak is likely to encroach on the means of communication at home (Lampl, 1999).

This monolingualization, which stigmatizes the minoritized language, leads not only to language loss but also to changes in identity and to the acceleration of assimilation. Sándor (2000) examined the factors of language maintenance and language loss with young people living in a settlement situated on the linguistic border and attending schools with either Hungarian or Slovak as the language of instruction. The children came from Hungarian or mixed marriages, but for all of them the dominant language at the beginning of their schooling was Hungarian. She found that the children who were educated in Slovak schools were more likely to change their identity and become Slovak-dominant bilinguals by the time they grew up.

OUTCOMES OF THE TWO KINDS OF SCHOOLING

There have been several investigations (Drábeková, 1993; Lanstyák & Szabómihály, 1997; Sándor, 1998; Vančo, 1999) that map the language use of Hungarian schoolchildren living in Slovakia in the Hungarian-language schools and in schools where Slovak is the language of instruction. When the performance of Hungarian students in Slovakia was compared with that of monolingual Hungarian children in Hungary, it was found that bilingual children going to schools where Hungarian was the language of instruction had more in common with the control group in Hungary than with bilingual children going to Slovak schools (Lanstyák & Szabómihály, 1997).

Vančo (2002), in a study of speech comprehension, suggests that in spite of the insignificant difference in Hungarian sentence comprehension between students in the two types of schools in Slovakia, there was a significant difference in terms of text comprehension, which attests to a weaker level of language processing in those being instructed in their second language rather than their first. While these two studies do not prove anything by themselves, what they and other studies from many parts of the world suggest is that minoritized-language maintenance is more likely within a minoritized language school system that promotes additive bilingualism. Minority education has two major tasks: It has to maintain the language and culture of the minority, and it has to establish a working bilingualism that the minority feels is not a burden, but rather some kind of treasure.

CONCLUSION

During the past 80 years, members of the Hungarian minority in Slovakia have managed to preserve their educational system, which is not only a sign of their desire to maintain their language but also a prerequisite for their bilingualism.

Because of the influence of the majority language, Slovak, the range of registers that the Hungarian minority uses in everyday language is not as varied as that used in Hungary. Moreover, while the Hungarian vernacular as used in Hungary is highly prestigious, the contact-induced variety used by the Hungarian minority in Slovakia has lower prestige. These differences between the bilingual and monolingual varieties of Hungarian stem from the fact that bilingual speakers of the language live in a different situation and consequently have different exposures and produce different language behaviors.

Recognizing this shrinkage of language registers and the shifts from monolingual Hungarian to different degrees of bilingualism to dominant Slovak, it is safe to state that there are two options for maintaining the viability of the Hungarian language beyond its use for interpersonal and familial affairs. The first option is to long for an ideal situation in which speakers will use the standard variety of Hungarian as naturally as the monolingual Hungarians do. The desire to do so may come from strong ties with the Hungarian nation, where the mother tongue plays a crucial role, or from a monolingual and ethnocentric point of view that is found not only in Slovakia and Hungary, but all over Europe.

The alternative option is for speakers to acknowledge that they are a community with its own language variety that is influenced, on the one hand, by the language of the majority and, on the other hand, by the standard variety of the home country. This option will pave the way for education and contribute to the multilingualism of Slovak society. It should enable students not only to maintain the minoritized language and culture but also to deal with bilingual situations. Within this context, researchers in linguistics have the task, first, of describing in detail and from many points of view the domains and situations of language use, and, second, of acting as language activists and professional leaders of language planning.

REFERENCES

Bauer, E., & Bauer, G. (1997). A kisebbségi iskola kulturális dilemmái [The cultural dilemmas of minority schools]. *Korunk, 10,* 101–110.

Csepeli, G., Örkény, A., & Székely, M. (2000). The steadiness and transformation of national-ethnic identity. *Minorities Research, 2,* 46–63.

De Groot, C. (2005). The grammars of Hungarian outside Hungary form a linguistic-typological perspective. In A. Fenyvesi (Ed.), *Hungarian language contact outside Hungary—Studies on Hungarian as a minority language* (pp. 351–370). Amsterdam: John Benjamins.

Drábeková, Z. (1993). A magyar-szlovák kétnyelvü diákok szlovák szókincsének néhány sajátosságáról [Some features of Slovak vocabulary of Hungarian–Slovak bilingual students]. *Hungarológia, 3,* 129–139.

Grosjean, F. (1992). Another view of bilingualism. In R. J. Harris (Ed.), *Cognitive processing in bilinguals* (pp. 51–62). Amsterdam: Elsevier Science.

Gyurgyík, L. (1994). *Magyar mérleg. A szlovákiai magyarság a népszámlásási és népmozgalmi adatok tükrében* [Measuring Hungarians: The Hungarians of Slovakia, as reflected in census and migration data]. Pozsony: Kalligram.

Gyurgyík, L. (2006). *A szlovákiai magyarság demográfiai, település-és társadalomsszerkezetének változása az 1990-es években* [The demographic, settlement and social changes of Hungarians in Slovakia in the 1990s]. Pozsony: Kalligram.

Lampl, Z. (1999). *A saját útját járó gyermek. Három szociológiai tanulmány a szlovákiai magyarokról* [The child that goes his own way: Three sociological studies on Hungarians in Slovakia]. Bratislava: Madách-Posonium.

Lanstyák, I. (2000). *A magyar nyelv Szlovákiában* [The Hungarian language in Slovakia]. Budapest and Pozsony: Osiris and Kalligram–MTA Kisebbségkutató Mühely.

Lanstyák, I., & Szabómihály, G. (1997). *Magyar nyelvhasználat–iskola–kétnyelvüség (Nyelvi változók a szlovákiai és magyarországi középiskolások néhány csoportjának nyelvhasználatában)* [Hungarian language use–school–bilingualism (Language variables in language use in some groups of secondary school students in Hungary and Slovakia)]. Pozsony: Kalligram.

Lanstyák, I., & Szabómihály, G. (2005). Hungarian in Slovakia. In A. Fenyvesi (Ed.), *Hungarian language contact outside Hungary—Studies on Hungarian as a minority language* (pp. 47–88). Amsterdam: John Benjamins.

Sándor, A. (1998). *A kétnyelvüség és a nyelvcsere összefüggése egy szlovákiai magyar beszélőközösségben* [The relationship between bilingualism and language shift in a Hungarian speech community in Slovakia]. In I. Lanstyák & S. Simon (Eds.), *Tanulmányok a magyar—szlovák kétnyelvüség köréből* [Papers about bilingualism] (pp. 116–135). Pozsony: Kalligram.

Sándor, A. (2000). *Anyanyelvhasználat és kétnyelvüség egy kisebbségi magyar beszélőközösségben, Kolonban* [Language use and bilingualism in a minority speech community, Kolon]. Pozsony: Kalligram.

Simon, S. (2002). Szlovákiai magyarok és nyelvtörvények [Hungarians in Slovakia and the language laws.] In M. Kontra & H. Hattyár (Eds.), *Magyarok és nyelvtörvények* [Hungarians and language laws] (pp. 25–52). Budapest: Teleki László Alapítvány.

Simon, S., & Kontra, M. (2000). Slovak linguists and Slovak language laws: An analysis of Slovak language policy. *Multilingua, 19*, 73–94.

Skutnabb–Kangas, T. (1984). *Bilingualism or not: The education of minorities*. Clevedon: Multilingual Matters.

Skutnabb-Kangas, T. (1997). *Nyelv, oktatás és kisebbségek* [Language, education and minorities]. Budapest: Teleki László Alapítvány.

Thomason, S. G. (2005). Typological and theoretical aspects of Hungarian in contact with other languages. In A. Fenyvesi (Ed.), *Hungarian language contact outside Hungary—Studies on Hungarian as a minority language* (pp. 11–27). Amsterdam: John Benjamins.

Thomason, S. G., & Kaufman, T. (1991). *Language contact, creolization and genetic linguistics*. Berkeley: University of California Press.

Vadkerty, K. (2001). *A kitelepítéstől a reszlovakizációig* [From deportation to re-Slovakization. Pozsony: Kalligram.

Vančo, I. (1999). Bujkáló anyanyelv. Tanítási óra alatti kódváltás, szlovák tannyelvü iskolában [Mother tongue in hiding: Code-switching during a lesson at school with Slovak as the language of instruction]. In I. Lanstyák & G. Szabómihály (Eds.), *Nyelvi érintkezés a Kárpát-medencében, különös tekintettel a magyarpárú kétnyelvüségre* [Language contact in the Carpathian basin with special regard to Hungarian-paired bilingualism] (pp. 87–94). Pozsony: Kalligram.

Vančo, I. (2002). A beszédészlelés és a beszédmegértés vizsgálata magyar–szlovák kétnyelvü gyermekeknél [Research on the speech perception and comprehension of Hungarian–Slovak bilingual children]. In I. Lanstyák & S. Simon, (Eds.), *Tanulmányok a kétnyelvüségről* [Papers about bilingualism] (pp. 71–92). Pozsony: Kalligram Könyvkiadó.

Vančo, I. (2005). *The Hungarian language in education in Slovakia*. Ljouwert/ Leeuwarden: Mercator-Education.

Zel'ová, A. (1992). The integration of the Hungarian minority in Slovakia: The language problem. In J. Plichtová (Ed.), *Minorities in politics: Cultural and language rights* (pp. 155–158). Bratislava: Czechoslovak Committee of the ECF.

6

Multilingual Primary Schools in Germany

Models and Research

Ursula Neumann and Hans-Joachim Roth

This chapter reports on a new development in Germany: Over the past 10 years bilingual primary school classes for grades 1–4 (grades 1–6 in Berlin) have been initiated. First the historical development that led to the founding of these classes is described. Then the results of their evaluation are presented. Subsequently, a school experiment conducted in Hamburg involving the language pairs Italian–German, Portuguese–German, Spanish–German, and Turkish–German is detailed. Included is a description of the pedagogical concept of the bilingual classes and the methodological design of the accompanying study. The development of the children's writing skills in both languages after 2 years in school is then discussed.

Berichtet wird über eine neue Entwicklung in Deutschland, wo in den letzten zehn Jahren an einzelnen Schulen bilinguale Grundschulklassen für die Jahrgänge 1 bis 4 (bzw. in Berlin bis Jahrgang 6) eingerichtet wurden. Dazu werden zunächst die wenigen vorliegenden Evaluationsergebnisse vorgestellt. Anschließend wird auf einen entsprechenden Schulversuch in Hamburg eingegangen, an dem die Sprachenpaare Italienisch–Deutsch, Portugiesisch–Deutsch, Spanisch–Deutsch und Türkisch–Deutsch beteiligt sind. Dargestellt werden das pädagogische Konzept der bilingualen Klassen, die methodische Anlage der Begleituntersuchung und die ersten Ergebnisse zur Entwicklung der Schreibfähigkeiten der Kinder in ihren beiden Sprachen nach Anlauf von zwei Jahren.

With the immigration of workers and refugees, Germany has developed into a multilingual society. The number of children growing up in families with a background of migration is approximately one in four; in cities, it is about one in three. At home, most of them hear and/or use languages other than German. Their socialization is bilingual.

Nevertheless, the prevailing habitus in public and at school is monolingual (Gogolin, 1994). The most important predictors of success in school, as international comparative school performance studies (Deutsches PISA Konsortium, 2001; Mullis, Martin, Gonzales, & Kennedy, 2003) have shown, are the level of competence in oracy and literacy in German. Germany has achieved relatively low scores in these studies. The social, linguistic, and psychological resources in languages other than German that children acquire with their families through the home languages are not integrated into the school environment in any significant way. Languages being taught as second languages are those with high social prestige, such as English and French. Latin has regained some significance lately. Some schools offer Spanish, but Turkish, Russian, and Farsi, languages spoken by the majority of immigrants in Germany, are not to be found in the school curriculum.

This policy regarding languages is juxtaposed with bilingual schools, where two languages are taught from the beginning of primary school. In this chapter we will distinguish between language of instruction (LoI) as the use of one or two languages for the transmission of knowledge, and the term *language teaching*, where "grammar, vocabulary, and the written and oral forms of a language constitute a specific curriculum for the acquisition of a second language other than the mother tongue" (UNESCO, 2003). In most cases of bilingual schooling, half the children in a class are proficient in only one of the languages, whereas classes are held in both languages. However, there are distinctions between different models as to how languages are utilized within the class. The Institute for Comparative and Intercultural Studies was appointed by the school administration to conduct a scientific evaluation of one of these experimental school settings. It was the Institute's aim to determine whether immigrant and minority children's language competence develops better under the conditions of bilingual schooling or in monolingual settings, and whether children speaking only German at the beginning can be supported in becoming bilingual. The aims of the school administration were somewhat wider: finding out whether bilingual schooling is effective in promoting bilingualism and in leading to better competence in German in children from a migrant background, or whether promoting bilingualism for German children is holding them back academically.

In this chapter, we provide an overview of the development of bilingual education in Germany. We will discuss how German schools reacted to linguistic diversity among pupils in the past and consider how they should react in the future. Therefore, we will present the current debate on the promotion of bilingualism in Germany. Subsequently, we will describe different models of bilingual education in German primary schools. The results of the evaluation of three bilingual models will follow this description. Then the evaluation of the Hamburg Experiment will be presented and discussed.

DEBATE ABOUT THE PROMOTION OF BILINGUALISM IN GERMANY

The innovative establishment of bilingual schools takes place within an ongoing debate about whether multilingualism should be publicly promoted as an expression of Germany as a multicultural society.

A monolingual habitus, a set of acquired patterns of thought, behavior, and tastes, runs through German schools, expressing itself in the beliefs and attitudes of students, parents, and teachers, as well as in the general structures of the school system. Starting with a relatively short (4–6 years) period in primary school, where learning takes place in a German-language setting, children then move on to their chosen form of secondary school. At that point, schools offer children a comparatively wide range of languages to study as subjects. On a nationwide scale, the dominant language at the secondary level is English. On a political level, the principle of federalism places the general responsibility for educational policy in the hands of the individual states (Bundesländer).

In keeping with the monolingual habitus, until the present time children of migrants were not seen as bilingual, but rather as children with support needs in the German language. With the increasing immigration of workers in the 1970s, so-called preparatory classes (Vorbereitungsklassen), which taught German as a second language, were instituted. They served to reduce the sole reliance on submersion as a way of introducing the German language to schoolchildren (Skutnabb-Kangas, 1986). This development of teaching German as a second language included organizational aspects as well as curricula, learning materials, and a specific training program for teachers. Based on bilateral agreements between Germany and the countries from which so-called guest workers (Gastarbeiter) used to be recruited, mother tongue instruction (muttersprachlicher Unterricht) is now available. Instruction provided in the mother tongue is a combination of religious education and "Sachunterricht" (i.e., a subject combining social studies and natural science) (Gogolin, Neumann, & Reuter, 2001). Along with the discussion in 1999–2000 about simplifying naturalization and the new law of immigration that came into effect on January 1, 2005, the aims and objectives of mother tongue instruction have been questioned. It is assumed to be in the public interest to foster a German nation-state and its democratic constitution. In other words, the government has to take care of proper instruction in the German language, whereas multilingual education—comparable to religious education—is not within the confines of government responsibility. Rather, multilingualism is a matter confined to the private sphere.

At the same time, on a political and public level, education decision makers have understood that early contact with languages other than German might make their acquisition easier and lead to better results in foreign languages like English and French at secondary school. In ordinary German schools now, classes in English start as early as Grade 3, with variations in border regions where French and Polish take the place of English. Some primary schools even offer English starting in Grade 1. In most cases, this takes the form of playfully introducing elements of language within the normal classes, for example, for 15 minutes a day. This practice, however, is completely independent of practices of language instruction for bilingual children from migrant families.

Occasional attempts to use the native languages of migrant children in the early teaching of foreign languages were made in the state of North-Rhine-Westphalia. However, this so-called interactive language learning (Begegnungssprachenunterricht), where language models of the language other than German were migrant children, did not gain acceptance. The main reason for its failure was that parents wanted the other language to be English.

BILINGUAL APPROACHES IN PRIMARY SCHOOL

Bilingual primary schools are still rare in Germany. While bilingual classes in secondary schools are quite common—mostly with French or English as the second language of instruction—only 6 of the 16 states offer classes in primary schools where children are able to learn how to read and write in two languages right from the outset. In Table 6.1 we present the range of languages offered by bilingual primary schools in Germany.

Most primary schools in Germany are run by the state and some of them recently have taken up bilingual programs. Most of them are situated in Berlin, where the Staatliche Europa-Schulen Berlin (SESB) offers 15 locations and 10 different languages in combination with German to teach children bilingually. The SESB should not be confused with the European Schools, which are official educational establishments controlled jointly by the governments of the member states of the European Union (for more on the European Schools, see Beardsmore, 1995). They are legally regarded as public institutions on the basis of an intergovernmental protocol signed in 1957. There are three European Schools—all offering the languages Dutch, English, French, and Italian. By contrast, the Greek schools are not European Schools, but are funded by the Greek government. Other private schools are run by nongovernmental associations.

Table 6.1. Languages offered by bilingual primary schools in Germany

Language	State-Run Schools	European Schools	Private Schools
Dutch		3	
English	7	3	2
French	6	3	
Greek	2		11
Italian	4	3	
Japanese			2
Polish	2		
Portuguese	2		
Russian	1		
Sorbian	6		
Spanish	5		
Turkish	4		

Source: Personal knowledge and such sources as the homepage of the Association for Early Multilingualism in Day-Care Centers and Schools [Verein für frühe Mehrsprachigkeit an Kindertageseinrichtungen und Schulen e.V]: <http://fmks-online.de>

Note: The Sorbs are an official autochthonous minority.

The founding of bilingual schools by the government was based on various factors. These schools were founded mainly to establish Berlin's role as the new capital and to promote the European ideal. Half of the children in these bilingual classes speak a language other than German. But although the second most common native language of primary school children in Berlin is Turkish, only schools with English, French, Italian, and Spanish were planned. The location offering Turkish had to be promoted painstakingly by interest groups, mostly well-educated Turkish parents. The foundation of bilingual primary schools in Hamburg, however, was implemented with the support of the consulates of Italy, Portugal, and Spain, which agreed to provide additional teachers for instruction through the medium of their languages. As in Berlin, the two Turkish classes were founded after a 3-year delay. And it was no easy task to find primary schools willing to participate in the experiment, for fear of getting a bad reputation.

In the Berlin model, the children in a class are assigned to two language groups. Literacy is introduced in their native language, and the second (or partner) language is taught as a subject. Content subjects are taught to linguistically heterogeneous groups in the non-German partner language, whereas mathematics is taught in German. In this model, both languages are treated as equal, and the amount of time devoted to the second language is gradually increased. The staff is made up of equal numbers of teachers from each language. On the children's report cards, the languages are treated differently: The various aspects of the first language are assessed with four grades, while there are only two grades for the second language.

In the Hamburg model, the teachers of the non-German languages of instruction are civil servants of their respective countries of origin, so there are no additional costs for the German school administration. These teachers are in class for 12 lessons a week and are responsible for teaching subjects in addition to the language they offer. The schools are free to decide on how to use the additional resource the teachers represent. They may want to divide the classes or have the teachers work as a team. The literacy classes take place in both languages, either concurrently or sequentially. The children are not separated into language groups as in the Berlin model. The children are grouped heterogeneously, and first- and second-language instruction is integrated. Report cards assess the children's success in the partner language with one grade, in addition to the five grades given for the different aspects of German. Therefore, the two languages are not equal, with German dominating considerably.

The past 2 years have seen the introduction of more bilingual primary school classes, mostly following the example of the Berlin model. The basic ideas correspond to the dual-language programs observed in several schools in New York 10 years ago (Lindholm-Leary, 2001). There are, however, still very few bilingual materials. The teachers manage with monolingual materials, partly from their home countries and partly developed in Germany for use in native-language instruction.

RESEARCH ON STUDENTS' LANGUAGE DEVELOPMENT IN BILINGUAL MODELS

There are no European studies offering an overview of the relation between success in school and language acquisition like those in the United States (Cummins, 2000; Ramirez, Yuen, Ramay, & Pasta, 1991; Thomas & Collier, 1997) or in New Zealand (May, Hill, & Tiakiwai, 2006). There are, however, a few studies on a smaller scale, where region and subject matter are taken into account, that suggest that first-language support has no negative consequences for the acquisition of a second language (Felix, 1993). As a rule, however, support will have a positive impact (Verhoeven, 1994; Westerbeek & Wolfgram, 1999). Nevertheless, support in a first language and its positive influence on a second language are closely linked to a sufficient duration and the coordination of first- and second-language teaching (de Bot, Driessen, & Jungbluth, 1989, 1991). The most successful models are those offering an effective and consistent delivery of bilingual instruction. When the delivery of bilingual instruction is consistent, both mathematics and second-language achievement tend to be better and children seem to catch up in their first-language development within 3 to 4 years when compared with monolingual children. The data on achievement of bilinguals suggest a strong relation between literacy and mathematics (Reich & Roth, 2002).

There is little systematic knowledge about multilingual German school experiments, as evaluations are not conducted on a regular basis (see Nehr, Birnkott-Rixius, Kubat, & Masuch, 1988, and Felix, 1993, for results of the coordinated alphabetization model developed and used in Berlin; for an evaluation of the Krefeld model, see Dickopp, 1982, and Reich & Roth, 2002). Available results on two-way bilingual projects are briefly presented below.

German–Italian School in Wolfsburg

The German–Italian School in Wolfsburg is attended by groups of Italian, German, and German–Italian children. There are three teachers who teach two classes in one grade. One of these teachers is an Italian native speaker. During the Italian lessons, the class is divided into two halves: One half of the class studies Italian, while the other is taught German or mathematics. In some cases, two teachers work together as a team (Sandfuchs & Zumhasch, 2002).

An evaluation of the German–Italian school covers data for the 4 years of primary school (Sandfuchs & Zumhasch, 2002). Student records were evaluated, and external tests were used to assess competency in reading, orthography, and mathematics. The authors point out that given the methods available, they had no choice but to use test instruments calibrated for children monolingual in German. At the time of the data collection, a special instrument to assess children's learning was developed in Italian. The main test results showed that monolingual German children achieved better marks in German than bilingual children; this held true for children from families where both parents or one parent came from Italy. The children with Italian as their family language scored better in Italian.

Overall, the results in German were outstanding. The majority of the respective groups reached the highest level of the reading test ("HAMLET 3-4") (see Lehmann, Peek, & Poerschke, 1997), even though there were differences among the three groups: 81% of the German, 64% of the Italian, and 72% of the German–Italian children were "unreservedly reliable readers" (the norm being 65.9%). Even the group with the lowest results is near the norm. However, 25% of the bilingual children required special support in German reading and orthography. In mathematics, the marks of the German children were better than the Italian students' scores; the performance test, however, suggested less pronounced differences.

This study also examined the school's social atmosphere. The students regarded the conduct of the teachers as positive and supportive; feelings of integration and good relations with fellow students were underlined. The overall satisfaction with the situation at school was higher among the children with a migration background than among the German children.

The authors point out the success of the intercultural approach and emphasize that German children are by no means being placed at a disadvantage in bilingual school models. The tendency toward less successful performance among the children with an immigrant background is explained partly by imprecisely measured factors of social status and insufficient support at the lower levels of performance.

German–Spanish Class in Nürnberg

The Nürnberg model was evaluated by examining the free writing of a Grade 3 Spanish–German class (Kupfer-Schreiner, 1994). Schools that followed this model offered children with an immigrant background language classes in their native language (Spanish, Turkish, or Italian) in addition to classes in German. These native-language classes were integrated into the regular curriculum and covered 7 hours a week.

The analysis included features such as orthography, syntax, and vocabulary. Kupfer-Schreiner found that the learning process for German was influenced by the starting point with respect to language. The bilingual Spanish–German group showed the most noticeable improvement in performance; children with other family languages—children from so-called Aussiedler families (German families from abroad, who speak Russian in most cases)—who had not been specially supported in the school context showed the smallest improvement. However, they had had the best results initially.

For Spanish, the researcher found an enormous improvement in the orthography of the bilingual group and calls it a "parallel development" of the languages. Parallel development means that the bilingual children reached nearly similar competences in both languages. Nevertheless, the learning process did not follow a linear course for all students, but quite often developed in stages. Teaching did not appear to necessarily have a direct and immediate effect, but it is suggested that the effect might be felt in later stages when it fit into the learning strategy of the children. Hence,

Kupfer-Schreiner took into consideration the possible long-term effects of teaching in studies of language acquisition.

The development of literacy is highly rule-based. Students develop individual "critical rules" guiding their learning process. Contrasting features of languages, for example, the differences between upper- and lowercase in German and Spanish, are learned more easily and are used productively in the individual learning process.

In the area of vocabulary development in German, Kupfer-Schreiner found a high increase with adjectives and a smaller increase with prepositions and adverbs. In the Spanish texts, a decrease of active vocabulary could be noted; the same held true for prepositions and adverbs. In spite of these findings, Kupfer-Schreiner highlights the children's obvious general linguistic improvement and their increasingly creative use of both languages.

Europa-Schulen in Berlin

The Europa-Schulen in Berlin were studied using a critical analysis of an experimental design (Zydatiß, 2000). Zydatiß also reported on the findings of a pilot study. Graefe-Bentzien (2001) found that the language development of an Italian–German class showed that in a bilingual setting, competence in the first language was not affected by the controlled simultaneous acquisition of two languages. The level of basic skills (i.e., listening, speaking, reading, and writing) acquired during the first 2 years of school was in accordance with the age-appropriate average of the monolingual control group. This held for the Italian language group as well, although considerable weaknesses in Italian were found among the bilingual students. German as a second language showed continuous improvement. However, the author cautions that the results are preliminary, as the students have not yet finished primary school (Graefe-Bentzien, 2001). A partial result that might inform further work is that neither the preschool attended nor family background are factors explaining progress in learning. What turned out to be of importance were general behavior in communication and performance in concept formation, which was studied using topics from the life and social sciences.

EVALUATION OF THE HAMBURG EXPERIMENT

The evaluation of the Hamburg Experiment included classes for children with a language background of Italian (one class, 23 children), Portuguese (one class, 23 children), and Spanish (two classes, 44 children). Oral language development and literacy in the family language and German as well as parental attitudes and the development of new practices in bilingual instruction were examined (Gogolin, Neumann, & Roth, 2001, 2003; Hansen, 2001; Owen-Ortega, 2003; Roth, 2002). Oral speech samples were evaluated using a procedure developed by Hans H. Reich following Harald Clahsen's profile analysis. Originally developed for German, it was adapted for Italian, Spanish, and Portuguese. A procedure developed by Mechthild Dehn was used to evaluate the orthography. It was adapted to suit the specifics of the different graphemic systems. External processes of performance control following the Progress in International Reading Literacy Study (Bos et al., 2004) were used in Grade 4.

Summary of the Preliminary Findings

Heterogeneity went beyond the four languages formally included in the project. In some families, more than two languages were used in everyday communication. In all, eight additional family languages were found. Thus, the experiment mirrors the multilingualism of the student population in Hamburg (Bühler-Otten & Fürstenau, 2004).

There was reasonable progress in the development of reading comprehension; with only a few exceptions, the children reached high results in the test used.

The acquisition of German by the second-language learners with respect to reading comprehension was also reasonable; after 2 years, the results for this group were not far from those of the bilingual and monolingual German children. This confirms research findings that suggest that second-language performance is enhanced by the promotion of the first language (Reich & Roth, 2002; Thomas & Collier, 2002).

Reading comprehension in Italian, Portuguese, and Spanish in Grade 3 was still highly dependent on the linguistic preconditions at the beginning of primary school.

Children who were bilingual at the beginning of primary school tended to develop a balanced bilingualism in reading comprehension; children whose dominant language was German also showed progress toward bilingualism in their reading skills.

The success of monolingual German children in the partner language (the language of instruction other than German) seemed to be highly dependent on factors other than linguistic preconditions (e.g., the gender distribution in the class).

The presence of a sufficient number of bilingual children was of great importance as well; if there were too few, the acquisition of the partner language by the class as a whole was far less effective.

Pedagogical Perspectives in Bilingual Instruction

Linguistic heterogeneity was an additional challenge for the teachers involved. Preliminary results of the Hamburg study point to the possibility that even children who are bilingual in other than the taught languages can profit from the model. If this finding turns out to be sound, it might support results from research in language acquisition and cognitive science suggesting that metalinguistic awareness is important for learning more than one language successfully. Bilingual instruction may foster the cognitive potential for language acquisition in bilingual children, even if it relates to only one of the languages spoken by the child (in this case, German).

All classes showed a dominance of German. This finding does not imply, however, that the children did not like learning the partner language or were not eager to do so. The students in all classes were highly motivated and made good progress, although this progress was more pronounced in the written than in the oral language. In some classes more than in others, linguistic models were lacking. The most important linguistic model was the teacher. All teachers followed the principle of "one language–one person" and avoided using the partner language. This left the children without the chance to observe strategies of language acquisition, examples of language learning phenomena, or instances of language switching. This was compounded by teachers' feelings that they might not be accepted by the children when using the partner language or that they lacked competency in using it. The impact on the children of having two bilingual teachers became overt when the German partner of the teaching team changed in one of the classes we were monitoring. The former teacher spoke only a little Spanish, while the new teacher was proficient in the language. After the change, observations showed that the new teacher addressed her Spanish colleague in Spanish and spoke Spanish with the children as well. The latter reacted by using Spanish more frequently when speaking in class and during student activities. The language climate in the class shifted toward a decreasing dominance of German and a noticeable bilingualism.

The role of German as the more important language became visible as well when both the German teachers and their team partners used German to discipline the children. The non-German teacher switched from Italian, Portuguese, or Spanish to German in order to reprimand a child, get the attention of all children, or give an instruction, even though she usually made every effort to act monolingually in class. On the other hand, it almost never occurred that the German teacher, given a similar situation, switched to the partner language, even if she had mastered the language.

Only a small amount of time is allocated to the comparative examination of the languages in order to discover grammatical and semantic similarities and differences. As different pedagogical approaches are being tested in the classes, it can be observed that cooperative forms like team teaching lead to language awareness and corresponding progress in learning. There seem to be positive effects for both cognitive understanding and fluent communication when a team of teachers who are competent in both languages teach the class mainly as a whole. The continuous presence of both languages in the form of teacher language models seems to heighten the children's ability to take in specific bilingual practices. This also results in an economical use of time: Necessary repetitions and consolidations do not have to include the complete linguistic material, but only the parts relevant at that moment. This approach has positive consequences for children's communicative fluency in both languages and the syntactic structure of their speech.

Development of Writing After Two Years of Schooling

Observation of the written language production of primary school children in bilingual classes has been rare. There are no adequate research methods, criteria for analysis, or standards that can be used as a basis for measuring the acquisition of written language. At the end of Grade 2, a point at which written language acquisition can be regarded as complete, this study took samples of freewriting based on a given picture story ("cat and bird") from all children in both languages (German and Italian, Portuguese, or Spanish, respectively). The quantitative evaluation was based on the following categories:

- number of words (words)
- number of sentence-like segments (sentences)
- mean length of sentences (MLS)
- mistakes in orthography (orthography)[1]
- mistakes in capitalization (capitalization)
- mistakes in grammar (grammar)

The means for each category for each of the four classes can be found in Table 6.2. Considering the mistakes made in writing in the texts, differences between the classes are noticeable.

Looking at the length of the texts in German, there are distinct differences among the four classes. The Italian class produced by far the longest texts (95 words), followed by the Spanish 1 class (74 words); the results for the Spanish 2 class (65 words) and the Portuguese class (64 words) are quite close and well below the others. This sequence is confirmed by the

Table 6.2. Results for the four classes

Category	Italian $N = 22$	Portuguese $N = 23$	Spanish 1 $N = 22$	Spanish 2 $N = 24$
German Texts				
Words	95.00	64.00	74.00	65.00
Sentences	12.55	10.35	9.71	9.25
MLS	7.6	6.7	7.3	6.7
Grammar	1.86	0.96	0.57	2.54
Orthography	14.61	10.48	9.00	11.29
Capitalization	4.41	3.87	3.14	5.50
Italian/Portuguese/Spanish Texts				
Words	44.00	54.14	44.43	47.50
Sentences	8.09	9.00	8.29	8.33
MLS	5.23	6.03	5.29	5.48
Grammar	6.36	2.29	6.19	0.54
Orthography	7.18	9.33	7.10	6.00

complexity of sentences (i.e., MLS): 7.6 and 7.3 for the first groups and 6.7 for the latter. There is no statistical connection between membership in a group and its MLS, since the variation within the groups is high (M = 7.1; SD = 1.5). Remarkable, however, is the strong connection between length and complexity. Students writing longer texts used longer sentences as well. An increase in quantity was accompanied by an increase in quality. These increases in quantity and quality were statistically significant ($r = .57$, $p < 0.01$), suggesting a connection between students being able to produce longer sentences and being able to produce clearer messages despite the complexity of the sentences.

The texts in the partner languages reveal a comparable finding: Groups with a higher number of words also had a higher MLS. Again, there is no statistical connection between being in a certain school and the MLS, but a highly significant connection between the length of a text and the MLS, higher even than in the German texts ($r = .81$, $p < 0.01$). The explanation can be found in competency differences for the partner language (i.e., children without previous knowledge of the partner language tended to write shorter and less complex texts). Nevertheless, while the relation was statistically significant ($r = .60$, $p < 0.01$), it does not account for all of the variation, as some of the children who started school without any knowledge of the partner language wrote more complex texts and some of the bilingual children did not.

There is no connection between complexity and frequency of mistakes (all types) in the German texts. However, there are relationships between amount of text, complexity, and a smaller number of grammatical mistakes in the partner language for the Portuguese class, but not for the whole of the sample (cf. Roth, 2003). Table 6.3 gives the results according to various linguistic preconditions.

No systematic difference in text complexity was found between the children who were bilingual at the beginning of school and those who were monolingual. The only significant data found for the German texts relate to grammatical phenomena: Children with a previous knowledge of the partner language (groups B and D) make significantly more mistakes. This

Table 6.3. Results for four linguistic preconditions

Category	A Monolingual in German *N* = 40	B Monolingual in partner language *N* = 7	C Bilingual with different family language *N* = 7	D Bilingual in German and partner language *N* = 33
German Texts				
Words	75.41	67.75	75.67	74.03
Sentences	10.32	9.63	11.44	10.53
MLS	7.34	6.23	6.68	7.07
Orthography	10.12	14.75	8.44	12.94
Capitalization	4.56	4.38	3.00	4.22
Grammar	0.68	6.00	1.00	1.59
Italian/Portuguese/Spanish Texts				
Words	35.78	63.88	39.56	62.67
Sentences	7.70	10.38	8.22	9.23
MLS	4.54	6.00	4.75	7.06
Orthography	5.50	9.12	4.67	10.40
Grammar	5.58	2.13	2.11	2.40

is because quite a number of children entered school without any knowledge of German (group B). Although there is quite a difference in the other language groups, their performance has to be recognized. After all, even those children who started acquiring German in Grade 1 (group B) are able to produce the main part of their texts error-free. The difference is even smaller with orthography and especially capitalization; these seem easier to learn than grammar. There is no connection with text length and text complexity.

The results for texts in the partner languages are quite different. The MLS is clearly related to a previous knowledge of the partner language at the beginning of school (at the 0.01 level); the same holds for the number of words. Grammatical mistakes are significantly less frequent among the children who are proficient in the partner language (groups B and D). The better performance of group C may be because these children were already bilingually socialized within their families and therefore developed higher linguistic awareness. It can be assumed that bilingual education at school allows the transfer of this metalinguistic competency into the process of literacy development.

The result regarding orthography is striking: A positive relation was found here as well (i.e., children with competencies in the partner language, groups B and D, made significantly more orthographical mistakes than those in groups A and C). This result is in accordance with the significant relation between text length and average number of mistakes ($r = .45$, $p < 0.01$), which is obvious. Generally the children who are proficient in the partner language seem to be more familiar with orthography. Perhaps teachers of the partner languages do not pay as much attention to orthography with these children, while focusing on the children in groups A and C.

What kinds of relationships can be found in the results for both languages? For the whole sample, there is a connection between the number of sentences in the German texts and in the respective partner-language texts ($r = .31$, $p < 0.01$), but there is no corresponding relationship for the MLS in these texts. This might suggest that only a few children write in a balanced bilingual way, whereas the majority shows differences between the two languages. Taking oral proficiency into consideration, this result verifies the dominance of one language for most of the children. After 2 years of school, a result like this should not be stressed too much. After all, of the 87 children in the sample, only 33 started school being proficient in both languages. A moderately significant relationship between the MLS in the German and in the partner-language texts can be found only for the children from groups B and D ($r = .35$, $p < 0.05$) (i.e., it is still true that a balanced bilingualism in the production of written texts is an area that needs further development).

The strongest relationship between the two languages is in orthography ($r = .34$, $p < 0.01$). Children with either good or poor skills in orthography are likely to reproduce them in the other language. This indicates a certain degree of independence between orthography and text complexity. However, it also shows that in bilingual instruction, special support is not necessary for those children who enter the dual-language model without knowledge of the partner language. The promotion of orthographic skills should begin without regard to the linguistic preconditions. On the other hand, text competency seems to be an area of learning that has to be developed in both languages separately; transfer from one language into the other could be found only in the Portuguese class, not in the whole sample.

Explaining Heterogeneous Achievement in the Partner Languages

One of the most salient results was a significant difference between the classes with regard to written and oral language proficiency. Each student had been followed from Grade 1. One of the remarkable results for the complete time span is that students in the Italian and Spanish 1 classes performed at a considerably lower level than those in the Portuguese and Spanish 2 classes. Two influencing factors identified by regular classroom observations may help to explain this. In the Italian and Spanish 1 classes, the lack of balance in the class with respect to gender on the one hand, and linguistic preconditions on the other, was found to be a factor in the divergent results for the partner languages (Gogolin et al., 2003, 2004; Neumann & Roth, 2004). The Italian class was productive only for the bilingual children, while a group consisting mainly of boys who started school as monolingual German, and who did not have a bilingual role model of the same gender, more or less refused to deal with Italian; the variation regarding the MLS in Italian is the greatest by far. In the Spanish 1 class, only a few children were distinctly competent in Spanish when they entered school in grade 1; the language teaching was therefore more like foreign-language teaching than bilingual instruction, and it took more than 2 years to transition to a bilingual or dual-language setting so that Spanish could be used as a classroom language. Correspondingly, the variation regarding the MLS is the lowest within an otherwise low level of Spanish. At the end of Grade 4, language proficiencies (orality and literacy) in these two classes were significantly lower than in the Portuguese and Spanish 2 classes.

A second factor is the difference between the classes with regard to organization. Both of the classes with higher performance were in heterogeneous language groups where a team of teachers and, as a consequence, a high frequency of contrastive language teaching was available to the learners. This way of teaching required more frequent and freer use of the partner language.

Exactly how these factors—imbalances in gender or linguistic preconditions and the extent of team teaching—are related and how much of the overall variation they account for cannot be found within a statistical analysis. Hypotheses are corroborated, however, that the successful acquisition of a partner language requires a balanced composition of the learning groups and a relatively high proportion of bilingual phases.

CONCLUSION

At present, the few bilingual primary schools in Germany offer an opportunity to study language acquisition and the instructional methods that facilitate first- and second-language acquisition. Current results suggest that the consequences of bilingual teaching are primarily positive: The children learn both languages, although the positive impact on the German language is the most pronounced. Even the children who make the least progress are able to write texts in the new language and speak fluently about topics of interest. All children acquire a good basis for learning further languages, as becomes obvious in the English classes in Grade 3.

These schools offer an attractive alternative to parents who are looking for a high-quality way either to further their children's abilities in the two languages spoken in the family and their surroundings or to give their children a head start on secondary education. This has a "soothing" effect on educational policy. The issue of minorities and their right to have their language taught to their children in state schools is not being touched.

It remains our scientific responsibility to show that in our society neither a lack of cognitive capacity nor pedagogical complexity is the reason that bilingual children or children with a background of migration fail in school. The linguistic situation is much more complex than the concept of bilingual schools is able to reflect. Nevertheless, these schools are models of a fruitful consideration of multilingualism and of the processes of teaching and learning, the possibilities of which have not yet been exhausted. They should be used in the interests of the vast majority of children from migrant families, whose language rights are being flouted today.

NOTE

1. For the Romance languages, mistakes regarding diacritics were counted as well; these are not used here, since the number and frequency of use vary

among the languages. The means for the four classes are IT = 2.73, PO = 4.67, S1 = 6.95, S2 = 7.52.

REFERENCES

Beardsmore, H. B. (1995). The European School experience in multilingual education. In T. Skutnabb-Kangas (Ed.), *Multilingualism for all* (pp. 21–68). Lisse: Swets & Zeitlinger.

Bos, W., Lankes, E-M., Prenzel, M., Scwippert, K., Valtin, R., et al. (2004). *IGLU. Einige Länder der Bundesrepublik Deutschland im nationalen und internationalen Vergleich* [Some landers of the Federal Republic of Germany in a national and international comparison]. Münster: Waxmann.

de Bot, K., Driessen, G., & Jungbluth, P. (1989). *De effectiviteit van het onderwijs en eigen taal en cultur. Prestaties van Marokkanse, Spaanse en Turkse leerlingen* [The effectiveness of instruction in the language and on the culture of origin: Achievements of Moroccan, Spanish and Turkish students]. Nijmegen: Institut voor Toegepaste Sociale Wetenschappen/Institut voor Toegepaste Taalkunde.

de Bot, K., Driessen, G., & Jungbluth, P. (1991). An evaluation of migrant teaching in the Netherlands. In K. Jaspaert & S. Kroo (Eds.), *Ethnic minority languages and education* (pp. 25–123). Amsterdam: Swets & Zeitlinger.

Bühler-Otten, S., & Fürstenau, S. (2004). Multilingualism in Hamburg. In G. Extra & K. Yağmur (Eds.), *Urban multilingualism in Europe: Immigrant minority languages at home and school* (pp. 163–191). Clevedon: Multilingual Matters.

Cummins, J. (2000). *Language, power and pedagogy: Bilingual children in the crossfire.* Clevedon, UK: Multilingual Matters.

Deutsches PISA Konsortium. (Ed.). (2001). *PISA 2000. Basiskompetenzen von Schülerinnen und Schülern im internationalen Vergleich* [PISA 2000: International comparison of basic competencies of students]. Opladen: Leske und Budrich.

Dickopp, K. H. (1982). *Erziehung ausländischer Kinder als pädagogische Herausforderung. Das Krefelder Modell* [Education of foreign children as a pedagogic challenge: The Krefeld Model]. Düsseldorf: Schwann.

Felix, S. (1993). *Psycholinguistische Untersuchungen zur zweisprachigen Alphabetisierung. Gutachten im Auftrag der Berliner Senatsverwaltung für Schule, Berufsbildung und Sport* [Psycholinguistic study of bilingual alphabetiziation: Report on behalf of the Berlin Senat Administration for School, Vocational Training and Sport]. Passau: Lehrstuhl für Allgemeine Linguistik der Universität Passau.

Gogolin, I. (1994). *Der monolinguale Habitus der multilingualen Schule* [The monolingual habitus of the multilingual school]. Münster: Waxmann.

Gogolin, I., Neumann, U., & Reuter, L. (Eds.). (2001). *Schulbildung für Kinder aus Minderheiten in Deutschland 1989–1999. Schulrecht, Schulorganisation, curriculare Fragen, sprachliche Bildung* [School education for children from minorities 1989–1999: School law, school organization, curricular matters, linguistic education]. Münster: Waxmann.

Gogolin, I., Neumann, U., & Roth, H. J. (2001). *Auswertung der ersten Sprachstandserhebung der portugiesisch–deutschen Klasse, Schuljahr 2000/01* [Evaluation of the first language assessment of the Portuguese–German class: School year 2000/01]. Hamburg: University of Hamburg.

Gogolin, I., Neumann, U., & Roth, H. J. (2003). *Bericht 2003. Schulversuch bilinguale Grundschulklassen in Hamburg* [Report 2003: Experimental bilingual primary school classes in Hamburg]. Hamburg: Arbeitsstelle Interkulturelle Bildung, University of Hamburg.

Gogolin, I., Neumann, U., & Roth, H. J. (2004). *Bericht 2004. Schulversuch bilinguale Grundschulklassen in Hamburg* [Report 2004: Experimental bilingual primary school classes in Hamburg]. Hamburg: Arbeitsstelle Interkulturelle Bildung, University of Hamburg.

Graefe-Bentzien, U. (2001). *Evaluierung bilingualer Kompetenz. Eine Pilotstudie zur Entwicklung der deutschen und italienischen Sprachfähigkeiten in der Primarstufe beim Schulversuch der Staatlichen Europa-Schulen Berlin (SESB)* [Evaluation of bilingual competence: A pilot study regarding the development of language proficiency in German and Italian in primary school within the school experiment of the Staatliche Europa-Schulen Berlin (SESB)]. Unpublished doctoral dissertation, Freie Universität Berlin. Retrieved August 8, 2008, from http://www.diss.fu-berlin.de/2001/14/index.html

Hansen, C. (2001). *Bilingualer Schriftspracherwerb am Beispiel einer italienisch–deutschen Modellklasse einer Hamburger Grundschule* [Bilingual acquisition of literacy: An example of an Italian–German model class in a primary school in Hamburg]. Unpublished paper for the first state examination, University of Hamburg.

Kupfer-Schreiner, C. (1994). *Sprachdidaktik und Sprachentwicklung im Rahmen interkultureller Erziehung. Das Nürnberger Modell. Ein Beitrag gegen Rassismus und Ausländerfeindlichkeit* [Language didactics and language development in multicultural education: The Nürnberger Model—A contribution against racism and xenophobia]. Weinheim: Deutscher Studienverlag.

Lehmann, R. H., Peek, R., & Poerschke, J. (1997). *HAMLET 3–4*. Weinheim, Germany: Beltz.

Lindholm-Leary, K. (2001). *Dual language education.* Clevedon: Multilingual Matters.

May, S., Hill, R., & Tiakiwai, S. (2006). *Bilingual education in Aerotea/New Zealand: Key findings from bilingual education/immersion: Indicators of good practice.* Hamilton, NZ: University of Waikato. Retrieved August 9, 2008, from http://www.educationcounts.govt.nz/publications/schooling/5075

Mullis, I. V. S., Martin, M. O., Gonzales, E. J., & Kennedy, A. M. (2003). *PIRLS 2001 international report: IEA's study of reading literacy achievement in primary schools.* Chestnut Hill, MA: Boston College.

Nehr, M., Birnkott-Rixius, K., Kubat, L., & Masuch, S. (1988). *In zwei Sprachen lesen lernen—geht denn das? Erfahrungsbericht über die zweisprachige Alphabetisierung* [Learning to read in two languages—Is that possible? A field report on bilingual alphabetization]. Weinheim: Beltz.

Neumann, U., & Roth, H. J. (2004). Bilinguale Grundschulklassen in Hamburg—

Ein Werkstattbericht [Bilingual primary school classes in Hamburg—Work in progress report]. *Grenzgänge, 11*(21), 29–56.

Owen-Ortega, J. (2003). *Schriftspracherwerb bilingualer Kinder am Beispiel einer spanisch–deutschen Klasse unter besonderer Berücksichtigung ihrer Strategien des Orthographieerwerbs in der Alphabetisierungsphase* [Literacy acquisition in bilingual children: An example of a Spanish–German class with a focus on strategies of learning orthography during the phase of alphabetization]. Unpublished paper for the first state examination, University of Hamburg.

Ramirez, D. J., Yuen, S. D., Ramay, D. R., & Pasta, D. (1991). *Final report: Longitudinal study of structured English immersion strategy, early-exit and late-exit transitional bilingual education programs for language-minority children.* San Mateo, CA: Aguirre International.

Reich, H. H., & Roth, H. J. (2002). *Spracherwerb zweisprachig aufwachsender Kinder und Jugendlicher. Ein Überblick über den Stand der nationalen und internationalen Forschung* [Language acquisition in bilingual children and young people: A review of national and international research]. Hamburg: Department of Education and Sports.

Roth, H.-J. (2002). *Il gatto va sull'albero—va sull'albero il gatto. Satzmuster und Sprachstand italienisch–deutscher Schulanfänger* [Il gatto va sull'albero—va sull'albero il gatto: Sentence patterns and language level of Italian–German school beginners]. Institute for Comparative and Multicultural Education, University of Hamburg.

Roth, H.-J. (2003). *Bilinguale Alphabetisierung und die Entwicklung von Textkompetenz am Beispiel einer portugiesisch-deutschen Klasse im zweiten Schuljahr* [Bilingualistic teaching to read and write and the development of comprehension of texts as illustrated by a Portuguese-German class of second graders]. In: /Zeitschrift für Erziehungswissenschaft/ 2003, Heft 3, S. 378–402.

Sandfuchs, U., & Zumhasch, C. (2002). Wissenschaftliche Begleituntersuchung zum Schulversuch Deutsch–Italienische Grundschule Wolfsburg—Reflexionen und ausgewählte Ergebnisse [Scientific monitoring of the school experiment German–Italian Primary School Wolfsburg—Reflexions and selected findings]. *Interkulturell, 1/2,* 104–139.

Skutnabb-Kangas, T. (1986). Multilingualism and the education of minority children. In T. Skutnabb-Kangas & J. Cummins (Eds.), *Minority education: From shame to struggle* (pp. 9–44). Clevedon: Multilingual Matters.

Thomas, W. P., & Collier, V. (1997). *School effectiveness for language minority students.* Washington, DC: National Clearing House for Bilingual Education.

Thomas, W. P., & Collier, V. (2002). *A national study of school effectiveness for language minority students' long-term academic achievement, final report.* Retrieved August 9, 2008, from http://www.crede.ucsc.edu/research/llaa/1.1_final.html

UNESCO. (2003). *Education in a multilingual world.* Paris: Author. Retrieved August 9, 2008, from http://unesdoc.unesco.org/images/0012/001297/129728e.pdf

Verhoeven, L. (1994). Transfer in bilingual development: The linguistic interdependence hypothesis revisited. *Language Learning, 44*(3), 381–415.

Westerbeek, K., & Wolfgram, P. (1999). *Deltaplan en het tij. 7 jaar taalbeleid primair onderwijs* [Deltaplan on a high: Seven years of Rotterdam language politics in primary education]. Rotterdam: Het Projectbureau/CED.

Zydatiß, W. (2000). *Bilingualer Unterricht in der Grundschule. Entwurf eines Spracherwerbskonzepts für zweisprachige Immersionsprogramme* [Bilingual tuition in primary school: Outline of a concept of language acquisition for bilingual immersion programs). Ismaning: Hueber.

7

Multilingual Education in Germany

Discourses, Practices, and Experiences in Two-Way Immersion

Gabriele Budach

This chapter looks at multilingualism in schools from a German perspective. Even though foreign language teaching remains the dominant form of representing other languages than German in the school curriculum, new forms that take into account societal multilingualism have started to emerge. Over the last 15 years an increasing number of bilingual programs have spread across Germany putting into practice ideas related to two-way-immersion or dual language education. The chapter focuses on one Italian-German bilingual program in Frankfurt/Main, where Italians represent the third-largest migrant community. The program was started by an initiative of parents, mostly linguistically mixed couples, who expressed their interest in an education that included both Italian and German languages and cultures for their children. Students from mixed, Italian-only, and German-only backgrounds are schooled together in a program that attempts to offer an alternative to monolingual schooling and socialization in just one national, dominant language and culture—German. The chapter presents findings from a four-year ethnographic study and suggests ways and consequences of bilingual teaching and learning as they unfold in the program. Based on observation and interviews, the study explores how the children construct the social identities of "German" and "Italian." The social identities appear to be complementary and reside in children's backgrounds as well as in roles that they adopt in bilingual learning routines as part of a developing bilingual learning culture in the school. In this chapter particular attention is paid to bilingually designed tasks and weekly plans. The analysis shows how these learning arrangements and tools help children to develop and reinforce specific role-based identities drawing on and valuing their diverse linguistic repertoires.

Der vorliegende Text betrachtet Mehrsprachigkeit und Schule aus einer deutschen Perspektive. Zwar überwiegt im deutschen Schulsystem noch immer

---

der traditionelle Fremdsprachenunterricht als Form des Ausbaus von Mehrsprachigkeit, doch nach und nach gewinnen auch Modelle an Boden, die Mehrsprachigkeit von Kindern mit Migrationshintergrund einbeziehen. So sind in den letzten 15 Jahren eine Reihe von Projekten entstanden, die auf unterschiedliche Weise das Konzept der two-way-immersion *oder* dual language education *umsetzen.*

Il testo tratta di un tale progetto bilingue à Francoforte sul Meno una città, dove gli italiani formano la terza grande minoranza linguistica. Il progetto emerse da una iniziativa di genitori bilingui che cercavano di mettere a disposizione ai loro figli un'educazione in italiano e in tedesco. Le classi bilingui in cui vengono accolti bambini di origine italiana, tedesca e bambini con repertori linguistici anche più diversificati presentano uno spazio alternativo che confronta l'ideologia del monolinguismo.

I dati esposti fanno parte di uno studio etnografico e qualitativo che viene condotto da due anni in una scuola elementare. Lo studio serve a illustrare meglio le pratiche dell' insegnamento bilingue e le conseguenze che ne sorgono per la costruzione di identità e di saperi in un ambiente che valorizza risorse linguistiche oltre che la lingua dominante.

*Die bisherigen Ergebnisse der Analyse ergeben, dass eine solche Lernkultur im Entstehen ist, die vor allem Italienisch und Deutsch einen besonderen, gleichwertigen Stellenwert zuweist. Emergono due tipi di identità; un'*identità italiana *und eine* deutsche Identität *che sono complementari nel corso dell'apprendimento bilingue. Der Entwicklung dieser Identitätsmuster förderlich erscheint der Einsatz bestimmter lernerzentrierter didaktischer Instrumente, wie des Wochenplans oder zweisprachig konzipierter Partneraufgaben. Il piano di lavoro settimanale e i compiti che vengono concepiti in due lingue sembrano essere metodi didattici che sostengono una cultura di aiuto e rinforzano l'apprendimento individuale tenendo conto anche dei saperi e delle risorse linguistiche che di solito vengono marginalizzati o esclusi.*

This chapter focuses on multilingualism and language education from a German perspective. In particular, it looks at two-way bilingual immersion (dual-language education) and explores some of the ways in which this fairly new model plays out as an approach to developing multilingualism. I will examine three aspects: (1) the German sociolinguistic context that is raising controversy about multilingualism as a goal of schooling and as a social reality; (2) the story of one particular bilingual project that portrays the competing interests and conditions for implementing multilingual education; and (3) some preliminary results from an ethnographic study that illustrate the impact of bilingual education on social identification and ways of learning. Within the framework of a community of practice, the findings suggest that two-way immersion creates a set of specific practices in which the majority and the minoritized languages are equally valued. These practices allow for identities and ways of learning that integrate the diversity of linguistic resources and potentially challenge dominant views of language hierarchies in the society.

APPROACHES TO MULTILINGUAL EDUCATION

Multilingualism is gaining ground in German language education. Thus, it often is voiced in public discourse that being bi- or multilingual is beneficial in many ways, but there is disagreement about the best way of achieving this goal. In the past, language programs were designed for those wanting to learn a foreign language (L2 or L3). Multilingual resources that children from a migrant background brought to the classroom were rarely taken into account. However, in a number of European countries there have been interesting attempts to build multilingual and multicultural curricula (Candelier et al., 2004; De Pietro, 2001) and programs in teacher education (Sjögren & Ramberg, 2005), some of them funded by the European Union. In diversifying monolingual curricula, beneficial effects are expected for two reasons: (1) early contact with other languages is supposed to raise language awareness and thereby facilitate the learning of foreign languages (Candelier, 2001; Hawkins, 1984); and (2) children from linguistic minorities enjoy situations in which their language is valued as a resource (Bernaus, Mesgoret, Gardner, & Reyes, 2004).

Yet these arguments rarely figure in German political debates on educational policy. This has to do with the dominant status of German as the only language of instruction in schools and the underlying ideology of monolingual state nationalism. However, there is a struggle over language policy and language education in which competing interest groups are involved.

On the one hand, there are representatives of the German majority who think of multilingualism in terms of languages that are added to the dominant L1. Their goal is to implement programs that allow for early and better teaching of more foreign languages for children of German background in order to improve their chances in a unified European labor market and provide a good basis for intercultural communication. Linguistic, social, and psychological resources that belong to the cultural baggage of linguistic minorities are seen as hindering the acquisition of German and tend to be less valued, especially if they do not involve languages of global recognition such as English, French, or Spanish. There are, however, language activists speaking in the interest of language minorities and advocating for the maintenance of heritage languages. To some of them, mostly middle-class parents, dual-language education (Freeman, 2001) in German and the respective minoritized language seems to be the perfect solution, given the fact that proficiency in German is a necessity and being bilingual provides an economic advantage over monolinguals. Others stress the importance of educational provision in L1, especially for the benefit of those children of migrant background who have difficulty succeeding in the German school system. Their linguistic problems often are analyzed by school officials as learning difficulties. This makes them probable candidates for special education, which takes place in a separate institutional branch. As recent school statistics show, migrant children, especially those from the third-largest migrant group, Italian, tend to be more affected by this mechanism of misdiagnosis and social selection (www.statistik-hessen.de/themenauswahl/bildung-kultur-rechtspflege/index.html).

The necessity for multilingual programs in German schools grows out of a sociolinguistic situation that is quite complex. While there are autochthonous minorities, that is, minorities historically associated with geographical space within the German nation-state, like the Sorbs, a Slavonic ethnic group living in the eastern part of Germany, or the Danish and Fries minorities in the northern part of Germany, there are also migrant communities of significant size, such as the Turks (about 3 million all over Germany), ethnic groups from the former Yugoslavia, and Italians, Spaniards, Greeks, and Portuguese who came to Germany as contracted migrant workers during the years of the economic boom after World War II. In terms of language education, regional legislation allows for schooling in the first languages of autochthonous minorities in regions where they are sufficiently numerous. The right to education in the languages of the migrant communities has not been officially established by any legislation. Some states of Bundesländer, however, offer afternoon classes in heritage languages, also known as community languages, mainly on a voluntary basis. However, a noticeable decline in these efforts is currently under way due to the takeover of a number of German states by conservative governments.

Over the past 20 years, a series of language programs have been set up that mainly serve the needs of the German majority and their interest in learning foreign languages. These include *early foreign-language* teaching (mainly in English or French) starting in Grade 3 (or 1) and *Content Language Integrated Learning (CLIL) programs* (Beardsmore, 1993), also called second-language enrichment (Genesee, 1987), that teach the L2 or L3, mainly English or French, as well as use it as a medium of instruction for at least one subject, such as history, geography, chemistry, or biology. CLIL programs usually start in Grade 7, following a period of intensive English or French classes.

Since the 1990s, a growing but still comparatively small number of two-way bilingual programs have been established at the elementary level. All of them use two languages of instruction, but a distinction can be made between (1) *dual-language* programs that start out developing biliteracy concurrently without separating children with strong or weak balanced bilingualism, and (2) those that teach literacy sequentially, which means that they divide children with different levels of achievement and start by teaching literacy in L1 before introducing L2.

Looking at the degree of institutional implementation, we become aware of the ways in which official language policy prioritizes certain projects over others. While early foreign-language teaching and CLIL programs are already part of many regional school curricula and benefit from institutionally allocated subsidies, dual-language programs still have to struggle over funding and the provision of human resources. This difference in treatment also reveals a difference in status, although all of the language programs mentioned above are still undernourished in terms of curriculum planning, teacher training, and the development of instructional materials.

As in many other contexts (Freeland, 1999), tracing the history of bilingual programs reveals that there is competition between *top-down* and *bottom-up* strategies, which represent different ways in which social actors can intervene in negotiating and orchestrating educational policy. CLIL programs first were established in the spirit of rising German–French friendship after World War II, and as such they are the product of a top-down strategy; in contrast, the first two-way immersion programs (for the Turkish in the 1980s) grew out of a community movement in heavily Turkish areas in Berlin. After a couple of years, however, this successful initiative was stopped by the senate in Berlin and replaced by a new program that suggested the creation of bilingual elementary schools. As the outcome of a top-down strategy, this project started off with more "valuable" languages such as English and French, which better suited the guidelines for a new European language policy (Staatliche Europaschule, 2009).

Having talked about different views of language education on a national level, we need to discuss a third entity that was mentioned earlier. This is the European Union (EU) and its respective institutions, as the language policy of the EU has an important impact on Germany, which is one of its member states. This third player enriches the picture by adding a level of international networks that overarches national language policy. As a result, there are three sources of discursive production that participate in setting the agenda on language policy for Germany, and their priorities compete and partly overlap: (1) the national educational institutions that prioritize the interests of monolingual Germans and German as the majority language and main language of instruction; (2) the institutions of linguistic minorities that advocate the acceptance and maintenance of minoritized languages; and (3) the European Council and the European Commission as international institutions that orient their language planning toward the goals of peacekeeping and the political and economic integration of the European Union. According to a multilateral model that values cultural and linguistic diversity, the EU institutions promote multilingualism (especially the languages of EU member countries) and respect for the minoritized languages spoken inside the European Union. As part of its political guidelines, the EU also encourages early foreign-language learning and the learning of minoritized languages. Instructional language choices are more a matter of teacher availability and curricular needs. For more information on the latter, see Declaration of the Conference of European Ministers of Education (Council Resolution, 1997), which asks for the introduction of early foreign-language learning and for the international collaboration of schools offering these programs.

Although the three players are not equal in power, their co-presence allows for different alliances and the enhancement of new legitimizing discourses. As a consequence, we can observe that in some cases the EU language policy serves as a reference for migrant communities in their attempt to implement bilingual programs. This is not true for all migrant communities, however, since the EU legislation prioritizes the languages of member states, excluding, for instance, claims of the Turkish community as Turkey is not yet part of the EU.

In what follows, I address the issue of one school project in which I have been doing fieldwork since September 2003; it is a two-way, dual-language German–Italian program in an elementary school in Frankfurt/Main.

FROM THE BOTTOM UP: HISTORY AND LOCAL CONTEXT OF A GERMAN–ITALIAN PROJECT

Presently, German–Italian bilingual projects in Frankfurt exist in three regular public schools, including two primary schools and one secondary school (*Gymnasium*). All of them originated from a bottom-up initiative by parents who were looking for an opportunity to provide their children with bilingual education. With the support of the local Italian community in Frankfurt, parents from both Italian and binational backgrounds founded a parents association in 1995. In 2002, the Italian minority was the third-largest, following the Turkish and Spanish immigrant communities, with 698,799 members (Fondazione Migrantes). To prepare the ground for a bilingual school project, the association conducted a series of persistent interventions to convince regional ministries, the school administration, the schools, and the Italian consulate in Frankfurt of the need for the project. Soon the initiative was supported by the Italian state. It encountered difficulties, however, in dealing with a quite inflexible school bureaucracy that was reluctant to adopt any change interfering with its established administrative practices. Furthermore, since the project operates on an international level involving Italian authorities, who send and pay the Italian teachers, its management is complex and logistically demanding, as obstacles, such as delays in appointing the Italian teachers, are encountered more frequently than in regular schools.

After 2 years of intense negotiation and numerous negative reactions from schools, such as "Italian would be a less interesting option than English," or "Italian kids are too noisy," the first bilingual class started in a regular public primary school as a pilot project. Half of the children were monolingual Germans from the rather wealthy neighborhood where the school is located. The other half were mostly bilingual children from a socially mixed Italian background who were recruited from all over Frankfurt, including the outskirts.

According to the two-way immersion design, Italian and German are used equally as languages of instruction. The two teachers team teach for 5 hours a week in order to create a balanced bilingual and bicultural environment. Literacy is introduced from the beginning in both languages to all of the students, regardless of their social and linguistic background, language profile, or proficiency. In 2001, when the first class finished primary school after 4 years, a secondary school in the neighborhood continued the program in a slightly different manner. As a response to the still-increasing demand, a second primary school project started in September 2003.

Attention will be devoted to the German–Italian school, where our research group[1] has followed the students and program development since the first year of implementation. The project deliberately grounds its legitimacy in a variety of social interests. It is explicit about the aim to serve the needs of both the German majority and linguistic minorities, namely, the Italian minority. The following extract, which shows the integrative philosophy of the school, is taken from an official application document submitted to the Hassian Ministry of Education, which approved the project:

> Taking into account the multilingual and multicultural background of many pupils of elementary schools, especially in urban areas, our school establishes a bilingual German–Italian branch. Thereby, we respond to the multilingual environment and understand multilingual resources as an educational potential. Our objective is

> to thereby enhance the general language skills and help develop a competent bilingualism. This should have a positive impact on the individual development, the school success and the job opportunities of our pupils. We align ourselves with the goals of the European Union to maintain the diversity of cultures and languages in a unified Europe. (unpublished document; for further information on the project, see www.schulserver.hessen.de/frankfurt/holzhausen; my translation)

Beyond the official text, the head of the school stated that she wanted a project that cross-cuts language and social boundaries. She envisioned the project as attracting a wide range of clients looking for an alternative to either private schools or special education.

Given the linguistic and social heterogeneity of children, parents, and schoolteachers, many different expectations are raised. Only a few schools in Germany are completely bilingual. In most cases, there is only one bilingual class each year, which creates an exceptional status and increases the level of complexity inside the school, especially when it comes to creating opportunities and distributing resources in an equitable way. The German–Italian school on which our record is based has a good deal of experience in coping with this kind of diversity, because it has also run a Greek–German bilingual project since the late 1970s and offers afternoon classes in the heritage languages Greek, Turkish, and Croatian. Yet, every project of this kind carries the hopes and concerns of administrators, teachers, and parents, which appear to be similar across countries and sociolinguistic settings (Dewaele, 2003).

From the parental perspective, the German parents are happy to provide their children with an early multilingual experience and the opportunity to learn another language at a very early age. However, they worry that their children won't catch up with their monolingual peers in a regular secondary school in the event that the bilingual project is not continued after elementary school or they decide on another school option.[2] The Italian parents are pleased and grateful to finally have access to an institutionalized bilingual Italian program that guarantees the introduction of their home language into German schooling and the acquisition of literacy in both Italian and German. Some of them, however, worry that their children will be left behind in the acquisition of Italian by the German children who do not yet know the language.

From the teachers' perspective, the experience of team teaching provides an opening toward new ways of teaching that include the institutional and cultural traditions of another school system. On the other hand, there is the anxiety of meeting the standards of the monolingual curriculum, where there are no bilingual standards, and of facing the challenges of team teaching, which puts into question approved and cherished ways of doing things.

Listening to the concerns of teachers reveals two dimensions where actions have to be taken in the years to come. Changes must be adopted in curriculum planning as well as in teacher training that take into account the differences in cultural and institutional backgrounds. Teacher professional development is starting slowly for CLIL on the secondary level, but almost no programs exist for the primary level. There are significant deficiencies in the development of bilingual curricula, and there are only a few empirical studies on the practices and effects of bilingual education in Germany. To inform this fairly new field of research, the scientific community can draw on studies carried out mainly in Canada and the United States (e.g., Calderón & Slavin, 2001; Christian, 1994; Christian, Montone, Lindholm, & Carranza, 1997; Cloud, Genesee, & Hamayan, 2000; Freeman, 2001; Genesee, 1987; Howard & Christian, 2002; Lindholm-Leary, 2001; Montague, Marroquin, & Lucido, 2002; Pérez, 2004; Pérez & Torres-Guzmán, 2002; Sugarman & Howard, 2001; Swain & Lapkin, 1982). Although these references provide important insights for further research, there is a need to create German corpora, a large set of documentation, that enable us to compare and to differentiate local and global conditions. As empirical research in dual-language education has started only recently in Germany (Gogolin, Neumann, & Roth, 2001, 2003; Gogolin, Neumann, Roth, & Hyla-Bruschke, 2001; Hansen, 2001; Neumann & Roth, 2004; Owen-Ortega, 2003; Roth, 2002, 2004), a deeper understanding of local conditions and experiences is needed. Since most of the current studies are quantitative and focus on measuring bilingual language proficiency, little is known about teaching and learning processes yet. Therefore, the focus of the present study is qualitative and addresses the issue of how teaching and learning unfold as social practices in the multilingual classroom. Thus, it will be important to understand what counts as meaningful forms of bilingual teaching and learning, and who benefits from these experiences, how, and in what ways.

RESEARCH METHODOLOGY

Research on bilingualism in a school context has been conducted from different perspectives. Depending on the research questions that are asked, studies adopt different understandings of language and language learning. There is a view that understands language learning as the acquisition of a set of skills that can be described and represented in a number of previously defined social and/or linguistic variables (Alanís, 2000; Gibbons & Ramirez, 2004; Oller & Eilers, 2002). Another view understands language learning as a social practice that unfolds in social interaction involving different levels of participation and recreating relations of power (Edelsky, 1996; Edelsky, Altwerger, & Flores, 1991; Martin-Jones & Saxena, 2003). This second view is also central to the idea of a community of practice (Lave & Wenger, 1991; Wenger, 1998), which provides an interesting theoretical framework for the present study. Eckert and McConnell-Ginet (1992/1998) have described a community of practice as follows:

> A community of practice is an aggregate of people who come together around a mutual engagement in some common endeavour. Ways of doing things, ways of talking, beliefs, values, power relations—in short, practices—emerge in the course of their joint activity around that endeavour. A community of practice is different as a social construct from the traditional notion of community, primarily because it is defined simultaneously by its membership and by the practice in which that membership engages. Indeed, it is the practices of the community and members' differentiated participation in them that structures the community socially. (p. 490)

This definition applies to the present study of a dual-language program in different ways. One aspect relates to the idea of specific practices that emerge through joint activities including both Italian and German as languages of bilingual learning. There is a need for the project to establish such practices, as it aims to give both languages legitimacy and to develop knowledge in both languages and cultures among all the students (Unger, 2001). Furthermore, such practices are not common either for many of the German students and teachers or for German society as the dominant surrounding environment. In order to make bilingualism a current practice for all of those who participate in the project, such practices have to become a substantial element of the teaching and learning routines.

A second aspect addresses the question of membership within the bilingual community of practice. Creating a linguistic environment in which bilingual practices are enacted as learning routines has an impact on the ways in which children identify socially. Children in the bilingual project negotiate language in interesting ways, wherein some of the categories of social identification they use are clearly linked to particular kinds of activities in which they engage. In these activities, having different individual linguistic repertoires is important and leads members to attribute to the speaker specific roles that are not only conventionalized but also reproduced in new and similar situations. Although there might be other ways of identifying that are meaningful for the children in different situations, the bilingual culture of the school project triggers an understanding that Italian and German are languages of equal status. It also potentially challenges established language hierarchies in the German-dominant society.

A third aspect addresses the issue of participation. Membership and degree of participation structure the community socially. Since participation is crucial when learning is understood as a social process, the bilingual project has sought to develop forms of teaching and learning that encourage participation by involving the individual students' linguistic repertoires (Foster, 1998). One type of activity that seems to support a relatively high level of participation from students with different backgrounds is bilingually designed tasks that require cross-linguistic peer collaboration. Encouraging activities that enlarge social participation also can lead to challenging or reversing established systems of belief and social hierarchies when knowledge that is generally less valued, for instance, competency in Italian, becomes an important resource for performing a task.

The study presented here aims to understand the whole process through which this new community of practice is coming to life. One important focus is school-based activities. Bilingual language practices and the ways in which they emerge, develop, and connect to other social categories, such as gender and social class, are therefore a central element of the study. An important goal is to understand the role of parents, school administrators, political authorities, and the Italian community in constructing and maintaining conditions that are crucial for the survival and development of the German–Italian bilingual project.

The empirical section of this chapter focuses on two questions that are directly linked to classroom activities, but also reach beyond the walls of the classroom. The first addresses the issue of how children position themselves socially, adopting or imagining specific roles that come from their experience in the bilingual project and are partly distinct from the social roles generated by the dominant society.

The second question addresses the issue of how bilingual language practices can be enhanced by including them in daily teaching and learning routines, for instance, as forms of tasks. Here, attention is paid to bilingually designed tasks that involve the participation of a cross-linguistic peer group contributing knowledge in Italian and German. The examples presented illustrate how bilingual learning is set up and what forms of individual learning occur when peer-group partners are working jointly to complete a bilingually designed task, but are learning different things.

The data presented here are of a qualitative nature and were collected during the first 2 years of schooling in 2003–2004. The data include participant observations of classroom activities that were videorecorded and/or stored in field notes, as well as artifacts from a portfolio activity that I asked the children to do during the summer holidays in 2004 and that they presented to the class at the beginning of the new school year. In this task I asked the children to choose five (or more) items from all the learning materials used in Grade 1 (drawings, texts, worksheets, etc.) and to think about their choice in relation to three questions: (1) why did I choose this item? (2) what do I like or dislike about it? (3) what did I learn using or making it? The children were to have conversations about their choices with their parents, and the parents were to take notes. Thus, two sets of data were collected: the student work and the parents' notes. The data also include retrospective interviews with 22 children that were conducted in pairs (the interviewer and two students). The interviews dealt with the portfolio of each child and attempted to elicit reflections on the children's bilingual learning experiences or even recreations of them.

CREATING A BILINGUAL COMMUNITY OF PRACTICE

When a dual-language program is implemented, a particular community of practice is created. This process relies on the mutual engagement of different social actors, including at least three levels of participation. The first level includes students and teachers as the main actors in classroom-based activities. Although the classroom itself represents a community, it is at the same time dependent on external conditions that reach into the classroom and cause the bilingual project to resonate back. These external conditions are shaped by social actors on a second level, including educational institutions and agents of the state bureaucracy that institutionalize curricula and ways of doing, thereby structuring the ways in which teaching and learning are enacted. On the third level are the parents, who come from different linguistic and social backgrounds. They engage in a variety of linguistic and social practices with their children, the teachers, other parents, and, occasionally, the representatives of municipal and state authorities. As a result, different levels of practice, including different social actors, topics, and aims of social action, can be observed.

Implementing a dual-language program involves "practices, routines, artefacts, symbols, conventions, stories, and histories" (Wenger, 1998, p. 6) that are new to the regular school system. This chapter shows how some of these new practices, conventions, artifacts, and stories come to life, and how they contribute to the idea of a bilingual community of practice. The first section of analysis addresses the issue of how participating in bilingual practices shapes or reshapes the positioning of the children in relation to their classmates and the world (Arce, 2000). It illustrates the argument that bilingual learning practices, by developing forms of cross-linguistic collaboration between students, increase respect for languages other than German and for classmates with multilingual repertoires. In the second section, the analysis explores ways in which bilingual practices in the classroom can be developed and sustained by making them an interesting experience for students with different needs (Wiese, 2001).

Negotiating Identity and Language Status

Identities can be based on a variety of factors, among which language is central. In the bilingual project, linguistic resources are important and contribute to allocating social roles that the students take on in the course of learning. However, their linguistic repertoires are complex, including more languages than German and Italian, but not all of them are used as a basis for social identification. This raises the question of why certain languages or linguistic repertoires are more likely than others to emerge as categories of identification. How does this relate to social practices and the ways in which a specific repartition of linguistic repertoires is valued in these practices? In what follows, I will argue that the ways in which children in the class identify and are identified are related to the ways in which languages are valued in the class and learning practices are structured linguistically. The co-presence and equal footing of German and Italian as languages of instruction lays the foundation for creating linguistic identities in these two languages that are considered by the students to be equal in status. These identities are generated and reinforced by specific practices of bilingual schooling, such as bilingually designed tasks, in which students repeatedly enact either a German or an Italian part, according to their linguistic repertoire. Due to the linguistic focus of the bilingual setting, other languages seem to be less relevant and tend to be left out in the students' identity constructions, as they are not part of regular learning routines. This is true for specific situations and interactions that I observed. However, there are other occasions where these languages, such as Persian, English, or Dutch, are given attention. They appear, for instance, when children are presenting their home reading to the class, bringing in material such as a community guide for Persians living in Frankfurt or a children's book in Dutch. Multilingual resources also become apparent while children are playing in the schoolyard or in the changing rooms, trying out their whole range of linguistic repertoire or guessing about those of their classmates.

The first example I want to discuss, Example 7.1, is taken from a pair interview and shows how the children identify themselves as German or Italian based on their linguistic repertoire. However, rather than being connected to an idea of ethnic or national collectivity, their positioning appears to be related to the roles that they adopt in the learning process.

With my first question, I seem to suggest that both boys are German. In fact, both do speak fluent German. Nevertheless, Matteo (all names are pseudonyms) refuses that classification, insisting on being identified as

Example 7.1. How task-based expert roles create identity

BENJAMIN: und das war die Sendung Matteo und Benjamin	BENJAMIN: that was the program Matteo and Benjamin
GABI: und jetzt die letzte Frage an die beiden Herren hier drüben auf der Bank, wie findet denn ihr das dass ihr auch mit italienischen Kindern zusammen seid hier in der Klasse?	GABI: and now the last question for the two gentlemen sitting over there, how do you like it to be with Italian children in the class?
BENJAMIN: gut	BENJAMIN: I like it
MATTEO: aber ich bin doch Italiener	MATTEO: but I am Italian
GABI: ja ja	GABI: oh yeah
BENJAMIN: und ich bin deutsch	BENJAMIN: and I am German
GABI: ja ja	GABI: oh yeah
MATTEO: ja deswegen helfen wir uns auch immer, weil das schön ist, ich kann ihm bei Italienisch helfen, er kann mir bei Deutsch auch sehr gut helfen	MATTEO: that's why we help each other all the time, because it's nice, I help him with Italian and he can help me with German
GABI: mh	GABI: mh
MATTEO: das macht so viel Spaß ge?	MATTEO: that's so much fun, isn't it, Benjamin?
BENJAMIN: zusammen arbeiten macht immer Spaß	BENJAMIN: working together is always nice
GABI: mh	GABI: mh
MATTEO: nur manchmal streiten wir uns, ge?	MATTEO: only sometimes we argue, right?

Italian, while Benjamin claims to be German. Both seem to have a stake in that investment because it becomes "part of who they are" (Wenger, 1998, p. 97). Matteo states the rationale for this identity choice, saying, "that's why we help each other all the time," and Benjamin adds that "working together is always nice." In this way, they express forms of membership and the source of their identities in the bilingual community of practice. Membership is ensured by participating in bilingual practices in which they work collaboratively and assume a linguistically defined role. Being Italian and being German are embodied as legitimate positions because they are valued through the language use in these practices. At the same time, choosing distinct identities that relate to linguistic capital in German or Italian underscores the condition under which interlinguistic collaborative work is possible. Matteo seems to make a connection between tasks that require both languages and the distinct linguistically defined roles that it is necessary to adopt in order to successfully complete these tasks. Furthermore, both students stress that they like engaging in collaborative cross-linguistic, peer-group work. They thereby sustain the rules set up in the bilingual project that aim at creating a culture of cooperative learning. Thus, it can be concluded that the boys' identities are emerging, at least partly, from specific learning practices and that their membership in the community is negotiated through participation in these practices.

Interestingly, the two main categories of identification are either German or Italian, although most of the Italians, including Matteo, are bilingual. Being bilingual, on its own, did not seem to be a relevant category, because it did not seem to raise distinctions that were relevant to the completion of bilingually designed tasks. In this case, where there are no monolingual Italian speakers in the class, bilinguals, as opposed to Germans, are identified according to their linguistic capital and their capacity to perform the Italian role in bilingual tasks.

For the project in general, the negotiation of status around the different kinds of linguistic resources is a permanent endeavor. It is quite surprising, though, to see how children deal with the different language repertoires of their classmates. In a situation like this, one might expect that children would discover and use language inequalities to play out relations of power in their own interest. I did, however, observe instances in that children didn't try to exercise power over one another, but tried instead to foster a language of common understanding and to develop collaborative strategies for sharing their unequal knowledge and equalizing differences. They faced the challenge and reacted naturally, looking for help where they could find it among their peers. This could be interpreted as another outcome of attempts to build a culture of collaborative learning.

Still, there are differential benefits and challenges that the community of practitioners has to account for. While children from a majority background enjoy the benefits of increased interest in other languages and of developing an understanding for those who grew up with more than one language, they also experience feeling what it means to be a minority and to be linguistically excluded. Minority students enjoy the legitimacy of their first language while acquiescing to the fact that German is established as the main language of communication among the students. However, bilingual learning also creates problems as children start off with different social and linguistic backgrounds. Example 7.2 illustrates that it is not always comfortable to rely on someone else's resources rather than possessing them oneself.

Karen is a monolingual German child and quite a bright student, but sometimes she doesn't feel comfortable asking for help and then suffers from not being able to complete a bilingually designed task on her own.

Example 7.2. Karen, a monolingual German, imagines to be bilingual

KAREN: ich find's toll dass ich Italienisch lerne	KAREN: it's gorgeous that I learn Italian
GABI: und dass da auch schon Kinder in der Klasse sind die das schon können	GABI: and that there are kids in the class who already speak it
SABINE: ja	SABINE: [another German girl] yes
KAREN: das ist auch schön nur manchmal	KAREN: this is also nice only sometimes
SABINE: weil dann hat man Hilfe	SABINE: [interrupts] because they can help you
KAREN: nur manchmal möcht ich gern'n italienisches Kind sein weil ich gern Italienisch können möchte	KAREN: only sometimes I would like to be an Italian child because I would like to know Italian

That is why she wishes to be a competent speaker of Italian, putting herself in the imaginative position of being an Italian child, who, in her understanding, doesn't have to face these problems. In doing so, she adds a new fictive role to the set of possible social identifications that emerge through bilingual practices, putting herself in someone else's position and guessing on the social consequences of having a different linguistic repertoire.

Practices and identities as they are enacted in the classroom also have an impact on social identification beyond the classroom. Participating in different communities of practice, such as school, family, or groups of friends involved in leisure activities, provides experiences in different social worlds that can have contrasting ways of using and valuing language. The school provides an experience that values bilingualism and thereby creates an alternative view that is different from that of the dominant society, which values German monolingualism. This creates some hope for a different understanding of multilingualism and its legitimacy in the future. But at the same time, this alternative view is confronted by the local and global language hierarchies, such as the hegemony of English, which prevails in many domains of mass culture.

In Example 7.3, Jacob shows how language issues from outside come into play in his classroom. Although the bilingual project creates the fiction of German and Italian as languages of equal status, the world outside, of course, can't be denied. The pressures of economically and socially grounded language hierarchies continue to resonate in the classroom. Jacob is one of the boys of Italian heritage. Since children of his age constantly are surrounded by English-speaking movies and music, English seems to have already gained a priority.

Prioritizing English as a language of preference, Jacob (otherwise the name would be spelled Jakob) already reproduces dominant views of

Example 7.3. Language hierarchies in the classroom

GABI: wie findet ihr's denn dass ihr jetzt beide Sprachen habt in der Schule?	GABI: how do you like it that you have both languages in school?
JAKOB: also mir wäre Englisch eigentlich besser aber Italienisch ist genauso gut	JAKOB: well I would like English better but Italian is as good

language hierarchies and the hegemonic power of English. Even though he rather plays around to tease me, it is clear that the dominant discourse on the importance of the English world has an impact on this 6-year-old. How his view of language hierarchies is evolving, and whether the bilingual project will contribute to challenging hegemonic views, remains another interesting issue to study. What can be observed at present is that the bilingual practices of the school start expanding into the children's homes as they interact with their parents. Parental and community involvement are seen as important factors in sustaining dual-language programs (Calderón & Rowe, 2003; Smith, 2001). In order to facilitate their children's learning, more than half of the German parents, mostly mothers, have decided to take part in an Italian-language course that is offered by the parents association as an evening class at the school. Since the beginning of the course, some mothers have discontinued attendance because of time constraints and/or decreasing interest. However, a significant number of German mothers continue and engage in learning practices with their children at home. Example 7.4 refers to such a practice, which takes place between Benjamin and his German mother, who participates in the evening Italian class.

Extending bilingual practices beyond the classroom is an important move to give the project a larger grounding. The practice mentioned above takes place in a setting different from school and involves a change of role for Ben-

Example 7.4. Extending bilingual practices beyond the classroom

BENJAMIN: ja das fand ich schön, weil man hier die Wochentage lernen konnte und dann hab ich der Mama zu Hause alle Wochentage beigebracht	BENJAMIN: that one I like because we could learn the days of the week [in Italian] and then I taught them all to my mum at home
GABI: wauh und hat sie sich was gemerkt	GABI: wow, did she remember some
BENJAMIN: ja das und das und das und das	BENJAMIN: yes that and that and that and that
GABI: was *lunedì*	GABI: here *lunedì* [Monday]
BENJAMIN: *lunedì, venerdì, sabato,* und *domenica*	BENJAMIN: *lunedì, venerdì, sabato* and *domenica* [Monday, Friday, Saturday, and Sunday]

jamin. In school, he is assigned to perform the German part (see Example 7.1); at home, he takes on the role of a teacher who is competent in Italian and thereby reverses the school routine. Being able to teach his mother, and telling me about it, appears to be a rewarding experience for him.

The examples in this section attempt to illustrate how identities emerge through bilingual practices and how they relate to ways in which linguistic resources are valued in these practices. The findings suggest that the monolingual identities of being Italian or being German are favored and equally valued, since they correspond to a distribution of linguistic capital that is needed to sustain forms of bilingual learning in the classroom. We also were able to see how classroom-based activities and systems of belief intertwine and contrast with other social spheres and views promulgated by the dominant society. Since identity-building and social positioning are dynamic processes, more research needs to be done on whether and how dominant ideologies of language can be challenged by dual-language education and in what ways.

Learning Through Participation

Recalling another important principle stated by Wenger (1998) and Eckert and McConnell-Ginet (1992/1998), learning is a social process and takes place through participation. That is why a dual-language program, like any other school program, needs to address the question of how to create opportunities that are likely to involve all students regardless of their different linguistic and social backgrounds. This aim is difficult to put into practice in any setting, but it is claimed that it is an essential condition for the success of bilingual programs. In fact, participation is a key issue in any educational setting; it only appears to be more salient in settings that are committed to systematically including more than one language but have to somehow accommodate the different levels of target languages brought in by the students.

In order to address the issue of participation, I will focus on two instruments used in the bilingual project, weekly plans (Freinet, 1994) and bilingually designed tasks. One of the basic principles of Célestin Freinet's pedagogy is the right to difference, respect for the individual, and responsibility for oneself and for others in the class. Pedagogical strategies that center on students and enhance collaboration and autonomous choices are favored. The use of weekly plans relies on the idea that a school day should not be completely structured and planned in advance. Students must have time to work on their own projects, when they choose their activities freely. In the bilingual project, the modification is that students freely choose the time and the partner, and the tasks included in the weekly plan are suggested by the teachers and are purposely designed as bilingual tasks.

Children find the weekly plans interesting to work with. I will argue that they are likely to encourage participation and thereby stimulate learning. I will then look at bilingually designed tasks as elements of weekly plans and argue that they open up possibilities for more participation that values resources in both German and Italian in specific ways. Moreover, I consider cases in which, at least to some extent, working in cross-language peer groups tends to reframe social positioning by revisiting common criteria and judgmental behaviors that define who counts as a stronger or a weaker learner. Finally, Example 7.8 will illustrate how cross-linguistic peer work unfolds around a bilingually designed task, creating an opportunity for children to learn different things according to their individual needs, linguistic resources, and levels of knowledge.

Weekly plans and bilingually designed tasks are pedagogical tools that support a child-centered approach to learning that takes into account the diversity of linguistic resources. It encourages children to learn from one another rather than rely on teachers as the sole language role models. In this way, the unequal distribution of linguistic repertoires is used as a resource to trigger children's participation and to create a collaborative learning culture in which differences in linguistic and cognitive achievement are equalized rather than emphasized.

The collaboration of paired bilingual groups is organized around weekly plans and bilingually designed learning tasks in the following ways. A weekly plan is used to assemble tasks from different areas, such as math, reading, and writing, and a certain amount of time throughout the week is reserved to work on it. During this time, children can decide autonomously on the time, subject, and partner for their learning. Worksheets and additional learning materials that are needed to complete the tasks included in the weekly plan are prepared by the teachers and made available in boxes for the students to pick up. The weekly plan as a learning tool was introduced after 1 month of schooling. Handling it requires a great deal of responsibility and autonomy. My observations, however, suggest that most of the children enjoyed working with weekly plans, and many of them chose one for their portfolio. In the interviews, the children not only revealed their ability to talk about the handling of this demanding tool but also pointed out how important it was for them to organize their activities autonomously with their peers. Moreover, they expressed their appreciation for the opportunity to create their own learning materials that drew on knowledge they had acquired previously.

Examples 7.5 and 7.6, drawn from interview data collected in September 2004 during the second year of the project, illustrate these findings. In Example 7.5, Karen, a German girl, speaks about taking responsibility for her learning and the pleasure and self-satisfaction she experiences with

Example 7.5. Autonomous learning with weekly plans

GABI: und was macht dir bei den Wochenplänen immer besonders Spaß?	GABI: is there something you like particularly with the weekly plan?
KAREN: dass man sich auch aussuchen kann welches man macht und ich find Wochenpläne einfach schön . . . und weil nicht vorgegeben ist und das da zuerst und das da und das und das da [klopft dazu auf den Tisch]	KAREN: that we can choose which one to do [first], I simply like weekly plans . . . and then because it's not set to do this first and then that and that and that [she knocks a few times on the table]

this opportunity. Karen communicates her dislike of interventionists and rigid styles of teaching. She enjoys creating her own structure according to her rhythm and immediate preferences.

Next, in Example 7.6, Sabine, another German girl, with whom Karen likes to work, appreciates this freedom, too. In addition, she points out her preference for the voluntary activities that are offered at the bottom of the plan for those who have finished the required part.

It was not only the brilliant students who invented riddles, worksheets, and other tasks that were reused by the teachers as didactic material for the whole class. Children who were slower and had more difficulties also participated in the creation of such materials, in both German and Italian. The fact that many children chose one or more worksheets produced by their classmates to include in their portfolio shows how much they identified with the work of their peers and how creatively they used the space that they had been given. As shown above, weekly plans are likely to trigger participation and creativity in both languages. They allow for learning opportunities and engagement in bilingual practices in different ways.

Within the work assembled in the weekly plans, the tasks are bilingually designed, integrating language learning in German and Italian with, for instance, science. These tasks also are bilingually labeled, identifying

Example 7.6. Creative learning with weekly plans

SABINE: Wochenplan hat mir immer gut gefallen, weil man da sich immer die Dinge aussuchen konnte, weil am am Ende immer sich da so Spiele ausdenken konnte	SABINE: I liked the weekly plan because we could always chose things and because at the end we could think up games [and riddles]
KAREN: hier, n' Rechenblatt das hat der Ronny gemacht, das fand ich schön	KAREN: this is a math worksheet, Ronny has done it, I liked it

an Italian student as "I" and a German student as "D" (for *Deutsch*). Completing the tasks requires the contributions of an Italian and a German child, which encourages language-crossing peer collaboration in which the different linguistic repertoires of two children are used. Example 7.7 suggests that privileging such activities also can enhance the engagement of marginalized students who are weaker learners and therefore tend to participate less. Encouraging their participation means counterbalancing dominant views on how to label social stratification and challenging criteria that are based on monolingual cognitive achievement.

Dana, who is German, and Lisa, who is Italian, have chosen each other as partners. Both are working on a task that consists of drawing lines between Italian words and corresponding images. For completing the task, reading skills and knowing Italian are both important. The interaction reveals that these abilities are unequally distributed between the participants. While Dana already reads German fluently, Lisa has serious problems with reading. On the other hand, Lisa is a competent speaker of Italian, while Dana lacks this knowledge. To complete the task, both contribute the resources available to them: Dana is able to provide the reading of the text, and Lisa is able to give meaning to the words in Italian. The different levels of reading proficiency are balanced because Lisa's knowledge of Italian, which is essential to the resolution of the task, is equally valued. This is an important experience for Lisa, since being a good or a bad reader plays a crucial role for first graders. According to that scale, Lisa is at the bottom, and she is aware of her position. The bilingually designed task provides her with a positive literacy experience where she feels satisfaction and demonstrates that she doesn't feel discouraged or blamed for being a bad reader. On the contrary, she approaches literacy with more interest and takes the risk of reading not only for herself, but in public and for another individual's consumption.

Example 7.7. Valuing complementary linguistic repertoire

GABI: kannst du das lesen?	GABI: can you read this?
DANA: nein ich weiß nicht was das heißt, Lisa weiß es, sie ist Italienisch [Lisa zeigt keine Reaktion]	DANA: no I don't know what that means, Lisa knows, she is Italian [Lisa shows no reaction]
DANA: [Dana versucht das Wort auf Italienisch zu lesen] *sa-pon-netta*	DANA: [Dana tries to read the word in Italian] *sa-pon-netta*
LISA: [Lisa wirft mit strahlendem Gesicht das Wort auf Italienisch ein] das heißt Seife	LISA: [Lisa jumps in and says the word in Italian, smiling all over her face] that means soap

This example is interesting because it suggests that cross-linguistic, peer-group work is a way of valuing marginalized linguistic capital and that it is likely to trigger the participation of those who usually remain excluded. Furthermore, this would suggest that there are conditions under which the unequal distribution of linguistic knowledge and skill can, if it is seen as a resource, counterbalance established hierarchies of social positioning to the advantage of those who usually are marginalized by them. However, it has to be noted that cross-linguistic, peer-group work does not necessarily evolve naturally. To unfold it as a valuable learning opportunity for students with different potentials, guidance by adults, the teachers or researchers, is needed (see my intervention in Example 7.7). A cross-linguistic peer collaboration without an adult's intervention can be found in Example 7.8. It accounts, in particular, for the diversity of individual learning processes that occur around resolving a bilingually designed task. Ronny, a German boy, and Carla, an Italian girl, are working on the same worksheet as Dana and Lisa in Example 7.7, but their interaction unfolds in a different way.

In this sequence, different interactional, linguistic, and cognitive processes occur in parallel forms. We can get a sense of how children collaborate, how they call for help, how they read to each other, how they correct each other, and how they build, correct, and formulate a new hypothesis. These children learn different things. Ronny acts competently in asking for help, and Carla acts competently in performing the role of teacher, giving only the amount of information that is needed to go to the next step. Ronny receives help in reading and pronouncing Italian words correctly, while Carla offers him the right acoustic pattern. Besides, Carla helps with the correct matching of words and pictures by correcting the mismatches. Traces of Carla's learning processes are apparent. Translating the Italian sequence *una saponetta pulita* into German, Carla reproduces the typical Italian word order with the adjective in postposition. A few moments later, Ronny asks her to do a structurally similar translation when he wants to know how to say *una sedia alta* in German. With his question, Ronny triggers a learning process because this time Carla puts the adjective in front of the noun, *ein hocher Stuhl*. Even if she doesn't choose the right grammatical form of the adjective, which is different from the adverb or copula form, she is able to correct herself and use the German word order correctly.

Other examples of positive experiences with weekly plans and bilingually designed tasks could be presented. Overall, these findings suggest that there are ways in which participation in bilingual practices can be encouraged by creating meaningful learning experiences for students (Budach, 2005). However, initial positive effects cannot be generalized yet. Therefore, it is important to conduct further research, paying close attention to

Example 7.8. How individual learning unfolds through cooperation

RONNY: was heißt das?	RONNY: what does this mean?
CARLA: was?	CARLA: what?
RONNY: [Ronny liest vor] *una sa-po-net-ta*	RONNY: [reads aloud] *una sa-po-net-ta*
CARLA: *saponetta*	CARLA: *saponetta*
RONNY: [versucht das Wort dem Bild zuzuordnen, zeigt auf den Stuhl] das?	RONNY: [tries to match the word with the right image, points to the chair] that one?
CARLA: nein Stuhl heißt *sedia* und das [zeigt auf die Seife] heißt *sapone*—Seife	CARLA: no chair means *sedia* and this [points to the soap] means *sapone*—soap
RONNY: mh und das? [zeigt auf *pulita*] *po*	RONNY: mh and this? [points to *pulita*] *po*
CARLA: *pu*	CARLA: *pu*
RONNY: *po-li-to*	RONNY: *po-li-to*
CARLA: *pulita*	CARLA: *pulita*
RONNY: was heißt das?	RONNY: what does this mean?
CARLA: sauber eine Seife sauber, eine Seife sauber. Ich gehe mal zu Luise gucken [verbringt einige Zeit bei einer Mitschülerin am Tisch]	CARLA: clean a soap clean [word order!], a soap clean. I go to look what Luise is doing [she spends some time at the neighboring table]
RONNY: Carla, Carla, komm, wir machen weiter [Carla kommt und liest, worauf Ronny zeigt]	RONNY: Carla, Carla, let's continue [Carla comes and reads aloud what Ronny is pointing to]
CARLA: *u-n-a s-edi-a alta* [zeigt auf die richtige Zeichnung] das hier	CARLA: *u-n-a s-edi-a alta* [points to the right picture] this one here
RONNY: und was heißt das?	RONNY: and what does this mean?
CARLA: ein hocher Stuhl	CARLA: a high chair

all students, including those who encounter no learning difficulties at all and those who have already received a recommendation for placement in special education. When looking at the experiences of all children, it will be important to ask whether they benefit, in what ways, and whether the program creates any difficulties for them. Thus, we can get a sense of how the bilingual community of practice is structured socially and to what extent it is possible to value linguistic diversity, to create more opportunities for participation, and to thereby make membership in that community more equitable.

CONCLUSION

At present, the political context in Germany seems to provide some space for developing bilingual education. This is particularly true for the two-way immersion programs that frequently grow out of bottom-up initiatives and the collective efforts of parental involvement. In my opinion, this is the result of converging political agendas to develop multilingualism, bringing together the educational interests of parents, migrant organizations, schools, the state, and the language policy of the European Union. On the one hand, legitimizing discourses that are produced by the different sides refer to common educational goals and tend to emphasize either the benefits of individual multilingualism or the need for an alternative to monolingual forms of schooling. On the other hand, more critical discourses that are grounded in the daily routine of bilingual projects tend to point to the difficulties and conflicts that arise from dealing systematically with linguistic and cultural heterogeneity.

Being aware of that complexity, initial findings of the study suggest that two-way immersion is an interesting alternative to monolingual forms of schooling. Making bilingual practices a part of daily teaching and learning routines seems to have a positive impact on social identification and ways of learning, since multilingual resources gain status as legitimate capital. Some findings even seem to suggest that, at least in some cases, bilingual practices in which the unequal distribution of linguistic repertoires is valued may challenge common criteria of social stratification by questioning cognitively based scales of achievement.

Preliminary results of the study also show that some forms of teaching and learning appear to be more appropriate than others in making bilingual practices an integral part of school culture. This study explored weekly plans and bilingually designed tasks as strategies of a child-centered approach. As the findings suggest, they are tools that seem to encourage participation by valuing unequally distributed linguistic repertoires and therefore to contribute actively to the creation of a bilingual community of practice. Furthermore, some findings underscore the potential of dual-language education for promoting linguistic diversity and developing an alternative view of language hierarchies that contrasts with that of the dominant society.

However, much more research on dual-language programs, their practices, and their outcomes is needed, since the institutional status of these programs is still fragile. There is a need to diversify the German school system, to develop multilingual and multicultural curricula, and to take into account the resources of an increasingly heterogeneous population. Therefore, it will be important for dual-language programs to gain recognition as a legitimate part of the German school system, leaving behind the image of experimental exoticism.

NOTES

1. Our group worked together with members of the research group Migration, Multilingualism and School, led by Professor Jürgen Erfurt, chair of Linguistics of Romance Languages.

2. In Germany, the school system divides after elementary school (4 years) into three different streams: (1) the *Gymnasium,* a high school leading to a diploma that allows for entry to a university; (2) the *Realschule,* which prepares for a degree that allows for an apprenticeship and professional preparation; and (3) the *Hauptschule,* which is for those who don't make it to the other types of schools. The German school system is highly socially selective, and the choice after elementary school is therefore most important. Another option for children with learning difficulties is to send them to special education programs. These are not integrated into the regular school system and take place in a completely separate institution from which a return to normal schooling is highly improbable.

REFERENCES

Alanís, I. (2000). A Texas two-way bilingual program: Its effects on linguistic and academic achievement. *Bilingual Research Journal, 24*(3), 225–248.

Arce, J. (2000). Developing voices: Transformative education in a first-grade two-way Spanish immersion classroom: A participatory study. *Bilingual Research Journal, 24*(3), 249–260.

Beardsmore, H. B. (Ed.). (1993). *European models of bilingual education.* Clevedon: Multilingual Matters.

Bernaus, M., Masgoret, A.-M., Gardner, R. C., & Reyes, E. (2004). Motivation and attitudes toward learning languages in multicultural classrooms. *International Journal of Multilingualism, 1*(2), 75–89.

Budach, G. (2005). Mehrsprachigkeit in der Grundschule? Betrachtungen zur Praxis von *Language Awareness* in einem bilingualen Projekt [Multilingualism in primary education? Practice of language awareness in a bilingual project]. In E. Burwitz-Melzer & G. Solmecke (Eds.), *Nie zu früh und selten zu spät. Fremdsprachenlernen in Schule und Erwachsenenbildung* [Never too early and rarely too late. Learning foreign languages in school and adult education] (pp. 43–52). Berlin: Cornelsen.

Calderón, M. E., & Rowe, L. M. (2003). *Designing and implementing two-way-bilingual programs: A step by step guide for administrators, teachers and parents.* Thousand Oaks, CA, and London: Sage.

Calderón, M., & Slavin, R. (2001). Success for all in a two-way immersion school. In D. Christian & F. Genesee (Eds.), *Bilingual education* (pp. 27–40). Alexandria, VA: TESOL.

Candelier M. (2006). L'éveil aux langues—une proposition originale pour la gestion du plurilinguisme en milieu scolaire [Eveil au langage—an original proposition for managing multilingualism in schools]. Contribution au Rapport mondial de l'UNESCO Construire des Sociétés du Savoir. In D. Cunningham, R. Freudenstein, & C. Odé (Ed..), *Language teaching: A worldwide perspective*, pp. 145–180). Belgrave: Fédération Internationale des Professeurs de Langues Vivantes.

Candelier, M., Andrade, A.-I., Bernaus, M., Kervran, M., Martins, F., Murkowska, A., Noguerol, A., Oomen-Welke, I., Perregaux, C., Saudan, V. and Zielinska, J. (2004). *Janua Linguarum—The gateway to languages. The introduction of language awareness into the curriculum.* Graz: European Centre for Modern Languages.

Christian, D. (1994). *Two-way bilingual education: Students learning through two languages* (Educational Practice Rep. No. 12). Santa Cruz, CA, and Washington, DC: National Center for Research on Cultural Diversity and Second Language Learning.

Christian, D., Montone, C., Lindholm, K., & Carranza, I. (1997). *Profiles in two-way immersion education.* McHenry, IL: Delta Systems.

Cloud, N., Genesee, F., & Hamayan, E. (2000). *Dual language instruction: A handbook for enriched education.* Boston: Heinle & Heinle.

Council Resolution on the Early Teaching of European Union Languages. (1997). Retrieved January 3, 2009, from http://eur-lex.europa.eu/LexUriServ/LexUriServ.do?uri=CELEX:31998Y0103(01):EN:HTML

De Pietro, J.-F. (2001). *Entre un projet initial et sa mise en œuvre: perspectives pour un curriculum intégré—Rapport du groupe de travail sur le curriculum.* [From the concept to its implementation: Suggestions for an integrated curriculum]. Evlang. Bruxelles: European Centre for Modern Languages.

Dewaele, J. M. (Ed.). (2003). *Bilingualism: Beyond basic principles.* Clevedon: Multilingual Matters.

Eckert, P., & McConnell-Ginet, S. (1992). Communities of practice: Where language, gender and power all live. In K. Hall, M. Bucholtz, & B. Moonwomon (Eds.), *Locating power: Proceedings of the 1992 Berkeley Women and Language Conference* (pp. 89–99). Berkeley: Berkeley Women and Language Group. (Reprinted in *Readings in language and gender*, pp. 484–494, by J. Coates, Ed., 1998, Cambridge: Blackwell.)

Edelsky, C. (1996). *With literacy and justice for all* (2nd ed.). London: Taylor & Francis.

Edelsky, C., Altwerger, B., & Flores, B. (1991). *Whole language: What's the difference?* Portsmouth, NH: Heinemann.

Foster, T. L. (1998). *Cooperative learning in a dual-language bilingual first-grade classroom: Peer partner selection and interaction across languages.* Unpublished doctoral dissertation, University of California, Santa Barbara.

Freeland, J. (1999). Can grass roots speak? The literacy campaign in English on Nicaragua's Atlantic coast. *International Journal of Bilingual Education and Bilingualism, 2*(3), 214–232.

Freeman, R. (2001). *Bilingual education and social change.* Clevedon: Multilingual Matters.

Freinet, C. (1994). *Les œuvres pédagogiques* (2 tomes). Paris: Ed. Seuil.

Genesee, F. (1987). *Learning through two languages: Studies of immersion and bilingual education*. Cambridge: Newbury House.

Gibbons, J., & Ramirez, E. (2004). *Maintaining a minority language: A case study of Hispanic teenagers*. Clevedon: Multilingual Matters.

Gogolin, I., Neumann, U., & Roth, H.-J. (2001). *Auswertung der ersten Sprachstandserhebung der portugiesisch deutschen Klasse, Schuljahr 2000/01* [Results of a first language proficiency test in a Portuguese-German class. Year 2000/01]. Hamburg: Univ. Hamburg (unpublished manuscript).

Gogolin, I., Neumann, U., & Roth, H.-J. (2003). *Bericht 2003: Schulversuch Bilinguale Grundschulklassen in Hamburg* [Report 2003: Bilingual primary education in Hamburg]. Hamburg: Univ. Hamburg, Arbeitsstelle Interkulturelle Bildung (unpublished manuscript.).

Gogolin, I., Neumann, U., Roth, H.-J., & Hyla-Brüschke, M. (2001). *Bericht über die wissenschaftliche Begleitung des Schulversuchs „Bilinguale Grundschule"* (Schuljahr 1999/2000 mit Ausblicken auf das Schuljahr 2000/2001))[Report and evaluative comments on the project "Bilingual primary school" (years 1999/2000 and prospective for 2000/2001)]. Department of Education, Hamburg (unpublished manuscript).

Hansen, C. (2001). *Bilingualer Schriftspracherwerb am Beispiel einer italienisch-deutschen Modellklasse einer Hamburger* [Bilingual literacy learning in primary education in an Italian-German class in Hamburg]. Grundschule: Department of Education Hamburg (unpublished manuscript).

Hawkins, E. (1984). *Awareness of language: An introduction*. Cambridge: Cambridge University Press.

Howard, E. R., & Christian, D. (2002). *Two-way immersion 101: Designing and implementing a two-way immersion education program at the elementary school level*. Santa Cruz, CA, and Washington, DC: Center for Research on Education, Diversity and Excellence.

Lave, J., & Wenger, E. (1991). *Situated learning: Legitimate peripheral participation*. Cambridge: Cambridge University Press.

Lindholm-Leary, K. (2001). *Dual language education*. Clevedon: Multilingual Matters.

Martin-Jones, M., & Saxena, M. (2003). Bilingual resources and "funds of knowledge" for teaching and learning in multi-ethnic classrooms. In A. Creese & P. Martin (Eds.), *Multilingual classroom ecologies* (pp. 107–122). Clevedon: Multilingual Matters.

Montague, N. S., Marroquin, C., & Lucido, F. (2002). A dual language curriculum for young children. In J. Cassidy & S. D. Garrett (Eds.), *Early childhood literacy: Programs and strategies to develop cultural, linguistic, scientific and healthcare literacy for very young children & their families, 2001 Yearbook*. Corpus Christi, TX: CEDER.

Neumann, U., & Roth, H.-J. (2004). Bilinguale Grundschulklassen in Hamburg. Ein Werkstattbericht. [Bilingual classes in primary schools in Hamburg: Notes from a workshop]. *Grenzgänge, 21*, 31–60.

Oller, D. K., & Eilers, R. E. (Eds.). (2002). *Language and literacy in bilingual children*. Clevedon: Multilingual Matters.

Owen-Ortega, J. (2003). *Schriftspracherwerb bilingualer Kinder am Beispiel einer spanisch-deutschen Klasse unter besonderer Berücksichtigung ihrer Strategien des Orthographieerwerbs in der Alphabetisierungsphase* [Bilingual literacy learning in a Spanish-German class with an emphasis on strategies of acquiring orthography]. Hamburg (unpublished manuscript).

Pérez, B. (2004). *Becoming biliterate: A study of two way bilingual immersion education*. Mahwah, NJ: Erlbaum.

Pérez, B., & Torres-Guzmán, M. E. (2002). *Learning in two worlds: An integrated Spanish/English biliteracy approach* (3rd ed.). Boston: Allyn & Bacon.

Roth, H.-J. (2002). *Il gatto va sull'albero—va sull'albero il gatto. Satzmuster und Sprachstand italienisch-deutscher Schulanfänger* [The cat goes up the tree–up the tree goes the cat: Syntactic pattern and language proficiency of German-Italian first graders]. Hamburg: Universität Hamburg, Arbeitsstelle Interkulturelle Bildung (unpublished manuscript).

Roth, H.-J. (2004). *Seguimos con el otro . . . Bericht zu den spanisch-deutschen Klassen im ersten Schuljahr. Zur Entwicklung der gesprochenen und geschriebenen Sprache* [Let's follow the other: Report on Spanish-German students in Grade 1. Notes on the development of speech and writing]. Hamburg: Universität Hamburg. Arbeitsstelle Interkulturelle Bildung.

Sjögren, A., & Ramberg, I. (2005). *Quality and diversity in higher education: Experiences from intercultural teacher education*. Stockholm: Multicultural Centre.

Smith, P. H. (2001). Community language resources in dual language schooling. *Bilingual Research Journal, 25*(3), 375–404.

Staatliche Europaschule Berlin (European State School Berlin). (2009). Retrieved January 3, 2009, from http://www.berlin.de/sen/bildung/besondere_angebote/staatl_europaschule/

Sugarman, J., & Howard, L. (2001). Two-way immersion shows promising results: Findings from a new study. *ERIC/CLL Language Link: An Online Newsletter from the ERIC Clearinghouse on Languages and Linguistics*. Retrieved June 26, 2008, from http://www.cal.org/resources/langlink/current2.html

Swain, M., & Lapkin, S. (1982). *Evaluating bilingual education: A Canadian case study*. Clevedon: Multilingual Matters.

Unger, M. (2001). Equalizing the status of both languages in a dual immersion school. *The ACIE Newsletter, 5*(1), 1, 2, 8, 12, 13.

Wenger, E. (1998). *Communities of practice: Learning, meaning, and identity*. Cambridge: Cambridge University Press.

Wiese, A. M. (2001). *"To meet the needs of the kids, not the program": Teachers constructing policy, program, and practice in a bilingual school*. Unpublished doctoral dissertation, University of California, Berkeley.

8

Multilingualism in Action

Language Education Policy in the Rapidly Changing Society of Taiwan

Chen-ching Li

This chapter examines the history, legacy, and prospects of multilingualism in Taiwan, from the island's early settlement by indigenous Austronesian peoples and subsequent occupation by Dutch, Portuguese, and Chinese forces, to Japanese rule at the dawn of the 20th century and the influx of mainland Chinese immigrants after World War II. It then explores in detail the postwar period, a time of rapid transition characterized by the internationalization of trade and advances in information technology, which have attracted growing numbers of foreign nationals to the island and, in turn, created a domestic demand for knowledge of foreign languages and cultures. Democratization of the political system, on the other hand, has led to a greater awareness of indigenous languages, leading to greater efforts to preserve oral traditions. The twin forces of internationalization and greater local awareness have combined to reshape the landscape of language education in Taiwan, producing a new generation that is at once more cosmopolitan and more aware of its linguistic and cultural roots.

Traditional Chinese

本文探討台灣語言多元政策的過往與未來。首先從歷史角度一窺台灣語言發展：從早期南島語系原住民的墾居，到荷蘭、葡萄牙、中國等殖民勢力的入駐，到二十世紀初日本的佔領，最後提及戰後來自中國大陸的外省移民遷入。接著將焦點放在二次大戰後的語言背景與演變。在這過程中，戰後的台灣由於進出口貿易發達、並且

Global Perspectives on Multilingualism, edited by María E. Torres-Guzmán and Joel Gómez.

資訊產業先進，因而吸引了大量的外籍人士來台就業，同時也使得台灣本地人對於外國語言與文化產生了興趣與需求。另一方面，台灣政治的民主化也使得民眾越來越重視本土語言，使得政府更致力於本土方言與弱勢族群語言的保存。國際化與本土化兩大力量共同勾勒出了台灣語言教育的版圖，也同時造就出了更具國際視野卻又更明瞭本土語言文化的台灣新生代。

GLOBAL REALITY OF MULTILINGUALISM

The growing importance of multilingualism is already having an impact on education reform initiatives in the multilingual society of Taiwan. Building on community multilingualism, educators envision a more harmonious nation in an increasingly diverse social and linguistic context.

In the wake of Taiwan's democratization, modernization, and education reform, and its recent ascension to the World Trade Organization, its role in promoting multilingualism will become much more prominent. As people worldwide become more aware of issues such as the digital divide, e-commerce, e-learning, cross-cultural learning, and the internationalization of education, the role played by multilingualism will become increasingly significant.

This new international awareness has prompted Taiwan to recruit more international professionals to work in its high-tech industry. The Taipei-based *United Daily News* (Hua, Li, & Chang, 2004) has written about a newly formed international community adjacent to Taiwan's Hsin-chu Science Park in which Indians, Koreans, Japanese, Malaysians, Americans, Europeans, and Australians live together harmoniously in an atmosphere of cultural and linguistic diversity. Multilingual ability and cultural awareness have enabled these professionals to work side by side, often in collaborative formats, within this high-tech city. The offspring of these expatriates, born and raised in this international community, also have grown to become multilingual.

In the face of continuous globalization in various economic and political sectors and a rapidly changing world dependent on high technology, Taiwan has been bracing for the diverse challenges of education reform on a large scale. National policy on the language rights of diverse ethnic groups and the growing number of immigrants from overseas also is being revised, and new laws have been enacted to safeguard equality for all in language education as well as social welfare. As a result, multilingualism has become a major issue not only with regard to school curricula but also in social commentary and day-to-day conversation.

In the sections below, I first will present a historical overview of multilingualism on the island of Taiwan, including its aboriginal roots and its brushes with Chinese, Japanese, and European colonial powers. This will be followed by a discussion of issues that loomed large in the mid-20th century, when the emphasis was on promoting the national language, Mandarin, while at the same time preserving local dialects and indigenous languages. Finally, I will examine the promotion of English-language education in Taiwan toward the end of the 20th century in the age of digitalization and globalization. How Taiwan manages to promote the languages of majority and minority groups, and to balance the languages of the hometown and global business, will determine whether it achieves the goal of multilingualism within its society.

HISTORICAL ROOTS OF MULTILINGUALISM IN TAIWAN

Taiwan is a linguistically and culturally diverse country whose majority population consists of Chinese settlers from China's Fujian and Guangdong provinces who began coming to the island in the early 16th century. Due to overpopulation and hardships in these two coastal provinces, Emperor Qianlong, the third ruler of the Qing dynasty (1736–1795), who was known for his appreciation of the value of extensive learning and global outlook, issued a decree in 1785 that officially allowed the Chinese to migrate to Taiwan. These early settlers spoke Taiwanese (also known as Southern Min), Cantonese, and the Hakka dialect. This population increased to 900,000 by 1790, and 2 million by 1810. In 1895, when Taiwan was handed over to Japan after the first Sino-Japanese War, there were 2.5 million Chinese living on the island.

Long before the arrival of these Chinese settlers, however, Taiwan had 11 tribes of indigenous peoples scattered throughout the island: the Atayal, the Saisiyat, the Bunun, the Tsou, the Thao, the Paiwan, the Rukai, the Puyuma, the Amis, the Yami, and the Kavalan. These tribes were speakers of Austronesian languages that were similar to Polynesian or Malay, but different from the languages of the Chinese immigrants. From early on, the linguistic landscape of Taiwan was a complicated one, and it often was affected by intranational and international developments.

The history of Taiwan is a story of both frustration and miracles. Isolated and poorly developed, the island was largely neglected before the 17th century. But during the age of exploration and maritime conquest by Europeans, it attracted world attention because of its strategic location and natural resources. The Dutch (1624) and the Spanish (1628) colonized parts of northern and southern Taiwan. Zheng Cheng-gong (also known as Koxinga), who was loyal to China's fallen Ming dynasty, defeated the Dutch in 1662 and set up a government on Taiwan to defy the Manchus, who had established the Qing dynasty in China. The Manchus conquered Taiwan in 1683 and ruled it until 1895, when it was ceded to Japan after the first Sino-Japanese War.

The Japanese rule of Taiwan between 1895 and 1945 was to have lasting consequences. In 51 years of colonization, Japanese language and culture were ingrained in the society of Taiwan, creating an intimate relationship between these two cultures that still has manifestations in today's world.

Taiwan was returned to China in 1945 at the end of World War II. Four years later, the Nationalist government lost the Chinese mainland to the communists and relocated to Taiwan. It was during this time that Mandarin Chinese became the language of instruction for all levels of schooling.

The pluralistic and multicultural forces that shaped the early history and linguistic development of Taiwan from the 16th century to the present have had an immense impact on the contemporary societal development of the island. It generally is agreed that there currently are four major ethnic groups, namely, the aboriginal peoples (2%), mainlanders (13%), Hakkas (15%), and Southern Min (70%). Democratic reforms initiated in the 1980s eventually led to the Language Equality Law, enacted in 2003, which grants equal status to languages spoken by different ethnic groups (see http://www.taiwannation.org.tw/republic/ rep31–40/no31_17.htm). The law, which marks a policy shift from an era when Mandarin was the only officially recognized language of Taiwan, is yet another sign of the island's growing celebration of multilingualism.

NATIONAL LANGUAGE POLICY AND MINORITY DIALECTS

To enhance nationwide communication and promote educational efficiency, the government of the Republic of China (Taiwan) founded the National Language Committee in 1946 to promote the learning of Mandarin Chinese, which had become the sole language of instruction in all levels of schooling. The principles and practices of teaching Mandarin that were promoted at the time followed the theories and recommendations of prominent linguists such as Y. R. Chao, Chi-hui Wu, Yu-pei Chao, Lee Hsian, and others, who saw the need for a national standard language and developed phonetic spelling systems and linguistic descriptions to aid in the promotion of the standard (see http://www.edu .tw/EDU_WEB/Web/MANDR/index.htm).

In contrast to the promotion of Mandarin Chinese in mainland China, only half of whose population spoke Mandarin as of 2004 (see http://www.moe.edu.cn/edoas/website18/info8989.htm), the promotion of Mandarin Chinese in Taiwan was so successful that as of 1991, 90% of the population spoke Mandarin (see http://www.npf.org.tw/PUBLICATION/ EC/092/EC-B-092-019.htm). Many of the young children in urban areas have shifted toward becoming monolingual, speaking Mandarin Chinese, but not Taiwanese or Hakka. This has prompted worries about the consequences of children abandoning their parents' native languages.

The successful democratic and social movements of the 1980s were conducive to reforms in education and language. The issue of language equality came to the forefront as Taiwan began to practice its newly acquired democracy. Advocates for different ethnic groups began to voice the need for learning and speaking their languages.

When the Legislative Yuan, the highest law-making body of Taiwan, enacted a new Language Equality Law in 2003, it mandated that all languages spoken in Taiwan be further protected and honored on an equal basis in all walks of public life. The preamble of this law reads as follows:

> The [Language Equality] Law has been enacted to safeguard the rights and freedom of all ethnic groups in using their language daily while participating in all public affairs in politics, economics, religion, education and culture. The domain of the Law is extended to the languages of minority groups, including Amis, Atayal, Paiwan, Bunun, Kavalan, Puyuma, Rukai, Tsou, Seediq, Yami, Thao, etc., as well as Hakka, Southern Min and Mandarin Chinese.

The languages of the aboriginal ethnic groups used to be neglected due to their small numbers and lower socioeconomic status. But since the enactment of the Language Equality Law, the teaching and learning of the 11 aboriginal languages, as well as the Southern Min and Hakka dialects, are being promoted. The ad hoc Education Reform Review Committee, appointed by the president of Taiwan (ROC), insisted that the languages of the aborigines and the Taiwanese dialects be taught in elementary school, alongside the teaching of English as a foreign language. There are indications that these minoritized languages may soon become compulsory subjects from elementary school onward.

The impact of national education reform in Taiwan is widely felt. As a result, two governmental agencies have been formed to meet the needs of minority ethnic groups: the Council for Hakka Affairs and the Council of Indigenous Peoples.

Council for Hakka Affairs

The Council for Hakka Affairs (CHA) was founded on June 14, 2001, based on the Organization Ordinance of the Council for Hakka Affairs and the Organization Law of the Council for Hakka Affairs, both of which were passed on May 11, 2000, by the Executive Yuan, the highest administrative body of the government of Taiwan, led by the premier, who, in turn, is appointed by the president.

The CHA was established in response to the fervent wishes of the Hakka community. Suppressed by mainstream cultures, the Hakka language is now facing extinction. In response to this, the Hakka community demanded that the central government establish an institute that would provide leadership in Hakka affairs and use the power of the state to sustain the Hakka language and culture.

In order to revive the Hakka language and culture, the CHA has formulated seven programs, including a Six-Year Plan for the First Step of the Revival and Eternal Growth of Hakka Language and Culture. In addition to organizing learning activities and recording Hakka customs, language, and culture, the CHA plans to subsidize Hakka literature, music, and art activities on a large scale.

In a span of 3 years, there has been some increase in the social spaces in which the Hakka language is being heard. Whereas Hakka was virtually absent from public broadcasting prior to the establishment of the CHA, there is now a Hakka television channel, and radio broadcasts in Hakka are now commonplace, especially in north-central Taiwan, where the Hakka community is concentrated. In education, the Hakka language has been adopted in the elementary and secondary school curricula. Thanks to the CHA, revival efforts are ongoing, and the Hakka language seems to be experiencing a renewal.

Council of Indigenous Peoples

Paragraph 11 of Article 10 of the Additional Articles of the Constitution of the Republic of China (Taiwan) states:

> The State affirms cultural pluralism and shall actively preserve and foster the development of indigenous languages and cultures. The State shall, in accordance with the desires of ethnic groups, safeguard their status and political participation. The State shall also guarantee, and provide assistance and encouragement for, indigenous education, culture, transportation, water conservation, health and medical care, economic activity, land and social welfare, measures for which shall be established by law. (http://www.taiwandocuments.org/constitution04.htm)

Prior to 1996, the highest government agency in charge of the general affairs of the indigenous peoples was the Indigenous Section under the Civil Affairs Department of the Ministry of the Interior. On November 1, 1996, the Legislative Yuan passed the Organic Law of the Council for Indigenous Affairs (see http://db.lawbank.com.tw/Eng/FLAW/ FLAWDAT0202.asp). On December 10 of the same year, the council was officially established so that the native languages of indigenous people could be duly preserved and promoted through educational initiatives. The functions of the Council of Indigenous Peoples in reviving native languages are similar to those of the Council for Hakka Affairs.

TRENDS IN MULTILINGUALISM IN TWENTY-FIRST-CENTURY TAIWAN

As a result of the laws and language reforms mentioned in the previous sections, Mandarin Chinese, Southern Min, Cantonese, Hakka, and the Formosan (indigenous) languages now enjoy a legally framed freedom that they did not have previously. Although Mandarin Chinese has been the language of school instruction, it must now compete with other languages and/or dialects as a means of communication in different subjects and domains. In recent years, Taiwanese and Hakka have been used widely in political and cultural activities, and the protection of indigenous languages is receiving much political attention. In the meantime, English and other foreign languages continue to be promoted as Taiwanese recognize the need for globalization and the internationalization of education in this era of knowledge-based economies. With the rapid development of science and technology sparking growth in the number of multinational corporations in Taiwan and the Chinese-speaking communities of the Asia Pacific region more broadly, the promotion of English and other foreign languages has received great attention at the national level. In one mandate of Taiwan's Executive Yuan, the efficient teaching and learning of English has become a major policy objective, a "national goal" to be achieved by 2008.

According to statistics compiled by the Ministry of Education (2004), out of a total student population of 5,376,947, about 90% are struggling with the learning of English as a foreign language. This includes 23.78% in colleges and universities, 25.36% in secondary schools (grades 7–12), 36.03% in primary schools, and 4.49% in kindergartens. The learning of English in Taiwan has become not just a fashion, but a social and economic necessity that has repercussions throughout the educational system. Consequently, young children in kindergarten are now learning English, many from teachers who are native speakers of English, part of the imported professional class that has increased dramatically in the past decade.

Language education policy in Taiwan has focused not only on the national language, Mandarin Chinese, and the languages of all the other ethnic groups, such as the Hakka and the indigenous peoples, but specifically on the role of English, which is regarded as a *lingua franca* for global communication. Since the early 1950s, English has become the dominant language of international business, higher education, information and communication technologies, popular culture, diplomacy, and more (Duff, 2004; Li, 2004). Thus, proficiency in English has become indispensable to all who intend to thrive in this modern world of cultural diversity and information technology. Social and economic development has intensified the proliferation of English in Asian countries.

To meet the challenge of efficiently learning the four language skills (listening, speaking, reading, and writing) of English, as well as the art of translation and interpretation, English-language educators all over the world have been searching for ways to help learners attain a higher level of proficiency so as to meet the needs of fast-growing businesses that operate in an international setting. English has become the international language of this era. Those who don't learn it will be disadvantaged. Thus, English-language teaching has been recognized as a formal discipline in institutions of higher learning in many countries.

Taiwan has established two major policies in relation to the promotion of English and second foreign languages. They are described in the following sections.

Extension of English Teaching to Third Grade

When English was first included in the Chinese curriculum at the turn of the 20th century, instruction started in Grade 7, and this was also the case in Taiwan. In 2001, however, this was lowered to Grade 5 by a directive from the Ministry of Education. In 2005, there was a further lowering to Grade 3. In metropolitan areas such as Taipei, English is now taught from Grade 1. Since 2000, a number of bilingual elementary schools have been established in urban areas, in which instruction is given in both Mandarin and English.

Second Foreign Languages in High School

To promote multilingualism, the teaching of Japanese, French, German, and Spanish has been implemented at the high school level on a voluntary basis. Starting in 1999, the Ministry of Education allocated a budget of NT$83,000,000 (US$2,515,151) to assist in the teaching of foreign languages in high schools. This 5-year project focused on three main areas: encouraging as many high schools as possible to offer second foreign languages; improving the quality of foreign-language teaching; and creating a sound environment for multilingual learning. According to the statistics of the Ministry of Education (2004), the number of schools offering second foreign languages increased rapidly, as shown in Figure 8.1.

The Ministry of Education decided to renew support for the teaching of Japanese, French, German, and Spanish in high schools for another 5 years (2005–2009). It is possible that the teaching and learning of these four foreign languages also will contribute to developing an appreciation for multilingualism in Taiwanese society.

CONCLUSION: PROSPECTS FOR MULTILINGUALISM IN TAIWAN

Duff (2004) has stated:

> With the intense globalization and human migration taking place within the Asia-Pacific region as well as beyond it, an appreciation of multiple languages and cultures and an ability to communicate effectively with people across languages, cultures, and communities is crucial. (p. 1)

Freeman (2004), speaking about the United States, has observed:

Figure 8.1. Schools offering a second foreign language

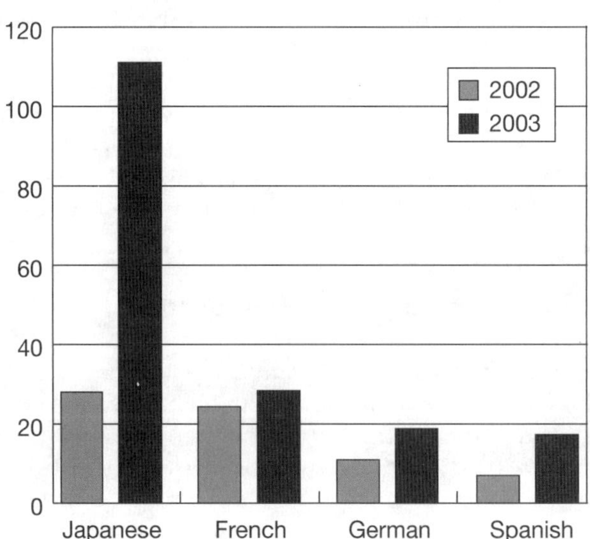

> Additive bilingual programs enable students (English language learners, heritage language speakers, and English speakers) to develop oral and written expertise in two languages, achieve academically, and develop intergroup understanding and relations. At the same time, they offer additional short-term and long-term benefits to students, their families, local communities, and the nation overall. (p. 325)

The Taiwanese situation discussed in this chapter resonates with both statements. Taiwan has been coping with the endless challenges of bringing itself into the world of modernity and globalization. With its rapid development in science and technology, as well as in global business networking, pushing the agenda of multilingualism is likely to assist Taiwan in ensuring a brighter future for its people at home and abroad.

REFERENCES

Duff, P. A. (2004). Foreign language policies, research and educational possibilities: A Western perspective. *Proceedings from the 3rd APEC Education Ministerial Meeting*, Santiago, Chile.

Freeman, R. (2004). *Building on community bilingualism*. Philadelphia: Caslon.

Hua, Y., Li, C., & Chang, N. (2004, August 9). The new portrayal of Taiwan: The input of multinational high-tech professionals into the local community. *United Daily News*, p. A3.

Li, C. (2004). Promising practice: English language teaching and foreign language learning in Chinese Taipei. *Proceedings from the 3rd APEC Education Ministerial Meeting*, Santiago, Chile.

Ministry of Education. (2004). *Educational statistics of the Republic of China*. Taipei: Ministry of Education (ROC).

9

Effective Transformation or Illusion?

Teacher Empowerment Through the Construction of Bilingual Education Programs in Colombia

Anne-Marie de Mejía, Harvey Tejada, and Sol Colmenares

In this chapter we discuss the notion of teacher empowerment as documented in a research study carried out in Cali, Colombia. The project on which this chapter is based was aimed both at developing proposals for an appropriate bilingual program for a school in the process of transition toward bilingualism, and also at facilitating a process of empowerment among those involved. In order to situate the project appropriately, we first describe the general sociolinguistic and cultural context of Colombia. We then make reference to findings arising from a discourse analysis of interactive data from group discussions in the project. These show that interstices exist that provide sites for the development of different practices of resistance and empowerment despite the rigidity that apparently characterized power relations among participants in the project. We conclude by suggesting ways in which legitimizing participants' voices may weaken vertical power relations and consider how the insights arrived at in this project may contribute to a greater awareness of these issues among those involved in developing bilingual or multilingual educational programs in the future.

Este capítulo surge a partir de una investigación colaborativa llevada a cabo en un colegio de la ciudad de Cali, Colombia. En la investigación, que fue realizada con dos propósitos fundamentales (desarrollar un programa bilingüe apropiado para el colegio y promover un proceso de empoderamiento entre los sujetos involucrados en la propuesta), se procesaron, a través del análisis del discurso, datos provenientes de las discusiones grupales del proyecto. Los resultados de ese análisis indican que, a pesar de la rigidez que parece caracterizar las relaciones de poder entre los distintos participantes del proyecto, existen intersticios donde se desarrollan prácticas de resistencia y

---

empoderamiento. El capítulo concluye sugiriendo formas en que las relaciones verticales de poder pueden ser debilitadas a través de acciones de legitimación de las voces de los participantes. Se considera, además, cómo las reflexiones a las que se llegó en este proyecto pueden contribuir a desarrollar niveles mayores de conciencia sobre estos temas entre sujetos involucrados en el desarrollo de programas bilingües o multilingües en el futuro.

SITUATION OF MULTILINGUALISM IN COLOMBIA

Colombia, which is a geographical gateway between Central and South America, was recognized officially for the first time as a multilingual and multicultural nation in the Colombian Political Constitution of 1991. Sixty different Amerindian vernacular languages and the English- and Spanish-based Creole languages (known as Islander English and *Palenquero*, respectively) were given co-official status with Spanish (the dominant language). In addition, bilingual education was recognized, for the first time, as the form of education to be implemented in these territories (www.banrep.gov.co/ regimen/resoluciones/cp91).

Although official recognition was hailed by many members of the minority-language communities as a great step forward, this did not immediately change ingrained attitudes toward these minoritized languages, particularly the Creole languages, which often are considered examples of badly spoken, or "broken," English or Spanish. However, as noted by Dieck (1998), there is recent evidence of change in this area, in that members of the *Palenquero* community of Palenque de San Basilio and the Islander English speakers of the Caribbean islands of San Andrés and Old Providence are beginning to revalue their languages, seeing them as a part of their cultural heritage that needs to be preserved.

In 1994, the Law of Education established a policy of ethno-education for minority communities in Colombia, characterizing this bilingual initiative as "a permanent social process of reflection and collective construction, by means of which the Indian communities would strengthen their autonomy within an intercultural framework" (Trillos, 1998, p. 73).

The other main tradition of provision for multilingual education involves bilingual programs for majority-language (Spanish) speakers in international languages, particularly English, which is a rapidly growing phenomenon. There is a dominant discourse in the country about "ínvesting" in English, and this language is associated by many Colombians with economic prosperity and positions of prestige (Valencia, 2005).

Consequently, English–Spanish bilingual education programs have a high profile among the Colombian middle and upper classes. This chapter will focus on bilingualism for Spanish-language speakers in the international language of English, as this is the field in which our research team has been working in recent years.

The rosy scenario associated with bilingual programs for majority speakers does not mean, however, that bilingualism is problem free. In a survey carried out in 2001 (Mejía & Tejada), it was found that there were four main difficulties associated with the development of Spanish–English bilingual schools in Colombia at the institutional level.

1. There is an almost complete lack of coherent school policies that justify language distribution throughout the curriculum on academic and contextual grounds, and that contemplate treating cultural aspects from a multicultural, bicultural, or intercultural perspective.
2. On the part of some teachers, school administrators, and parents, there is a perception of biculturalism or interculturalism as a threat to school philosophy and national identity, particularly in schools that have long-established roots or religious orientations. Similarly, there is some evidence of the foreign language being seen as a threat to the development of the students' first language.
3. In contrast to the previous point, there is a tendency for some institutions to focus almost exclusively on the foreign language and culture, while the development of the students' first language and culture is seen as of secondary importance.
4. There is a widespread need for appropriate teacher training and development to bridge the traditional divide between foreign-language teachers and subject (content) specialists.

In keeping with a focus that positions the school as a place of promise and resistance with respect to the world's linguistic diversity, in this chapter we will discuss issues arising from one particular collaborative research project carried out recently in a school in Colombia, where we were commissioned to develop an appropriate bilingual program, and in which we contextualized our interest in examining processes of empowerment among project participants. We will argue that in spite of the rigidity that seemed to characterize power relations among different participants, there is evidence that there are "interstices," or social spaces, that provide sites for the development of different practices of resistance (Martin-Jones & Heller, 1996) and empowerment.[1] We will go on to suggest that it is important to support such processes of teacher empowerment if multilingual education programs are to develop effectively in the future.

RESEARCH SITE AND METHODOLOGICAL ORIENTATION

The research site was a private Catholic school situated in the south of the city of Cali, the third-largest city in the country. In Colombia, many parents from higher socioeconomic groups send their children to private, fee-charging schools, as free public education is available to only a limited number of students, usually from the poorest sections of the population. The school had around 1,000 students at the time of the study, divided into three levels: preschool, primary, and secondary.

The school, originally founded by nuns, is concerned with promoting Christian ideals in its students, emphasizing moral values and the development of a strong sense of cultural identity. Although the school was a monolingual Spanish-speaking institution, the school authorities were conscious of the need for students to reach a good level of proficiency in English in order to be able to compete successfully in the job market. Consequently, the school recently had intensified the use of this language in the curriculum, with a view to developing a full English–Spanish bilingual program in the future.

Initially, the school had approached the Universidad del Valle to request a consultancy on how best to implement a bilingual education program. In this type of intervention, university staff usually are seen as outside experts who are brought in to conduct a study and write a report detailing results and recommendations for further implementation. In this particular case, the head teacher of the school requested help in strengthening the process of bilingual education at the preschool level as well as extending it at the primary level, with a view to eventually restructuring the whole school as a bilingual institution. However, our team of researchers was interested in examining the notion of empowerment in relation to curriculum construction, in line with ideas on empowering research proposed by Cameron and colleagues (1992), as we had begun to do in a previous project (Mejía & Tejada, 2001). We therefore persuaded the school to agree to a different type of intervention involving a collaborative research perspective and formed a group of co-researchers from both the school and the university.

While it might be suggested that persuading the school to agree to a novel type of research relationship was an imposition on the part of the university staff's agenda, it also might be argued that the university staff took up the challenge of justifying the merits of a collaborative project to teachers and school administrators, who were accustomed to a relationship of dependency on university expertise. Thus, the project was conceived in terms of two main objectives: (1) developing a bilingual education program appropriate for the needs of the school community; and (2) facilitating the empowerment of the participants.

It was decided to adopt a microethnographic research perspective, and a variety of data sources were used in the interest of triangulation. First of all, the weekly interactive discussion sessions of the Bilingualism Committee (consisting of members of the academic and administrative staff of the school and two staff members and a research assistant from the Universidad del Valle) were examined, with a view to analyzing how the process developed over time. We were particularly interested in examining the relative contributions of the university staff and the school participants, and looking at ways in which different areas of expertise were socialized and used in making curricular decisions. In addition, all participants were asked to reflect on their experiences in a diary every 3 or 4 months, registering how they felt about the process and mode of working, as well as how they felt they were contributing to the ongoing process of curriculum construction. Interviews with selected participants also were carried out at the end of the project in order to gain a better understanding of their views on the process of empowerment.

We followed the lead of Cameron and colleagues (1992) in their characterization of empowering research as research "on, for and with" (p. 22) the participants and in their use of interactive, or dialogic, research methodologies, which take into account the agendas of all the participants and emphasize the importance of sharing the knowledge generated with the community.

In the initial stages of project formulation, it was considered necessary to develop a working definition of empowerment that would orient the process. This was characterized in the following manner:

> Empowerment is the process through which the participants in the research become conscious of their capacities, potential, knowledge and experiences in the area, so that they can assume responsibilities in the development of autonomy and full participation in decision-making, not only during the research process, but also in the following phases of assessment and modification of the proposals in the light of the changes and new advances in national educational policies. (Mejía & Tejada, 2001, pp. 3–4; translated by chapter authors)

As can be seen, the emphasis in this definition is on process, rather than product, and therefore implies a longer time scale than often is considered appropriate in consultancies and other more "vertical" interventions. The process of consciousness-raising was seen as leading to a greater degree of responsibility and participation in decision making, both during the research and afterward. Furthermore, everyone taking part in the project was to be considered a participant. There was to be no division into researchers, on the one hand, and their subjects, on the other, in the process of curriculum construction.

The discourse analysis of the interactive discussion data was based on four defining categories: consent, resistance, asymmetry, and reciprocity. *Consent* can be seen as the acceptance of, or at least the nonopposition to, the use of power. In the project, this was evidenced by being in agreement with the ideas of other members of the group. *Resistance*, on the other hand, refers to any force that opposes or slows down an initiative or a plan. In the project this was exemplified when some of the schoolteachers did not agree with the university staff's decision not to accept the traditional role of "experts." The term *asymmetry* is used to indicate the lack of equilibrium existing among members of the group, especially in relation to position in the hierarchical structure of the school and the possession of specialized knowledge. *Reciprocity* refers to a mutual cooperative interchange of knowledge or experience. These four categories are closely linked to the concept of power, as discussed by Foucault (1980), Fairclough (1989), and others, and were considered essential characteristics of the notion of empowerment in terms of this project.

We will now report some of the results of the project in relation to the process of empowerment in general and then focus in more detail on differing participant perceptions of the relationships between the theory of bilingual education and the realities of classroom practice (Mejía & Tejada, 2001).

RESULTS OF THE PROCESS OF EMPOWERMENT

The detailed analysis of the interaction was carried out in the first instance using a number of discursive categories that emerged from the data. These were characterized as "you and us," directive speech acts, the act of decision making, the formulation of questions, reference to previous speakers, and types of reference to what had been read (the relationships established between theory and practice). The results of this analysis then were examined through the lens of the four defining categories mentioned above. For reasons of space, however, we will refer here to only two of the discursive categories used: directive speech acts and the relationships established between theory and practice. As our main focus in the project was on the examination of aspects of power and authority in relation to facilitating empowerment, we did not specifically focus on other characteristics of group interaction, such as different personality traits or learning styles.

Directive Speech Acts

The category of directive speech acts is based on Searle's (1980) definition, which characterizes these as acts carried out with the intention of having the interlocutor change the present state of things in order to achieve a future action. An example taken from our data involves a proposal by the head teacher addressed to the rest of the Bilingualism Committee to include in the minutes of future meetings decisions made in relation to the agreed topics: "I . . . would propose . . . that the minutes should include the points to be discussed . . . and the decisions taken in relation to these" (11–02–02) (Editors' note: All dates in this chapter are in day–month–year format).[2]

One interesting result of the analysis of speech acts is evidence of both consent and resistance to the notion of empowerment, often by the same participants, as can be seen in the following examples.

During the first phase of the project (September–December 2001), the university staff openly acknowledged the collaborative nature of the project and promoted the notion of empowerment, as can be seen in the following statement made by a staff member during the first meeting of the Bilingualism Committee:

> Nosotros entendemos muy bien lo que es asesoría y lo que venimos a hacer no es esto precisamente. Nosotros tenemos en construcción el concepto de empowerment, el trabajo conjunto, mutuo, de una parte y de otra, el intercambio saludable y crítico . . . experiencias de uno y otro lado. (10–9–01)
>
> *We understand what consultancy means and what we have come to do is not exactly that. We are in the process of developing the concept of empowerment, working together, a healthy, critical exchange . . . experiences from both sides.*

However, analysis of the transcripts of the meetings of the Bilingualism Committee reveals that it is in fact the university staff who produced the highest number of directive speech acts during Phase 1, as can be seen in Table 9.1. Out of a total of 117 directive speech acts from 13 participants, they are responsible for 61 (52.2%). Given that they were focusing on the advantages of adopting a policy of empowerment, it was expected that their directive role would be less prominent.

Thus, there is evidence of the coexistence of the phenomena of consent/resistance toward empowerment on the part of the university staff. There is an explicit discourse in favor of empowerment (consent), but at the same time there is implicit resistance to this, evidenced in the number of directive speech acts carried out by these participants.

It may be noted, however, that although the "powerful" participants (those members of the Bilingualism Committee who had directive status within the school hierarchy and those who were considered to be experts

Table 9.1. Directive speech acts according to participant

Participant Type	Phase 1		Phase 2	
	Number	**%**	**Number**	**%**
University				
Researcher 1	32	27.4	107	21.7
Researcher 2	29	24.8	58	11.7
Research Assistant	6	5.1	4	0.8
School Administration				
Head Teacher	14	12.0	63	12.8
Preschool Coordinator	1	0.9	21	4.3
Primary Coordinator	2	1.7	20	4.0
Secondary Coordinator	3	2.6	48	9.7
Head of English Department	14	12.0	71	14.4
Teachers				
Preschool Teacher 1	3	2.6	15	3.0
Preschool Teacher 2	3	2.6	53	10.7
Primary Teacher 1	4	3.4	13	2.6
Primary Teacher 2	3	2.6	8	1.6
Primary Teacher 3	3	2.6	13	2.6
Totals	*117*	*100.3*	*494*	*99.9*

Note: Percentages do not total to 100% because of rounding off.

because of their specialized knowledge) carried out a relatively large number of directive speech acts, they were also the people who explicitly advocated the adopting of an empowering, collaborative orientation, recognizing reciprocally the value of contributions from all members of the committee. The less powerful participants, for their part, revealed a relationship of complementarity by making reference to more powerful participants or recognized sources to back up their own directive speech acts.

In the second phase of the project (January–May 2002), however, while there is still an obvious asymmetry in the number of directive speech acts carried out by powerful participants in relation to the number attributed to other participants, there is some increase seen in the relative number of such acts on the part of other participants, such as the coordinators and one of the preschool teachers.

There is also evidence from the transcripts to suggest that some of the preschool and primary school teachers, drawing on their teaching experience, contributed actively to the formulation of curriculum proposals, particularly during this second phase. Thus, there is more evidence of reciprocity and complementarity in power relations among participants than in the first phase.

So while there are certain indications of linear progress in the process of empowerment, there is also evidence of a countercurrent of resistance to this notion, aimed at maintaining the traditional directive role of the university staff, based on their status as experts in the field. These two positions are exemplified in the following observations by the head of the English department:

> Mi expectativa [es que] por medio de este hacer, porque si es una investigación, no es que ustedes nos van a decir no enseñe tal cosa primero y después enseñamos tal cosa . . . hagan así, hagan asá. . . . Lo que les pido es que orienten y encaminen el trabajo para que nosotros podamos sacar nuestras propias conclusiones. Mi expectativa: empoderamiento de esta transformación. (10–09–01)
>
> *What I expect, as this is a research project, is not that you are going to say, teach this first, then teach that . . . do this, do that. . . . What I am asking is that you should guide the work so that we can draw our own conclusions. I expect empowerment from this transformation.*
>
> Al comienzo hubo una resistencia y de pronto los profesores no las expresan aquí pero decían ¿y entonces, ellos [los profesores universitarios] qué es lo que están haciendo? (02–07–02)
>
> *At the beginning there was resistance and maybe the teachers did not express it [openly] here, but [privately] they were saying, so what is it that they [the university staff] are doing?*

Theory and Practice

A second important aspect of bilingual curriculum development as evidenced in our study involved perceptions of the relationship between theory and practice, which were found to shed light on the processes of participant empowerment.

Focus on Changing Perceptions. From the beginning, the notion of theory became closely associated with topics that initially were suggested mainly by the university staff in response to questions and concerns expressed by the school participants, which were researched and discussed during the first phase of the project. The readings undertaken, particularly valuable in the search for principles or models to which examples of classroom practice could be related, were seen as constituting a basic common ground from which to begin the process of dialogue and discussion.

Authors such as Anna Camps (2001) in the field of pedagogy and Jim Cummins (2000) in the area of bilingualism have highlighted a dialectic conception of the relationship between theory and practice. According to Camps:

> Research in this field should lead to the development of theoretical knowledge which justifies and helps us to understand and interpret the activity of teaching and learning language, in other words, theorising . . . which in turn leads towards a new level of understanding of practice by grounding and transforming it. (p. 3; translated by chapter authors)

Cummins states:

> I see the relationship between theory and practice as two way and ongoing: practice generates theory, which in turn, acts as a catalyst for new directions in practice, which then informs theory, and so on. (p. 1)

In light of these notions, we will now examine how the participants positioned themselves toward the theoretical considerations introduced in the readings and discuss ways in which they related theory and practice.

Positioning Toward Theory. The data reveal that many participants valued the readings positively as "useful" and "pertinent," and categorized the authors as "ethical" and "honest." An example of how they felt about theory comes from an interview with the head of the English department.

> Nosotros no estudiamos las teorías del bilingüismo, nosotros nos fijamos en ejemplos porque fuimos a mirar colegios bilingües . . . pero en realidad claridad en lo que eran los conceptos y los fundamentos del bilingüismo yo no tenía. . . . Entonces a mí me aclaro muchísimas ideas . . . me dio un poquito de tranquilidad . . . me mostró que lo que nosotros de una manera empírica no estábamos tan desfasados. (02–07–02)
>
> *[In the past] we didn´t study theories of bilingualism, we looked at examples, because we went to visit bilingual schools . . . but in reality I was*

not at all clear about the concepts and bases of bilingualism . . . So [the project] clarified many things for me . . . I felt a little more reassured . . . it showed me that what we had been doing in an empirical manner was not so mistaken.

In many cases, these participants felt that the readings represented an instance of authority and were based on "true" information. The texts used helped to provide answers to concerns about bilingual processes. They also generated reflection and reassured participants by confirming previous intuitions or empirical practices. As one of the secondary school teachers said:

> Yo quedé muy contenta después de leer, me aclaró muchas dudas, me dio muchas seguridades, me mostró que vamos por el buen camino y que naturalmente como dice allí al final vamos . . . a encontrar problemas y todo pero pues en eso estamos para tratar de solucionarlos lo mejor posible. (8–10–01)
>
> *I was very happy after [studying] the reading, it clarified a lot of doubts and made me feel much more certain, it showed me that we are on the right track and that of course . . . we will come up against problems . . . but that we are here to try to solve them in the best way we can.*

In addition, the readings opened participants´ eyes to different possibilities and provided motivation for changing ideas and looking for alternatives suitable for the particular context or situation, as can be seen in the following extract:

> Yo insisto en que estas últimas conferencias de manera clara y definitiva pues nos llenan más de incertidumbre y nos . . . estimulan a qué miremos que vamos a hacer desde nuestros factores particulares. (16–10–01)
>
> *These last readings . . . lead us to question and encourage us to think about what we are going to do from the point of view of our particular situation.*

It is interesting to note that as participants seem to move from one position to another, at times they feel reassured, and at other times they feel uncertain.

In addition to these examples of consent to taking theoretical concerns on board, there were also moments when participants showed resistance to these notions, refusing to identify with them, as in the following example from an interview with one of the primary teachers. He rejected theory as static and used this to justify his contention that his participation was more active in the second (decision-making) phase than in the first phase, which was focused on discussion of the readings.

> Creo que al principio . . . no participaba . . . no participaba mucho pero ya al final creo que sí . . . porque era ya lo que me tocaba más a mi, digamos ya hablábamos del aula del desarrollo del hacer institucional allí entonces como que me tocaba más a mi. (02–07–02)
>
> *I think that at the beginning I did not participate . . . I did not participate much, but at the end I did . . . because it was what concerned me more . . . we were talking about the classroom, the development of institutional practices, so it concerned me more.*

Perceptions of Relationships Between Theory and Practice. There is also evidence of a marked tendency among the participants to establish relationships between ideas taken from the readings and developments in the institution, particularly in relation to classroom practice. As was perhaps to be expected, it was the school participants who did this more than the university staff (on 20 out of 22 interventions). In this way, the school participants made use of their own expertise derived from their pedagogical practice and initiated a dialogue with knowledge based on the readings, showing awareness of the need to contextualize much of what they had read. This is shown in the following observation from the head of the English department, after reading an article on the role of parents in bilingual education in Europe:

> Específicamente situándonos en Cali . . . no podemos pensar en que los padres van a tener el desempeño como lo tiene el padre francés o el padre inglés. (16–10–01)
>
> *Specifically situating ourselves in Cali . . . we cannot think that the parents will react in the same way as French or English parents.*

At other times, there is an observable tension between theory and practice. This is particularly evident when school participants express the view that while they realize that theoretical considerations are valuable, this does not diminish the importance of discussing classroom practice. This tension may be interpreted as a sign of resistance to theory that is seen as coming from "outside," and is not seen as helpful for the solution of pressing pedagogical problems. In the following extract, one of the preschool teachers explains why she thinks it is important to focus on practice.

> Hay problemas que hay . . . que resolver ya . . . [que] a mí me parece muy importante, muy interesante, la parte de teoría y me gusta . . . todo esto pero me preocupa que se vaya todo en teoría y nosotros necesitamos resolver cosas inmediatas que no se han resuelto. (1–10–01)
>
> *There are problems which have to be solved right now; I think the theoretical part is very important, very interesting . . . all of that, but what worries me is that everything revolves around theory, and we need to find solutions for immediate problems which have not been solved.*

This observation is reminiscent of Cummins's (2000) characterization of popular conceptions of theory as being "irrelevant to practice and the 'real world' . . . [and] dismissed as 'just theory'" (p. 2). In this case, the teacher sees the need for immediate application of theory to practice in order to resolve classroom difficulties, rather than considering theory as feeding into a reflexive view of practice.

On occasion, however, particularly in the second phase of the project, this tension seems to be resolved to some degree. Some of the school participants propose ideas that are susceptible to being researched, which necessarily involves reflection on practice and a systematization of experience. In other words, school participants seem to take on board the implications of theoretical considerations, an area that they usually felt was the sole responsibility of the university staff. This development thus may be seen as a step toward the valuing of their own voice and the voices of their fellow participants. In the following extract, it is possible to discern traces of a research question regarding the relationship between the first language and the foreign language. This primary teacher's hypothesis is based on the idea that teaching and learning methodologies should be the same for both languages.

> Si en la lengua materna se trabaja la producción textual también se debería incluir esa parte en inglés como metodología ¿no? (20–05–02)
>
> *If the textual production [approach] is used in the mother tongue, this should also be the methodology used in English, shouldn´t it?*

From the analysis of the transcriptions, as well as the participant diaries and the interviews, it is possible to note how the participants in the process of empowerment gradually begin to take ownership of theoretical concepts introduced through the readings and discussions. The different reactions toward the relationship between theory and practice reveal different stages in the process of conceptualizing these two notions. On the one hand, there is recognition of the interdependence of theory and practice, while on the other hand, there is evidence of the continuing belief that theory and practice are two separate entities.

Some participants realize that valuing the role of theory in reorienting pedagogical practice, as well as creating research hypotheses and reflecting on teaching and learning activities carried out in particular contexts, does not exclude the idea of a dialogic relationship between theory and practice, which implies processes of retheorizing from practice, and vice versa.

As participants develop greater awareness that the relationship between theory and practice is two-way and ongoing, there is a recognition that theory integrates observations and practices into coherent perspectives and that these perspectives, in turn, are modified by the interaction with practice. Many of the teachers' questions and observations in the second phase of the project are no longer based on a perception of what is sanctioned by authority, but instead are centered on their own classroom practice. They are, thus, far more aware of the value of their own ways of perceiving knowledge and of putting it into practice "in their own voice." The transformation of these individuals into subjects capable of "speaking with their own voice" (Gieve & Magalhaes, 1994, p. 133) is intrinsically bound up with the ways in which each person presents himself or herself to others and in the ways in which others see the person. As Taylor (1994) has recognized, we always define our identity in relation to what our significant others wish to see in us or, at times, in opposition to what they would like to see.

In the gradual development of ownership of theoretical concepts, there is a growing awareness among the participants that they are part of a process and, since it is a collective process, that the results depend on everyone, in contrast to the short-term results derived from more vertical interventions.

INSIGHTS FOR THE FUTURE

Bearing the above in mind, we may now inquire as to the significance of the results of one very localized research project for a globalized vision of multilingual education. In particular, we may ask about the importance of teacher empowerment, as discussed in this study, in helping to construct an educational site where multilingualism and multiculturalism can be effectively supported and expanded.

Various authors in the fields of bilingual education and English-language teaching (ELT) (Auerbach, 1995; García, 1993; Ricento & Hornberger, 1996) have argued for recognizing the importance of the role of teachers in promoting change, not only in the area of classroom practice but also in such areas as curriculum development, language policy, and societal goals. These areas traditionally have been thought of as the exclusive domain of "experts," as noted in the following observation by Ricento and Hornberger:

> In the ELT literature, the practitioner is often an afterthought who implements what "experts" in the government, board of education, or central school administration have already decided. The practitioner often needs to be "educated," "studied," "cajoled," "tolerated," even "replaced" by better prepared (even more compliant) teachers. (p. 417)

Teachers, too, often have been socialized into seeing themselves as passive recipients of ready-made curricula and policies that they have little power to influence. In the field of curriculum development, Auerbach (1995) sees what she terms the *ends–means* model as the dominant example of a process that usually begins with university-based researchers "identifying the body of 'knowledge' . . . to be covered." Curriculum content then is organized and sequenced into "chunks" of knowledge to be covered in a particular space of time. Thus, "despite the fact that it is couched in scientific terms, the ends–means approach serves as a mechanism of social control, disempowering for both students and teachers" (pp. 13–14).

An alternative, more empowering vision is to "place the classroom practitioner at the heart" (Ricento & Hornberger, 1996, p. 417), thereby facilitating processes of educational and social change and institutional transformations from a grass-roots, bottom-up perspective. Ofelia García (1993), in her work with bilingual teachers in New York, puts the onus for the development of this new perspective squarely on teachers themselves. In a strongly worded exhortation, she claims that

> [the teacher] must stop being an instructor, accepting of orders, of curriculum planned, of material given, and must claim her role as an educator, empowering the community she teaches by providing it with the appropriate knowledge and resources it needs. . . . Only then, will [teachers] feel empowered to transform practices that can, little by little, crack by crack, impact on societal goals. (p. 36)

García thus rejects a limited instructional role for teachers that does not take into account wider sociocultural and educational influences. Her vision of a "true" educator implies a critical commitment and active involvement in constructing knowledge that is valid for the wider community.

The different vision advocated by these researchers, then, depends on practitioners, school administrators, and university staff recognizing that all members of the educational community have the right and the duty to contribute to processes of effective change, and that change is not unidirectional. Top-down policy proposals should be complemented and extended by bottom-up initiatives, and grass-roots proposals should not be dismissed out of hand as inappropriate.

However, as we have indicated before, it is important not to underestimate the difficulties involved in facilitating processes of empowerment. As we have found, it is not a question of groups or individuals handing over power to others. Gieve and Magalhaes (1994) say that it is, rather,

> about "voice" and allowing the subjects' own voice to emerge, indeed promoting it. . . . [Empowerment is] the ability to value one's knowledge and meanings through a process of critical reflection on the meanings and knowledge of others. (p. 131)

In the bilingual curriculum project in Cali, the school participants did not ask to be empowered. In fact, they were quite happy to accept a traditional expert–nonexpert relationship. It was because the university staff decided to focus the project around the notion of empowerment that the school participants were, in a sense, forced (or at least strongly persuaded) to come to terms with the implications of assuming a much greater role and responsibility for decision making. There is, thus, a strange contradiction in the idea of "forcing" people to confront the issue of their own empowerment.

Ivanic (1994) maintains that collaborative research of the kind discussed in this chapter usually is advocated on ethical grounds: Participants can learn a lot from the research, decisions about methods are made jointly and so do not constitute too much of a burden or an intrusion, and the knowledge generated will be available to serve the needs of a wider community. She also feels that this type of approach can increase the quality of the research itself by developing richer methodologies that take into account the agendas and perspectives of all the participants involved.

Thus, we would submit that if we wish to ensure that research results really do inform the policy and practice of multilingual schooling and are not invisibalized as Skutnabb-Kangas (2004) suggests, we need to continue to blur various traditional dichotomies: between researchers and researched; between practitioners and curriculum designers; between theory and classroom practice. This blurring is in line with what Johnson (1998) sees as Derrida's contribution to "the relaxation of the rigid oppositional system which usually forms and constrains our understanding of the world" (p. 61).

In our experience, policy documents that inform curricular practices will not, on their own, transform educational systems. Agents of change are, in the last resort, individual teachers in their classrooms, who may or may not be convinced of the need to support multilingualism as a resource for their students. Our study indicates that a collaborative view of curriculum construction, involving different members of the school and academic communities, can lead to valuing personal expertise and thus promoting empowerment and "ownership" of change. We therefore would maintain that a collaborative approach to curricular construction in multilingual education settings, oriented toward facilitating empowerment among participants, is an effective way to create a vision of multilingual schools as sites where the world's linguistic diversity may be preserved, recovered, and expanded.

CONCLUSION

At the beginning of this chapter, it was pointed out that the power of dominant groups is not monolithic and that, in every situation where there are asymmetrical relations of power evident between groups or individuals, there are always interstices or social spaces in power structures where processes of empowerment may be situated (Martin-Jones & Heller, 1996). It is our contention that resistance and consent in the processes of bilingual curriculum construction take place in these interstices and suggest how participants are involved in a process of empowerment while attempting to reshape their mental schemata in order to give new meanings to their own perceptions and those of others, in a reflective, critical, and nonlinear fashion that reflects the netlike quality of the nature of power, referred to by Foucault (1980).

The nonlinearity of processes of empowerment has been underlined by Magdalena Léon (1997) in her writing about women's empowerment. She says:

> Empowerment is not a linear process with a beginning and an end that are defined in the same way. . . . Empowerment is different for each individual or group depending on his or her life, context and history. (p. 20; translated by chapter authors)

The evidence in our data for a fluctuating coexistence of consent and resistance to processes of empowerment gives empirical support to this statement and, at the same time, indicates the importance of assuming a nonreductionist position toward these phenomena.

Empowerment, as discussed in this project, is not about transferring power from the more powerful to the less powerful, but about the broadening of social spaces for collaboration. The results of our study have indicated both the complexity of this process and its differential nature, as shown by the reactions of various participants. The awareness of participants' own "capacities, potential, knowledge and experiences," envisioned in the earlier definition of empowerment, came about as a result of reflecting on the words of others (both in the readings and in the subsequent discussions) and through the recognition and validation of the differences in expertise among the participants. Throughout this process, it is possible to see signs of the transformation of individuals into subjects capable of "speaking with their own voice" and of individual voices becoming more prominent in the process of collective construction.

We therefore may conclude that there *is* evidence that empowerment in processes of bilingual curriculum construction is a reality, albeit a complex one, not an illusion. The weakening of established hierarchies of power that are based on knowledge and institutional status is more likely if participants get involved in the dynamics of marketing their own orders of discourse in an interactive situation where knowledge is redistributed, taking into account the agendas of all participants.

Promoting processes of empowerment demands great commitment on the part of all participants. As we found throughout the project, the invisibility and naturalization of power (Fairclough, 1989) make it difficult to change established role relationships and hierarchies and show how deeply ingrained the dominant researcher–researched paradigm is (Cameron et al., 1992). Participants often experience uncertainty, questioning, and resistance, which may result in increased insecurity and anxiety, but which also can lead to growth and change.

NOTES

1. The relationship between resistance and empowerment established in this chapter is based on Foucault's (1980) observation that power, by its very nature, engenders resistance and/or confrontation. In this view, the struggle between power and the resistance to power can lead to the transformation of established power relations. It is in this sense that we postulate that resistance can result in processes of empowerment.

2. Dates are the dates on which the data were collected.

REFERENCES

Auerbach, E. (1995). The politics of the ESL classroom: Issues of power in pedagogical choices. In J. Tollefson (Ed.), *Power and inequality in language education* (pp. 9–33). Cambridge: Cambridge University Press.

Cameron, D., Frazer, E., Harvey, P., Rampton, M. B. H., & Richardson, K. (1992). *Researching language: Issues of power and method.* London: Routledge.

Camps, A. (Ed.). (2001). *El aula como espacio de investigación y reflexión* [The classroom as a space for research and reflection]. Barcelona: Biblioteca de Textos.

Cummins, J. (2000). *Language, power and pedagogy: Bilingual children in the crossfire.* Clevedon: Multilingual Matters.

Dieck, M. (1998). Criollistica Afrocolombiana [Afrocolombian creole studies]. In L. A. Maya (Ed.), *Geografía humana de Colombia: Los Afrocolombianos* [The human geography of Colombia: Los Afro-Colombians] (pp. 303–338). Bogotá: Instituto Colombiano de Cultura Hispánica.

Fairclough, N. (1989). *Language and power.* London: Longman.

Foucault, M. (1980). *Power/knowledge.* New York: Harvester Wheatsheaf.

García, O. (1993). Understanding the societal role of the teacher in transitional bilingual classrooms: Lessons from the sociology of language. In K. Zontag (Ed.), *Bilingual education in Friesland: Facts and prospects* (pp. 25–37). Leeuwarden/Ljouwert: GCO/MSU.

Gieve, S., & Magalhaes, I. (1994). On empowerment. In S. Gieve & I. Magalhaes (Eds.), *Power, ethics and validity* (pp. 121–145). Lancaster: Lancaster University, Centre for Research in Language Education.

Ivanic, R. (1994). Collaborative research: Enriching the contribution or contaminating the data? In S. Gieve & I. Magalhaes (Eds.), *Power, ethics and validity* (pp. 116–120). Lancaster: Lancaster University, Centre for Research in Language Education.

Johnson, C. (1998). *Derrida. El estado de la escritura* [Derrida: The state of writing]. Bogotá: Editorial Norma.

Léon, M. (Ed.). (1997). *Poder y empoderamiento de las mujeres* [Power and the empowerment of women]. Bogotá: TM Editores.

Martin-Jones, M., & Heller, M. (1996). Introduction to the special issue on education in multilingual settings: Discourse, identities and power. *Linguistics and Education,* 8, 3–16.

Mejía, A. M. de, & Tejada, H. (2001). *La construcción de una propuesta curricular bilingüe para colegios monolingües en Cali* [The construction of a bilingual curricular proposal for monolingual schools in Cali]. Unpublished research report. Cali: Universidad del Valle.

Ricento, T., & Hornberger, N. (1996). Unpeeling the onion: Language planning and policy and the ELT professional. *TESOL Quarterly, 30*(3), 401–427.

Searle, J. (1980). *Actos de habla.* Madrid: Cátedra.

Skutnabb-Kangas, T. (2004). The one common feature in multilingual schooling: Politics and emotions rule while research results are invisibilised. *Proceedings from the International Symposium on Imagining Multilingual Schools,* Teachers College, Columbia University, New York.

Taylor, C. (1994). El multiculturalismo y la política del reconocimiento [Multiculturalism and the policy of recognition]. In A. Gutmann (Ed.), *Argumentos y debates y multiculturalismo* [Arguments and debates and multiculturalism] (pp. 25–74). Princeton, NJ: Princeton University Press.

Trillos, M. (1998). La educación indígena en Colombia. In M. Trillos (Ed.), *Educación endógena frente a educación formal* (pp. 69–95). Bogotá, Colombia: Universidad de los Andes, Centro Colombiano de Estudios de Lenguas Aborígenes.

Valencia, S. (2005). *English language teaching in Colombia: Changes in policy and practice viewed through a regional case study.* Unpublished doctoral dissertation, University of Wales at Aberystwyth.

10

Multiculturalism and Language Education in New Zealand

Past, Present, and Future

Roger Barnard

This chapter initially reviews historical immigration patterns that have led to New Zealand's present multiethnic diversity. It then considers language-in-education policies and practices in terms of (1) the language or languages used to deliver the curriculum and (2) the additional languages taught in schools. The limited extent of language education in New Zealand is discussed, and it is argued that even if there were greater provision for bilingual education, a more radical review of the principles of mainstream education would be needed. It is suggested that to promote a vision of multicultural schooling, mainstream education could appropriate certain metaphors from the Maori worldview. The implications of moving from vision to policy implementation then are considered, and the question is raised as to whether sufficient and appropriate resources will be found to do this effectively. The chapter concludes with the need for wider structural reforms if New Zealand is to become a harmonious multicultural society in the next few decades.

Ho te kaupapa o tënei wähanga ko te takenga maha ma te whakaako reo i Aotearoa. Hei tïmatanga körero, ka titohia te ähua o ngä tini hekenga mai i täwhähi i pënei rawa ai te kanorautanga o ngä iwi kei te whenua nei e noho tahi ana. Kätahi ka äta wetewetengia ngä kaupapa here me ngä whakatinanatanga i aua kaupapa e pä ana ki ngä reo i roto i ngä mahi mätauranga, arä, ngä reo e whakaakona nei te marautanga, me ërä atu reo e whakaakona ana i roto i ngä kura.

Ka körerotia te whäiti o te whakaako i ngä re i Aotearoa, me te kökiri i te whakaaro, ahakoa pea ka whakawhänuitia ake te wähi ki te whakaako reo, ki te mätauranga reorua, ko te mea nui me äta tirotiro höhonu ngä kaupapa katoa o te mätauranga i roto i te köawa matua. Ka whakaputaina te whakaaro, e kökiritia ai te whäinga o tënei mea, o te mätauranga takenga maha, me mätua tiki atu e te köawa matua ëtahi tirohanga, ëtahi tikanga i te ao Mäori, ä, ko aua tirohanga me aua tikanga ka äta körerotia i konei.

Kätahi ka wänangatia ngä ähuatanga o te whakatinanatanga i ënei whäinga, ä, ka toko ake te pätai he nui ränei, he tika ränei ngä rauemi kei a tätou e pai ai te whakatutuki i taua whakatinanatanga.

Hei whakaaro whakamutunga i roto i tënei wähanga, me tino whänui te whakahöu i ngä whakahaere mätauranga, e noho ai ngä iwi maha o Aotearoa hei hapori rangimärae i ngä tekau tau e heke mai nei.

There exists in New Zealand a tension between the melting pot of assimilation and the complexity of linguistic and cultural diversity. A central issue facing all states in the 21st century is whether the melting pot theory is either feasible or morally justifiable. If it is feasible, it can be so only by denying the language rights of minority communities—with the possible outcome of social division and perhaps conflict: We can think only too readily of the ethnic cleansing that regularly occurs in countries seeking to assert the rights of dominant linguistic or cultural groups. However, if the celebration of cultural diversity is morally more acceptable, is it feasible? The starting point for a truly multilingual and multicultural society—and it is *only* the starting point—is the language education provided in the nation's schools.

Within this chapter, I will review the historical immigration patterns that have led to New Zealand's present multiethnic diversity and the language-in-education policies and practices in schools. Appropriating certain metaphors from the Maori worldview (Bishop, 2003), I argue that even if there were greater provision for bilingual education, a more radical review of the principles of mainstream education would be needed. The questions remaining are whether sufficient and appropriate resources will be found to do this effectively and whether New Zealand will move to become a harmonious multicultural society in the next few decades.

IMMIGRATION TRENDS IN NEW ZEALAND

When Europeans—or *pakeha*, as they were called by the local inhabitants—first arrived on the shores of New Zealand in the late 18th century, they found that although there were slight dialect differences, the indigenous tribal people all spoke a commonly understood language—*te reo Maori*, the language of the ordinary people. In 1840, when European settlers were very much in the minority, the Treaty of Waitangi was signed between the British Crown and more than 500 indigenous leaders. According to this treaty, *tangata whenua*—the people of the land, as Maori people preferred (and still prefer) to designate themselves—were accorded the same rights, privileges, and responsibilities as other British subjects in New Zealand. The treaty also promised protection of Maori *taonga*—their cultural treasures, which included their language, *te reo* Maori. However, as more and more settlers arrived—by 1881 they outnumbered *tangata whenua* by more than ten to one—the English language increasingly dominated social, economic, and educational life. The effect of this was to reduce the number of domains in which, and functions for which, te reo Maori could effectively be used. At the same time, and in defiance of the treaty, legislation was passed specifically aimed at marginalizing land ownership by *tangata whenua*, reducing their political participation and diminishing their share of the benefits of the wider society (Bishop, 2003). By the 1930s, such actions had led to an increasing denigration of the Maori language and culture—to the point where not only *pakeha* but also *tangata whenua* tended to assume that the Maori people were an underclass, their culture primitive and unfit for the modern world—an obvious case of linguistic imperialism (Ansre, 1979, cited by Phillipson, 1992).

However, the years following World War II saw an upsurge of pride and self-awareness among *tangata whenua*, which was tied to a determination to assert their linguistic, cultural, and legal rights. Maori leaders pointed to the obligations of the Treaty of Waitangi and, in a bold step of reconciliation, the government in 1975 established the Waitangi Tribunal to deliberate and rule on alleged breaches of the treaty. In 1985, its powers were made retroactive to 1840 to provide restitution for the wrongs that had been done to Maori by previous administrations. This was one of a series of measures that, according to the historian Michael King (2003), so changed the face of New Zealand life that "their cumulative effect could legitimately be called a revolution" (p. 494). Another important milestone was the Maori Language Act of 1987, which stated that Maori—as an official language of New Zealand—may, if people so choose, be used in an increasingly wide range of public domains. Thus, although English is the majority language, it is not an *official* language of New Zealand (Peddie, 2003).

During the first 100 or so years of British rule, the vast majority of immigrants came from the British Isles. A few came from mainland Europe and elsewhere in the world, such as Hong Kong, although successive governments strongly discouraged, and sometimes penalized, immigration from Asia. Then in the 1960s, waves of immigrants came from the Pacific Islands—notably Samoa, Tonga, and Fiji—to fill low-skilled vacancies in the then-swelling job market. These *Pasifika* people were culturally, ethnically, and to some extent linguistically related to Maori and were expected to assimilate into the English-dominant New Zealand society, so no official recognition was paid to the preservation or development of their respective languages and cultures. In a break from the past "Whites only" policy, in 1987 (the same year as the Maori Language Act) the government made a radical change to its immigration policy, as a result of which well-skilled and/or well-heeled people from Asian countries have been encouraged to immigrate. There are now significant numbers of residents and citizens originating from Taiwan, India, Korea, and—especially since 1999—the People's Republic of China. These communities, like those from the Pacific, tend to congregate and form enclaves in large urban areas. As is the case with the *Pasifika* communities, there is growing evidence of language loss among the second generation of immigrants; however, there is no danger of most of the Asian languages themselves becoming extinct, as there are very large speech communities in their countries of origin. To add to the ethnolinguistic vitality of New Zealand, successive governments have maintained a commitment to the United Nations to accept approximately 750 refugees each year, and these have arrived in waves from Southeast Asia, Africa, the Middle East, and Eastern Europe. These new settlers are joined by about 1,000 refugees who come under the "family reunion" rationale on an annual basis as well as those who have sought and been granted asylum status.

Paradoxically, therefore, just as New Zealand society was coming to terms in 1987 with bilingualism and biculturalism, the nation's doors were opened to people from diverse languages and cultures. The 2001 New Zealand census reveals the current extent of multilingual and multicultural diversity in New Zealand and its schools, as shown in Table 10.1. The implication from the data is that the proportion of Maori and *Pasifika* schoolchildren is rising, while that of children of European descent is falling. In very large part, this has to do with the simple fact that the number of Maori and Pasifika women of childbearing age is increasing and their families are larger than those of Europeans. The number of immigrants and refugees from non-English-speaking backgrounds also is increasing. Thus, if

Table 10.1. New Zealand national and school population data

Ethnicity	National population	School population
European (*pakeha*)	72.0%	63.0%
Maori	14.0%	20.4%
Pasifika	6.6%	8.0%
Asian	6.5%	6.0%

Source: Peddie, 2003.

present trends continue, schools will become increasingly multilingual and multicultural.

MEDIUM OF INSTRUCTION IN NEW ZEALAND SCHOOLS

Various languages are used as media of instruction in New Zealand, each having a different history of policy and practice. In this section, attention will be paid first to the use of English and Maori as media of instruction, and then to the limited extent of instruction in community languages from the Pacific region and Asia. The section will conclude with a summary of the language instruction of New Zealand's Deaf community.

English

The choice of the medium of instruction is important not only because this will be the students' language of wider communication in society but also—and more important—because the language or languages selected will shape the learners' cultural worldview. Certainly until the 1980s, and even into the present, education policy in New Zealand has been overtly assimilationist. The New Zealand Curriculum Framework states, "Because English is the common language of communication in New Zealand, all students will develop the ability and confidence to communicate competently in English" (Ministry of Education, 1996, p. 11). Until recent years, little attention was paid in schools to the linguistic and cultural needs of children of *tangata whenua* or immigrant families from non–English-dominant backgrounds.

In the 1870s, after the introduction of state primary education, Maori leaders petitioned Parliament requesting that formal education for their children be conducted *only* in English (Simon, 1998). They believed education through the medium of English was more relevant than *te reo* Maori for their children and would allow them to fully participate in the modern sectors of New Zealand society. As a result of internal migration after 1945, increasing numbers of Maori children attended mainstream English-medium schools in urban areas. In many of these schools, the language and culture of *tangata whenua* were denigrated, and children sometimes were punished for speaking their own language. These children increasingly were considered to be "failing," although—given the hegemony of *pakeha* values and practices in pedagogy and assessment—the school system more accurately might be considered to be failing them.

> Judged by the system's own standards Maori children are not being successfully taught, and for that reason alone, quite apart from the duty to protect

> the Maori language, the education system is being operated in breach of the Treaty. (Waitangi Tribunal, cited by Bishop & Glynn, 1999, p. 28)

As Bishop and Glynn argue, "Research, pedagogy and assessment practices, instead of being part of the solution, have themselves become part of the problem" (p. 27).

With regard to immigrant children, the following statements from the New Zealand Curriculum Framework represent the current policy of the Ministry of Education:

> The prior knowledge, first language, and culture of each student should be respected and incorporated in English programmes. . . . Students from language backgrounds other than English should work towards the same objectives for English as native speakers, [although] they will approach the objectives differently and may at times be working at different levels from most of the class. (Ministry of Education, 1994, p. 15)

It is worthy of note that, in the 90-odd pages of "Teaching, Learning and Assessment Examples," no specific mention is made of different routes or levels appropriate for these learners, nor are suggestions made to teachers about how the planning and execution of their lessons might be varied to take learners from diverse backgrounds into account. Since then, however, the Ministry has produced teachers' handbooks for effective literacy practice in primary and secondary schools (Ministry of Education, 2003, 2004), which contain background information, summaries of research findings and theoretical underpinnings, and strategic (rather than finely detailed) guidance for implementing effective programs. Teachers are encouraged, through short seminars and workshops and in-house staff development programs, to develop the suggestions contained in these manuals.

Maori

In the early 19th century, missionaries established schools for the children of *tangata whenua* in which the medium of instruction was *te reo* Maori, but in which European and Christian values were promoted. Missionaries had considerable success in translating religious works into *te reo* Maori—thereby providing a written form of the language—but they may have had less success in their educational aims. According to one (unnamed) Maori historian quoted by King (2003), the Wesleyan missionaries "taught domesticity, agriculture and . . . prudery with little success, and Christianity with less" (p. 144). As noted above, later in the century there was a drive by Maori leaders for English-medium education. They assumed that the Maori language would be preserved through its use in traditional

Maori cultural settings (King, 2003); after all, at that time all *tangata whenua* could speak their mother tongue, and the language remained in a relatively healthy state until the 1930s. Subsequently, however, it came to be realized that there was a distinct possibility that the Maori language would be extinguished if steps were not taken to revive it. This was because fewer and fewer people were using the language in everyday contexts, and by the 1970s, it was realized that young Maori had effectively lost the language (Benton, 1979). Only the older generation—those over the age of 50—had sufficient competency to conduct their affairs in Maori (Waite, 1992), and they literally were dying out, and their language with them.

Therefore, in the early 1980s, a grass-roots Maori education movement started that led to the formation of hundreds of *kohanga reo*. These were preschool language nests in which young children of *tangata whenua* could be immersed in Maori language and cultural values with the full support of their *whanau* (extended families), who would be responsible for administering the new educational ventures (Irwin, 1990). Within 6 years, some 8,000 children were enrolled in *kohanga reo*, representing about 15% of Maori children under the age of 5. Such was their perceived success that Maori-medium primary schools (*kura kaupapa Maori*) were set up to take over where the language nests left off. As this trend continued, the Ministry recognized and supported these schools, not least by producing Maori-language versions of the national curriculum specifications for all seven essential learning areas. In the 1990s, a number of Maori-medium secondary schools (*whare kura*) and tertiary institutions (*wanaanga*) were established. However, by 2001 only 3% of students were in Maori-medium education (9,594 in 545 *kohanga reo*; 5,016 in about 59 *kura kaupapa Maori*—an average of approximately 18 children in each kohanga reo and 85 in each primary school) (Peddie, 2003). The following year saw slightly higher enrollment, but it was still the second lowest in the previous 10 years. It can be seen that as the number of Maori students is expanding, the enrollment in immersion programs is falling.

There has been a commitment by the Ministry of Education to support the development of Maori-medium education, but the enrollment has been disappointing. One of the problems associated with Maori-medium schools running parallel with the mainstream educational system is that underlying the Maori versions of the national framework is a hidden curriculum that reflects the dominant *pakeha* culture and fails to acknowledge, or even negates, Maori educational values and perspectives (Bishop, 2003). Edmonds (2001) has pointed to the problems in producing culturally authentic Maori curricula because of the general shortage of Maori teachers in the educational system generally, and the lack even among them of native-like competence in te reo Maori. Despite these difficulties, it is evident that *kohanga reo* and *kura kaupapa Maori* have revitalized the language in that some, albeit a minority, of the younger generation of *tangata whenua* can use *te reo* Maori to some extent in everyday life.

Thus there is now a dual-track system whereby Maori parents (and others) may elect to have their children educated through the medium of English in mainstream schools or else in Maori—at least to the end of primary school. By completing their primary education in Maori immersion classes, the children are inducted into *kaupapa Maori*, the collective vision or philosophy of *tangata whenua*, which includes both the underlying discourse structures and the specific terminology of the various school subjects. To the extent that the immersion is total, these students will not have been introduced to the dominant *pakeha* culture and discourses of learning, nor will they necessarily know the English terminology of mathematics, science, and so forth. On entry to mainstream high schools, therefore, they may be at a disadvantage in comparison with their peers who have been taught through the medium of English. Parents—and teachers—probably assumed that because these students would be exposed to, and use, English in their social environment, they would be able to apply their social language skills in mainstream classes. Such a view, however, does not take into account the distinction made by Cummins (1981, 2000) between basic interpersonal communication skills (BICS) and cognitive academic language proficiency (CALP). The former—BICS—can be developed in social situations such as the home, playground, or street. However, in order to cope with the intellectual demands of school subjects, CALP needs to be systematically developed and cannot be left to be acquired by osmosis.

Community Languages

As noted in Table 10.1, 14% of the school population are from *Pasifika* or Asian backgrounds. The Curriculum Framework states:

> Students whose mother tongue is a Pacific Islands language or a community language will have the opportunity to develop and use their own language as an integral part of their schooling. (Ministry of Education, 1994, p. 15)

In 2003, some 20 primary schools had Pacific-medium programs in which just over 1,600 students were enrolled; 18 of these were serving the Samoan community (Tuafuti & McCaffery, 2005), by far the largest *Pasifika* group in New Zealand. However, this total represents only 2.8% of all *Pasifika* students. In the same year, just over 2,500 preschool children were in about 100 language nests where the medium of instruction is one of the various *Pasifika* languages. This figure is the lowest total in 10 years, well down from peaks—approaching 4,000—in the mid-1990s (Peddie, 2003). No official provision has been made by government agencies for the children of Asian immigrants to receive an education in their mother tongue, although some schools do make rooms available for after-hours education in the first language. Outside the school system, little progress has been made by successive governments to identify, locate, and support community language schools, most of which are self-funded and are held in a range of formal and informal settings: schoolrooms, religious and community halls, sitting rooms, and garages (Shameem, 2003).

One other category of minoritized-language speakers can be considered briefly—the Deaf. For much of the 20th century, Deaf children were placed in mainstream classes and expected to follow lessons by lip-reading. The current situation is that more than 85% of Deaf and hearing-impaired children are now enrolled in mainstream classes as opposed to 5% in Deaf-unit classes in regular schools and 8% in one of the two Deaf Education Centres in New Zealand (Stockwell, 2000). Since the 1990s, rhetoric and practice in Deaf education in New Zealand have been altered by a paradigm shift from a deficit/curative view of deafness to recognition of the Deaf as a community with an autonomous language, New Zealand Sign Language (NZSL). In response, policy in the Deaf Education Centres has endorsed a bilingual-bicultural option that utilizes NZSL (McKee & Biederman, 2003). This policy was given impetus when in April 2006 legislation was enacted which made New Zealand Sign Language the nation's second official language. In 2007, new curriculum guidelines setting the direction for teaching and learning NZSL were sent to all early childhood centres and schools for teachers who wish to plan and implement NZSL programs with their students. The curriculum positions NZSL as a language of choice along with other languages offered in mainstream schooling, enabling hearing students to learn it as well.

SECOND-LANGUAGE TEACHING IN NEW ZEALAND SCHOOLS

In New Zealand, as elsewhere in the multilingual world, there is a perceived need for school students to acquire competence in more than one language. Within this section, consideration will first be paid to the provision of English and Maori as second languages. This will be followed by a discussion of the situation regarding community and foreign language teaching in the country. The section will conclude with a discussion of some of the constraints to effective second-language provision in New Zealand's schools.

English as a Second Language (ESL)

There are many students in New Zealand schools who need instruction or other support in English to enable them to access the curriculum, and these numbers are predicted to rise sharply (Department of Statistics, 2002). Upon enrollment in school, an assessment is made of the English-language competence of students from non-English-speaking backgrounds (NESB students), and for those who fall below a certain threshold, the school is provided with a limited amount of supplementary funding from the Ministry of Education. In 2002, official funding was made available for 18,309 NESB students in primary schools and 4,951 in secondary schools (Franken & McComish, 2003). This funding is provided for only 4 school years, and there are many other NESB students who have been in school for several years and still need language support, but for whom the schools are no longer able to obtain official funding. In 2003, the total number of students needing ESL support was estimated to be 42,420 (25,000 in primary schools and 17,420 in secondary schools), of whom about 9,700 were *Pasifika* students (May, Hill, & Tiakiwai, 2004). In addition to these students, there were some 14,000 international students, mostly in secondary schools, whose families paid full fees and for whom schools provided ESL instruction.

ESL support usually takes the form of providing instruction to small groups of learners outside regular classroom periods. In schools surveyed by Franken and McComish (2003), 60% of primary schools used this system, with some 27% supplementing it with in-class support; less than 5% provided ESL solely or primarily through in-class support. The amount of time allocated to pull-out instruction ranged from half an hour to 6 hours a week (Barnard & Lata Rauf, 1999; Franken & McComish, 2003). The situation in secondary schools was very similar, with most schools offering between 2 and 6 hours of pull-out English tuition instruction a week (Cameron & Simpson, 2002; Franken & McComish, 2003). Very few of the ESL programs at either the primary or secondary level were referenced to the mainstream curriculum. As the authors of the report to the Ministry point out:

> The practice of withdrawing small groups of students from a selection of different classes and class levels, places constraints in terms of addressing curriculum learning as few classes work on the same curriculum material at the same time. (Franken & McComish, 2003, p. 82)

As a consequence, NESB students with minimal or low English competency spend the rest of the school week in mainstream classes in a situation of incomprehensible input.

Maori as a Second Language

In the 1980s, an attempt was made to introduce a bilingual/bicultural perspective into mainstream schools through the development of *Taha Maori* (the Maori side) programs. According to Ritchie (1992), there was a great need for "attitude modification techniques" to reduce *pakeha* prejudices about the cultural values of *tangata whenua*, and it was hoped that the provision of factual information about Maori educational aspirations and expectations through such programs might begin an appropriate attitudinal shift among *pakeha* students and their parents. A second aim of these programs was to help Maori students "feel a greater sense of identity and self-worth" and "enhance their educational achievements as well" (Hirsch, 1990, p. 38). According to Bishop and Glynn (1999), while the intention of these programs may have been benign, the trivial and piecemeal ways that they were implemented belittled the principles of partnership enshrined in the Treaty of Waitangi. Another result of *Taha Maori* has been the development of curriculum documents in *te reo Maori* for the other learning areas as well as for the teaching of Maori as a second language.

When the Curriculum Framework was introduced and the development of specifications in *te reo Maori* was planned, it was expected that "students will have the opportunity to become proficient in Maori" (Ministry of Education, 1993, p. 10). Since then, there has been no systematic collection and analysis of data on students' progress and achievement in the medium of Maori, although there are statistics regarding uptake, or enrollment: "Over 20% of *all* school students were studying *te reo Maori*, but the vast majority studied the language for less than three hours a week" (Peddie, 2003, p. 21). Noting that "less than three hours a week" might mean as little as one or two brief sessions, Peddie goes on to say that in 2001 only 9% of high school students studied Maori as a subject—only 6% after the first year—and that almost 75% of all Maori students in the mainstream were not studying their language to the point where they might be expected to be reasonably proficient. As Glynn (2003) has pointed out, there has been a lack of clear policy direction and goal-setting for students learning Maori as a second language in mainstream schools.

Other Second Languages

The situation in New Zealand regarding the teaching of languages other than Maori or English as curriculum subjects is complicated by three interconnected factors. In the first place, unlike most other national educational systems, the study of a second language is not compulsory in New Zealand schools, and only recently has the Ministry of Education obligated schools to offer instruction in languages other than Maori and English as the eighth essential learning area. Second, many languages are competing for the limited available resources. Since 1995, the Ministry of Education has introduced curriculum documents for the following languages: Chinese, Spanish, Samoan, Japanese, German, Korean, French, Cook Island Maori, Tongan, Niuean, Tokelauan, and New Zealand Sign Language. The third factor, consequent upon the two above, is the low take-up and retention rates, making the annual cost per language student extremely high. The plethora of options has been accompanied by a reduction in the numbers of students studying second languages. For example, 2 years after the introduction of the Chinese curriculum statement in 1995, "the take-up rate for Chinese was only 0.4% of the secondary school population. That represented 948 students spread over five years of schooling in 34 different schools, an average of fewer than six pupils per school year in each school" (Johnson, 2000, p. 86). According to Peddie (2003), only 24.5% of the nation's high school population of just over 200,000 studied a second language. Such a low take-up rate is compounded by low retention. Half of the students reported by Peddie were taking short "taster" courses of about 40 hours in the first year of secondary school, and most students did not follow up these courses. Johnson (2000) gives average retention rates in secondary schools as follows: French, 7.5%; Japanese, 14.5%; German, 14%. The take-up of second languages in primary schools is even more limited: Peddie (2005) reports that just under 17% of all New Zealand primary students study a second language, 84% of whom are in Years 7–8, and only 3% receive more than 30 hours of instruction a year.

Various reasons can be adduced for these limited take-up and retention rates. One may be that over 80% of the population is monolingual in English (Peddie, 2003); consequently, New Zealand may still be, as Janet Holmes (1990) declared several years ago, a "determinedly monolingual country" (p. 19), unwilling to accept the need for bilingual education for the majority of students. Second, the proliferation of SLT (second language teaching) curriculum documents has led to a lack of clarity about objectives, standards, and proficiency levels. For example, there is as yet no common framework, as there is now in European schools (Council of Europe, 2000), to compare achievement standards across second languages. A third reason is that school curricula are already heavily loaded, and the addition of an eighth essential learning area makes syllabuses, especially those in primary schools, overcrowded.

There is also a major problem of teacher supply. Johnson (2000) has pointed to the fact that many schools in remote areas find it difficult to recruit language teachers. Indeed, there is a shortage of competent language teachers throughout the country. Evidence of this may be adduced from the diminishing number of students graduating from New Zealand universities majoring in a second language. According to Johnson (2000), "whereas 6% of all New Zealand graduates completed their degrees with a major in an international language in 1970, only 3.18% did so in 1997" (p. 522). Moreover, Johnson also reports that it is very difficult to establish the actual or relative linguistic competence of students graduating from language departments in universities: "Each university is free to establish its own concept of what constitutes progress, achievement and proficiency" (p. 247). One possible source of language teachers is among the immigrant communities, but according to Shameem (2003), there have been too few opportunities or resources provided for overseas-qualified teachers to work in New Zealand schools or to receive appropriate training to facilitate their entry to the workplace. In 2001, there were very few students from ethnic backgrounds other than English or Maori being trained as teachers for the New Zealand school system, and very few of these were being trained as language teachers (see Table 10.2).

Moreover, given the limitations of the 3-year bachelor of teaching program, "almost no meaningful instruction can be provided—even for general teachers—in second language acquisition and/or bilingual education" (May et al., 2004, p. 126). Among existing language teachers, there is little inservice professional development; even in the government-funded Second Language Learning Project, almost 60% of the respondents stated that no professional development took place in their schools to facilitate the project (Peddie, Gunn, & Lewis, 1999).

As noted above, the Ministry of Education now requires all primary—as well as secondary—schools to offer instruction in second languages. Many schools are offering more "taster" courses in foreign languages, notably Spanish, Japanese, German, and French. Typically, they are taught for about 40 hours a year outside regular school hours by teachers who may have very little competency in the target language or previous background in

Table 10.2. Ethnic background of student teachers in preservice primary and secondary teacher education, 2001

Ethnicity	Primary training	Secondary training
European (*pakeha*)	5,936 (70.2%)	1,227 (74.6%)
Maori	1,928 (22.8%)	260 (15.8%)
Pasifika	444 (5.3%)	75 (4.5%)
Asian	143 (1.7%)	83 (5.0%)
Total	*8,451 (100%)*	*1,645 (100%)*

Source: Ministry of Education, 2002.

language teaching. To facilitate its policy, the Ministry requires its regional language advisers to organize day-long professional development sessions for mainstream primary teachers who are willing to run these courses, followed by four or five school visits over the year to demonstrate and observe language lessons and the use of the resource packs that are provided to the teachers. This is the extent of professional development provided. While it is mandatory for schools to offer second-language instruction, it is not compulsory for students to actually learn another language. Given the present shortage of qualified and competent language teachers, Peddie (2005) suggests that it would be sensible if this compulsion were to be phased in over a period of about seven years. Even if more resources are invested in this policy over the next few years, it will still be a very long time before the majority of New Zealand's *pakeha* children and adults are competent users of more than one language.

A MUDDLED PAST AND TWO VIEWS OF THE FUTURE

Between 1975 and 1987, New Zealand society started to take steps to acknowledge and rectify previous injustices done to *tangata whenua*—and to a very large extent it is still struggling to come to terms with the implications of being a bilingual and bicultural society. Maori—and *Pasifika*—people are still highly overrepresented in negative social indices such as unemployment, sickness, poor housing, poverty, and imprisonment. In 1987, the nation opened its doors to a multicultural future with a radical change in immigration policy, and many thousands of Asian settlers are now residents or citizens. Ever since then—and especially after 2002, when Asian immigration reached a peak—there have been major debates about the respective rights, responsibilities, and values of *tangata whenua*, *pakeha*, and immigrants. This complexity and confusion are reflected in the nation's schools.

While the majority of Maori students are in English-medium schools, the Maori language and culture are taught in immersion schools. Only a minority of Maori students are enrolled in *kohanga reo* and *kura kaupapa Maori*. In the *whare kura* there are only a few adolescent students. In sum, very few students learn *te reo Maori* in mainstream schools. There are a very small number of Pasifika bilingual units, but very little instruction in Pasifika languages in the mainstream. Most Deaf children are enrolled in mainstream schools, but hardly any teachers are able to use New Zealand Sign Language. Very few students learn foreign languages in high schools, and even fewer in primary schools, although, as noted, some very modest steps are being taken in this regard.

Therefore, unless positive steps are taken to educate future citizens to appreciate the value of multilingualism and multiculturalism, the future may reproduce, or even increase, the tensions of the past. Maori people will continue to feel neglected, oppressed, and denied the rights accorded to them by the 1840 Treaty of Waitangi and reinforced by the 1975 Waitangi Tribunal. Many *pakeha* will consider the main effect of the Tribunal to be the distribution of benefits on the basis of ethnicity rather than according to actual needs. Minoritized linguistic and cultural groups will be resented, marginalized, and unsettled—their voices unheeded and their mother tongues lost to them. The majority of Kiwis will remain determinedly monolingual and monocultural, and issues of race, culture, and languages in New Zealand will be a dividing force.

An alternative future can be imagined in which New Zealand's children of all backgrounds—particularly those from monolingual *pakeha* families—will "grow out of the shell of their mother tongue and their own culture" (Kaikonnen, 2001, p. 64). Although such shells may afford protection from the shock of the culturally unfamiliar, they tend to constrict learners' intercultural development. Growing out of the "cultural shell" means the ability not only to appreciate the culture of other people but also to view one's own cultural beliefs, values, and practices through the prism of other points of view. Such an aim should be an integral element of second-language instruction, alongside other objectives such as linguistic and communicative competency (Barnard, 2005). However, even second-language programs more ambitious than those available in New Zealand can only complement the development of intercultural awareness promoted elsewhere in the school. What is necessary is a more radical review of the mainstream curriculum in New Zealand.

REIMAGING EDUCATION—THE APPROPRIATION OF METAPHORS

To promote positive multicultural schooling in New Zealand, educational theorists and practitioners might question some of the basic constructs of mainstream education. They could do this by appropriating metaphors used in parallel contexts. *Appropriation* in this sense means understanding the cultural values, ideas, and aspirations expressed by the metaphors of others and investing them with a personal meaning according to one's own particular frame of reference.

> The word in language is half someone else's. It becomes "one's own" only when the speaker populates it with his own intention, his own accent, when he appropriates the word, adapting it to his own semantic and expressive intention. (Bakhtin, 1981, pp. 293–294)

A metaphor, therefore, is a powerful tool that allows us to see our own reality through a prism, to see it in another light. A multidimensional perspective is offered to (1) reflect on existing beliefs and actions, (2) perceive alternative realities by examining others' metaphors, and (3) create a synthetic image by appropriating these metaphors to the existing context. Such appropriation allows the emergence of a hybrid and discursive "third space" that "challenges our sense of the historical identity of culture as a homogenizing unifying force" (Bhabha, 1994, p. 37).

In New Zealand, an obvious point of reference is the collective worldview (*kaupapa*) that underpins Maori educational praxis. Jones and colleagues (1995) have argued that the development of multiculturalism can be carried out only in relation to the bicultural relationship between *pakeha* and *tangata whenua*. According to Bishop (2003):

> Solutions to structural issues of power and control . . . can be addressed in mainstream classrooms by reference to Maori experiences of colonisation, resistance and educational initiatives in ways that will eventually benefit *all* students. (p. 223; emphasis in original)

A 2002 official report (Education Review Office) reviewed 52 *kura kaupapa Maori* and identified the greatest strengths of the programs to be the use of cooperative learning techniques, safe and effective classroom environments, and close relationships with the community. Smith (1997), Bishop and Glynn (1999), and Bishop (2003) have identified a number of interrelated metaphors as key constructs in Maori education; these include self-determination, cultural treasures, reciprocal learning, educational partnership, and extended families. Bishop and Glynn (1999) propose that they be applied to mainstream schools to promote the skills and understandings necessary for children to participate in the modern multilingual/multicultural world.

Tino rangatiratanga (*self-determination*)

Given their grass-roots origins, Maori-medium schools have always emphasized the need not only for parents and teachers but also for students to take a full part in key decision making with regard to administration, curriculum, and pedagogy. Bishop and Glynn (1999) argue that "the mainstream system is too entrenched in the passing on of knowledges-out-of-context to allow the development of flexible thinking" (p. 169). If New Zealand schools fully adopted pedagogical practices based on *tino rangatiratanga*, students would be enabled to develop flexibility, creativity, and responsible control in the learning process.

Taonga tuku iho (*treasures from the ancestors*)

Essentially, this means the recognition of the *tapu* (specialness) and *mana* (potential for power) of each child's cultural heritage, as opposed to adhering to stereotypical profiles. In Maori education, this was given force because of the discrimination that children of *tangata whenua* suffered—and still suffer—in mainstream education and society. In all classrooms, it is necessary to acknowledge and normalize the *tapu* and *mana* of every child, and at the same time to recognize that in today's world students are no longer monocultural, but live in intersecting dimensions. The mainstream curriculum needs to fully incorporate students' current and traditional treasures in order to "allow children to present their multiplicities and complexities and their individual and collective diversities" (Bishop & Glynn, 1999, p. 170).

Ako (*to teach and to learn*)

This metaphor for reciprocal learning is defined by Metge (1983) as "a unified cooperation of learner and teacher in a single enterprise" (p. 2). It means that the teacher is no longer viewed as the wellspring of all knowledge, but rather as a (leading) partner in educational conversations. According to Smith (1992), this principle emerged from the cultural traditions and socioeconomic circumstances of Maori communities, but it also may have derived in part from the modesty of many of the original teachers in *kohanga reo* and *kura kaupapa Maori*, whose pedagogical preparation and experience were somewhat limited. The application of *ako* to mainstream classrooms would democratize the educational process by reducing the power differential and cultural imbalance between teacher and learners—thereby potentially enabling teachers to learn from their students, and students to learn from one another, as well as from the teacher.

Kai piki ake i nga raruraru o te kainga (*overcoming home difficulties through partnership*)

Many Maori parents have been alienated from mainstream schools as a result of social discrimination, deficit educational experiences, and negative socioeconomic factors. Thus, a key plank of Maori-medium schooling is to involve parents as full partners in the educational venture, and thereby bridge the cultural gap between home and school. Appropriating this metaphor to the mainstream would involve making policy and practice as culturally responsive as possible and ensuring the participation of all parents, including, for example, those from immigrant communities, who otherwise might be marginalized by social, cultural, or linguistic distance from the dominant ethos.

Whanau (*extended family*)

This metaphor, based on the traditional kinship relationships of Maori society, has been extended in Maori education to refer to people working together for a common end. It involves a system of rights and responsibilities, commitments, and obligations that are fundamental to the collective (Metge, 1990). The attributes of *whanau* include "warm interpersonal interactions, group solidarity, shared responsibility for one another, cheerful cooperation for group ends . . . and [that] the group will operate to avoid singling out individuals for comment and attention, and to avoid embarrassing individuals who have not yet succeeded within the group" (Bishop & Glynn, 1999, pp. 83–84). If applied to the mainstream classroom, a *whanau* relationship would ensure that "a pattern of interactions would develop where commitment and connectedness is paramount, where responsibility for the learning of others is fostered and where the classroom becomes an active location for all learners to participate in decision-making processes" (Bishop & Glynn, 1999, p. 172).

These metaphors are clearly grounded in Maori *kaupapa*. However, as the authors cited above fully acknowledge, these images have been extended by appropriating constructs from other educational communities. Indeed, some of these metaphors resonate with some of those that underpin mainstream practices in New Zealand, but may have been neglected in recent years. By fully engaging in dialogue in Bhabha's "third space" with communities whose metaphors are being appropriated, educators can develop a multicultural community of practice (Wenger, 1998).

MOVING FORWARD: FROM REIMAGING TO IMPLEMENTATION

In order to envision ways of moving toward multicultural schooling, the Ministry of Education commissioned a number of research projects to identify key issues. These include studies relating to Maori participation and performance in education (Chapple, Jeffries, & Walker, 1997; Rau, 2003; Rau et al., 2001); the introduction of second-language instruction in primary schools (Gibbs & Holt, 2003; Peddie et al., 1999); issues relating to Pasifika education (Coxon et al., 2002); evidence of best practice in teaching diverse students (Alton-Lee, 2002; Franken & McComish, 2003); the educational needs of Deaf children (Stockwell, 2000); the experiences of international students (Ward & Masgoret, 2004); and international findings and approaches to bilingual education (May et al., 2004). The positive reception of such reports by the Ministry suggests that there is potential for developing, or at least encouraging, appropriate bilingual and multicultural education policies in the future.

For such policies to be really effective, a number of steps should be taken. Above all, there needs to be full dialogue between agents of the Ministry and educators within the different communities, with a view to synthesizing a coherent multicultural philosophy for national education. Systematic analyses of current and future language-learning needs and affordances should be carried out—including surveys of relevant languages to teach and the human, physical, and material resources required and available. Language communities should be assisted in maintaining, developing, and enriching their own languages and cultures, one outcome of which would be that bilingual resource people could be identified to serve as interpreters and community mediators in schools. In addition, competent bilinguals in the various communities could be recruited into the teaching profession and, if not already qualified, given appropriate and sufficient pedagogical preparation. It would be important to strengthen language-learning programs in tertiary institutions, so that more graduates would be to some extent bilingual and attuned to other cultures. The preparation and professional development of all teachers, not merely those teaching second languages, should extend well beyond training them to implement specific methods to achieve predetermined competencies. They should be encouraged to explore and appropriate cross-cultural educational metaphors such as those outlined earlier. If this was achieved, teachers could uphold a stance of "critical multiculturalism," which means that they would

> recognise and incorporate the differing cultural knowledges that children bring with them to school, *while at the same time* address and contest the differential cultural capital attributed to them as a result of wider hegemonic power relations. (May, 1999, p. 32; emphasis in original)

If all this took place, teachers would become sharply aware of the multilingual and multicultural diversity in New Zealand schools and be educated to make heuristic curricular decisions based on the needs and resources of their learners, on the opportunities for incorporating different languages and cultures into their classes, and on the constraints presented by the context in which they work. For this to be effective, school policies and curricula would need to be culturally inclusive and responsive, and realigned to address the balance of power within learning interactions. In the very long term, it just may be possible to envision a system wherein all children are sensitized to their own language as well as the languages of other cultures, where all children—not only those from minority communities—can become proficient in at least one other language, and where multiple languages as media of instruction may become available.

The above recommendations would require a considerable investment by the Ministry of Education, not only in primary and secondary schools but also—and perhaps especially—in tertiary institutions. For example, increasing the number of students in university language departments probably would require special funding, perhaps by way of scholarships to encourage the study of second languages by students and additional grants to enhance the quality and quantity of language instruction. Even more investment would be required for the professional development of student teachers; the present 3-year teaching degree is devoted to an understanding of the principles and procedures of the National Curriculum, and students have little time or opportunity to develop the wider perspective required by "critical multiculturalism." The reintroduction of a 4-year bachelor of education degree is needed, with multicultural issues placed in a central position in the curriculum.

CONCLUSION

As noted earlier, schooling is pivotal to the promotion of positive multicultural and multilingual awareness, attitudes, and activity among the nation's future citizens. However, educational policies and practices—however well informed by research, theory-driven, and imaginative—can be truly effective only if they are in line with structural reforms and a broad attitudinal change in society at large. In other words, the issue of multicultural competency across the nation needs to be moved higher on the national political agenda. Since the publication of Waite's (1992) seminal discussion document, issues relating to language policy have been delegated to the Ministry of Education, despite consistent calls (e.g., Crombie & Paltridge, 1993; De Bres, 2005; Kaplan, 1993; Peddie, 1997, 2005) for a national policy to be handled interdepartmentally, and preferably by the Prime Minister's office. Only through such high-level coordination can broad and effective consultation take place with all stakeholders—not merely in the education sector but also in other public institutions, as well as business, labor, and community and other organizations. At the same time, there needs to be a persuasive public awareness program on the value of multilingual and multicultural competency and incentives for the increased use of second languages in the workplace, mass media, and social settings. From research and consultation should emerge sensitive and effective national language policies. Given its place in New Zealand as a unique linguistic and cultural treasure still in need of careful nurturing—and its status as an official language—*te reo Maori* needs to have a separate, strong, and culturally responsive policy that is fully resourced. The same arguments might be applied to New Zealand Sign Language. There also needs to be a heuristic set of coherent policies for the other languages widely used in New Zealand and support for community-based language programs and cultural initiatives. These policies, while distinct, should be dovetailed so that insights, ideas, practices—and metaphors—current in one context can be appropriated to others. They also need to be supported with adequate resources and clear designation as to which agencies are responsible for detailed planning, implementation, and evaluation. Only then will it be possible to move from imagining multilingual and multicultural schools to a new realization. However, as may be adduced from the complex issues raised in this chapter, there is a very long way to go to move New Zealand from the dominance of *pakeha* culture in the 19th and 20th centuries to a broader, more inclusive set of pluralistic values in the decades to come in the 21st century.

REFERENCES

Alton-Lee, A. (2002, July). *Quality teaching for diverse students: Best evidence synthesis.* Draft for formative QA. Wellington: Medium Term Strategy Policy Section, Ministry of Education.

Ansre, G. (1979). Four rationalisations for maintaining European languages in education in Africa. *African Languages, 5*(2), 10–17.

Bakhtin, M. (1981). *The dialogic imagination.* Austin: University of Texas Press.

Barnard, R. (2005). The diverse aims of second language teaching: Implications for New Zealand primary schools. *New Zealand Journal of Educational Studies, 39*(2), 207–221.

Barnard, R. C. G., & Lata Rauf, P. (1999). Non-English speaking background pupils in Hamilton primary schools: A survey of learners, teachers and ESOL provision. *TESOLANZ Journal, 8,* 36–47.

Benton, R. (1979). *Who speaks Maori in New Zealand*? Wellington: Council for Educational Research.

Bhabha, H. (1994). *The location of culture.* London: Routledge.

Bishop, R. (2003). Changing power relations in education: Kaupapa Maori messages for "mainstream" education in Aotearoa/New Zealand. *Comparative Education, 39*(1), 221–238.

Bishop, R., & Glynn, T. (1999). *Culture counts: Changing power relations in education.* Palmerston North, New Zealand: Dunmore Press.

Cameron, S., & Simpson, J. (2002). ESOL teachers' perspectives on the provision for NESB students in Hamilton and Auckland secondary schools. *Many Voices, 19,* 16–23.

Chapple, S., Jeffries, R., & Walker, R. (1997). *Maori participation and performance in education: A literature review and research programme.* Wellington: Ministry of Education.

Council of Europe. (2000). *A common European framework of references for languages.* Retrieved July 26, 2007, from http://culture2.coe.int/portfolio//documents/0521803136txt.pdf

Coxon, E., Anae, M., Mara, D., Wendt-Samu, I., & Finau, C. (2002). *Literature review on issues facing pacific education.* Auckland: Auckland University Press.

Crombie, W., & Paltridge, B. (1993). Aoteareo: The way forward. A response to Aotearoa: Speaking for ourselves. In W. Crombie & B. Paltridge (Eds.), *Working papers in language education 1* (pp. 15–27). Hamilton, New Zealand: University of Waikato Language Institute.

Cummins, J. (1981). The role of primary language development in promoting educational success for minority language children. In California State Department of Education (Ed.), *Schooling and language minority students: A theoretical rationale* (pp. 3–49). Los Angeles: California State University.

Cummins, J. (2000). *Language, power and pedagogy: Bilingual children in the crossfire.* Clevedon: Multilingual Matters.

De Bres, J. (2005, May 4). Languages and cultures in Aotearoa New Zealand. Presentation by the Race Relations Commissioner, Massey University, Palmerston North, NZ.

Department of Statistics. (2002). *Census snapshot 13.* Retrieved May 27, 2005 from www.statistics.gvt.nz

Edmonds, K. (2001). Curricula through te reo Maori or te reo Maori through curricula? In R. Barnard & R. Harlow (Eds.), *Proceedings from the Conference Bilingualism at the Ends of the Earth* (pp. 23–27). Waikato, New Zealand: University of Waikato.

Education Review Office. (2002). *The performance of Kura Kaupapa Maori.* Wellington: Author.

Franken, M., & McComish, J. (2003). *Improving English language outcomes for students receiving ESOL services in New Zealand schools, with a particular focus on new immigrants.* Wellington: Ministry of Education.

Gibbs, C., & Holt, R. (2003). *The teaching of international languages in New Zealand schools in years 7 and 8: An evaluation study.* Wellington: Ministry of Education.

Glynn, T. (2003). Responding to language diversity: A way forward. In R. Barnard & T. Glynn (Eds.), *Bilingual children's language and literacy development* (pp. 273–281). Clevedon: Multilingual Matters.

Hirsch, W. (1990). *A report on issues and factors relating to Maori achievement in the education system.* Wellington: Ministry of Education.

Holmes, J. (1990). Community languages: Researchers as catalysts. *New Settlers and Multicultural Educational Issues,* 7(3), 19–26.

Irwin, K. (1990). The politics of kohanga reo. In S. Middleton, J. Codd, & A. Jones (Eds.), *New Zealand education policy today: Critical perspectives* (pp. 110–120). Wellington: Allen & Unwin/Port Nicholson Press.

Johnson, D. E. (2000). *International languages in New Zealand secondary schools and universities: Coherence, consistency and transparency.* Doctoral dissertation, University of Waikato, Waikato, New Zealand.

Jones, A., Marshall, J., Morris Matthews, K., Hinangaroa Smith, G., & Tuhiwai Smith, L. (1995). *Myths and realities: Schooling in New Zealand* (2nd ed.). Palmerston North, New Zealand: Dunmore Press.

Kaikkonnen, P. (2001). Intercultural learning through foreign language education. In V. Kohonen, R. Jaatinen, P. Kaikkonnen, & J. Lehtovaara (Eds.), *Experiential learning in foreign language education* (pp. 61–105). Harlow, UK: Pearson Education.

Kaplan, R. (1993). *New Zealand languages policy: Making the patient more comfortable.* Wellington: Ministry of Education.

King, M. (2003). *The Penguin history of New Zealand.* Auckland: Penguin Books.

May, S. (1999). Critical multiculturalism and cultural difference: Avoiding essentialism. In S. May (Ed.), *Critical multiculturalism: Rethinking multicultural and anticracist education* (pp. 11–41). London: Routledge Falmer.

May, S., Hill, R., & Tiakiwai, S. (2004). *Bilingual/immersion education: Indicators of good practice.* Wellington: Ministry of Education.

McKee, R. L., & Biederman, Y. (2003). The construction of learning contexts for deaf bilingual learners. In R. Barnard & T. Glynn (Eds.), *Bilingual children's language and literacy development* (pp. 194–224). Clevedon: Multilingual Matters.

Metge, J. (1983). *Learning and teaching: Ho tikanga Maori.* Wellington: New Zealand Department of Education.

Metge, J. (1990). Te rito o te harakeke: Conceptions of the whanau. *Journal of the Polynesian Society, 99*(1), 55–91.

Ministry of Education. (1993). *Te anga marautanga o Aotearoa.* Wellington: Learning Media.

Ministry of Education. (1994). *English in the New Zealand curriculum.* Wellington: Ministry of Education.

Ministry of Education. (1996). *New Zealand curriculum framework.* Wellington: Ministry of Education.

Ministry of Education. (2002). Tertiary statistics. Retrieved August 26, 2003, from http://www.minedu.govt.nz

Ministry of Education. (2003). *Effective literacy practice in years 1 to 4.* Wellington: Learning Media.

Ministry of Education. (2004). *Effective literacy strategies in years 9 to 13: A guide for teachers.* Wellington: Learning Media.

New Zealand Government Bill. (2004). Retrieved May 27, 2005, from http://www.brokkers.co.nz/bills/new_bills/b041241.pdf

Peddie, R. (1997). Why are we waiting? Languages policy development in New Zealand. In W. Eggington & H. Wren (Eds.), *Language policy: Dominant English, pluralist challenges* (pp. 120–146). Amsterdam: John Benjamins.

Peddie, R. (2003). Languages in New Zealand: Population, politics and policy. In R. Barnard & T. Glynn (Eds.), *Bilingual children's language and literacy development* (pp. 8–35). Clevedon: Multilingual Matters.

Peddie, R. (2005). Planning for the future? Languages policy in New Zealand. In A. Bell, R. Harlow, & D. Starks (Eds.), *The languages of New Zealand* (pp. 30–50). Wellington: Victoria University Press.

Peddie, R., Gunn, C., & Lewis, M. (1999). *Starting younger: The second language learning project evaluation*. Auckland: Auckland UniServices/University of Auckland.

Phillipson, R. (1992). *Linguistic imperialism*. Oxford: Oxford University Press.

Rau, C. (2003). *A snapshot of the literacy achievement of year 2 students in 80–100% Maori immersion programmes in 1995 and 2002–3 and the impact of teacher professional development on that achievement*. Wellington: Ministry of Education.

Rau, C., Whiu, I., Thomson, H., Glynn, T., & Milroy, W. (2001). *He ara angitu. A description of success in reading for five-year-old Maori medium students*. Wellington: Ministry of Education.

Ritchie, J. (1992). *Becoming bicultural*. Wellington: Huia Publications

Shameem, N. (2003). Community language schools: Teacher education needs in New Zealand. In R. Barnard & T. Glynn (Eds.), *Bilingual children's language and literacy development* (pp. 225–246). Clevedon: Multilingual Matters.

Simon, J. (Ed.). (1998). *The native schools system 1867–1969: Nga kura Maori*. Auckland: Auckland University Press.

Smith, G. H. (1992). Tane-nui-a-rangi's legacy . . . propping up the sky: Kaupapa Maori as resistance and intervention. *Proceedings from the Aotearoa/New Zealand Association for Research in Education/Australia Association for Research in Education Joint Conference*, Deakin University, Victoria, Australia.

Smith, G. H. (1997). *Kaupapa Maori as transformative praxis*. Unpublished doctoral dissertation, University of Auckland, Auckland, New Zealand.

Stockwell, W. (2000). *Establishing Deaf children's educational needs*. Unpublished report for Specialist Education Services, New Zealand.

Tuafuti, P., & McCaffery, J. (2005). Family and community empowerment through bilingual education. *International Journal of Bilingual Education and Bilingualism, 8*(5), 1–24.

Waite, J. (1992). *Aoteareo: Speaking for ourselves*. Wellington: Learning Media.

Ward, C., & Masgoret, A. M. (2004). *The experiences of international students in New Zealand: Report on the results of the National Survey*. Wellington: Ministry of Education.

Wenger, E. (1998). *Communities of practice: Learning, meaning, and identity*. Cambridge: Cambridge University Press.

Afterword: Multilingualism for Understanding

iZemia's Unity in Linguistic Diversity

María E. Torres-Guzmán and Joel Gómez

When we began this book's journey, we were searching for new metaphors that would help us reframe the national debates on bilingual education within the United States. The search for, or stumbling upon, the iZemia story was fortuitous, as it has the historically grounded force that simultaneously offered us a fresh way of thinking about linguistic and cultural diversity (Encino, 2007). iZemia proposed that there was unity in linguistic diversity and that this diversity was of benefit for the whole of society (Dascal, 1999). We propose it as a metaphor for unity in linguistic diversity as a way of launching the concept of *multilingualism for understanding*.

In our use of the iZemia story as a metaphor, we are attempting to establish continuity with the past. But as Encino (2007) proposes, it may be more like going back in time to recover a disruption that might help us illuminate the future. iZemia's story is disruptive of the reigning "common" understanding of multiple languages as portrayed in the Tower of Babel metaphor. It was from this starting point that we based the concept of *multilingualism for understanding*. We relied on Dascal's multiple philosophically based arguments for linguistic diversity—that is, the practical, the ethical, the ontological, the epistemological, and the cognitive foundations—to illustrate how the different arguments contribute to understanding how multilingualism is manifested in different parts of the world. In attempting to understand a phenomenon like multilingualism, we also used a conceptualization of understanding as going beyond that which we already know (Wiggins & McTighe, 2006) to recreate and regenerate the knowing that comes from our past and present histories of participation in the world.

Multilingualism for understanding refers not only to the phenomenon of multilingualism itself, but also to the processes and outcomes of becoming and enacting multilingualism in our everyday lives. It furthermore proposes that we think about policies and practices of multiple languages not only as based on our and other people's legacies, but also as a necessary condition for ensuring a "glocalized" (García, Skutnabb-Kangas, & Torres-Guzmán, 2006) democracy that goes beyond the neoliberal promotion of diversity to one that is grounded in social justice. We recognize not just the present but also the past as a resource for envisioning a future for multilingualism. What it means with respect to the application of multilingualism for understanding in education is that policies and practices must be based on flexible and expanded ways of understanding multilingualism.

Here, we attempt to summarize the understandings derived from the multiple cases of multilingualism worldwide. We first highlight ways in which the contributors in this volume are pushing on the fluidity with which we can see and present the world of multilingualism to others—whether in definition, in instructional designs, in connections with the world, or in connection with other fields. This is followed by a summary of the threads that cross the different contexts and also the obstacles and constraints we still face and will have to overcome to make multilingualism for understanding a reality. We would like to acknowledge that in the selection of the threads, we build not only on the scholarly contributions in this volume, but also on the work of numerous scholars of multilingualism (Block, 2007; Cummins, 2001; Hornberger, 2004; Ricento, 2000).

PUSHING THE CONCEPT OF MULTILINGUALISM

We first will focus on what we see as the contributors' extension of the concept of multilingualism, as the contributors appeal to a more inclusive and fluid view of the use of more than one language in everyday situations, including classrooms. We understand the contributors are envisioning multilingualism for the future as inclusive of the disruptive and incommensurable of the past legacies (Encino, 2007). They have something to say with respect to the possibilities of multilingualism at a time in which we also acknowledge and question the reality of globalization and democratization. Thus, they bring forth the necessity of examining the relationship between diversity and social justice as we project into the future (Banks, 2003; Ladson-Billings, 1995; Nieto, 2002). We also feel that their work calls for the expansion of multilingualism based on the intricate links between language and culture. These links highlight the need for looking not just back at the past or forward at the future, but sideways to our communities within the present, to find a more feasible and viable imagined future.

Multilingualism, the Phenomenon

The contributors to this volume challenge the definition of multilingualism, defined by Cenoz and Genesee (1998) and Cook (1995) as the "capacity to use several languages appropriately and effectively for communication in oral and written language" (cited in Wildsmith-Cromarty, this volume). Bloch does so as she helps us understand how the conditions of South Africa raise questions about the definition. First, she calls attention to the privilege English faces within the educational setting. In the case of South Africa—as in many other parts of the world—English, the ex-colonial language, presently plays the dual roles of *lingua franca* and linkage to the globalized world of the markets and the media. English carries a privileged position despite the fact that many other regional and vernacular languages are legally recognized. A second and perhaps more distinguishing condition of South Africa, is that it represents a print-scarce environment in which reliance on print has not been seen as necessary in carrying out everyday life events. Thus, children do not experience the urgency of learning how to read and write as part of their socialization into functioning within their community's adult life, as is the case in highly literate societies. Both of these contextual features—the scarcity of print and privileging of English among a primarily non-English-speaking population—create conditions within schools where most of the oral communication between teachers and students occurs in the African mother tongue. The written text, within its power differential, is in English.

At the other extreme, as Barnard mentioned, are the needs of the Deaf community, the nonoral sign language. More research has to be conducted and disseminated to understand the Deaf community, as their claim is that the visual and written languages used in schooling are distinct and thus their education is bilingual. This is yet another community excluded when we use the traditional definition of multilingualism.

One must acknowledge that the definition of bilingualism as education in two or more languages and/or two or more literacies is an attempt to be specific about the phenomenon of bi/multilingual education. As Wildsmith-Cromarty pointed out, the definition proposed assumes having two or more languages in which the individual can reach oral and written proficiency. Considering the range of realities, from the multilingualism of South Africa to the multilingualism of the Deaf, Wildsmith-Cromarty (this volume) describes bi/multilingual education globally as the use of "more than one language in order to fulfill various communicative purposes," and multilinguals as those "who have specific configurations of linguistic competencies that reflect unique interactions among the languages" within the instructional setting. In the United States, advocates of bilingual education have not pressed for a broad definition, as many fear that the largest recipient population will be shortchanged (Valdes, 1997). These fears might have a sociohistorical basis, but it is important that as we learn about the different forms of multilingualism, we acknowledge that advocating for multilingualism for understanding broadens the constituencies for which its existence will matter in the form of policies and practices within our nation's public schools.

Definitions of Multilingualism

Omoniyi also considers the definition of multilingualism, for two reasons. One is because multilingualism traditionally references minoritized-language education and he proposes expanding the vision of multilingualism to include an "invisible" community—the expatriate and "third culture kid" who is hybridized and may or may not speak the languages of the "new Europe." Second, he does not find bi/multilingual education per se. What he finds are ways in which the expatriate and national elites need to become, and benefit from becoming, bi/multilingual as they project into their envisioned future as adults within the new Europe, Africa, and/or the world. The way they become bi/multilingual within the educational system, however, is through language learning as subject matter.

In contrasting the elite schools' and public education's needs for bilingualism, Omoniyi brings into focus the distinction between elite and folk bi/multilingualism (Grosjean, 1982). This distinction serves to differentiate what population is served by what type of bi/multilingual education, as there are distinct needs and thus distinct benefits. In the first case, as in the schools examined by Omoniyi, the objective was the learning of the languages that would benefit the young people in their future projected world. The goals of folk bi/multilingualism were more closely associated with the acknowledgment of past exclusions of those communities from which the children came and the present need to access learning as well as the projected future participation in the dominant society.

Within this volume, the contributors speak to such bi/multilingualism within language communities like the Maori in New Zealand, the African-language communities within Africa, the Hakka in Taiwan, and the Sorbs, the Danish, the Fries, and the long-term Turkish workers within Germany. However, there is a blurring of those boundaries with populations that have had glorious pasts but discriminatory and silenced presents, such as the Hungarians in the Slovakian state. Another blurring occurs with the expatriates in Nigeria. They have been privileged in relation to the African continent, but are at a disadvantage in relation to children who are being educated within and for the "new Europe." Another blurring of multilingualism occurs in many countries where the need for English learning, in the hope of participating in the world market economy (Lo Bianco, 2002), becomes the basis for multiple languages in schools. Similarly, multilingualism becomes a necessity, and blurs the elite/folk distinction, in the multistate configurations such as the European Union. The world of bi/multilingualism no longer can be an elite folk distinction where folk bilingualism is compensatory. The phenomenon of learning and using multiple languages depends as much on the individual learning/using the languages as on the context of learning/using the languages. Hornberger (2004) proposes bilingual continua, but we would say that such continua apply to the individual and institutional levels of analysis. We would propose a multilingual continuum for the policy levels of analysis. This must be more like a continuum of language freedoms and of participation—albeit partial—in a glocalized society.

The new configurations of multilingual schooling within the German society are testimony to educational programs that incorporate not just those that have been excluded in the past, but also the children of the dominant society as they face the need for multilingualism within the European Union. Neumann and Roth find that both sets of populations—those from the dominant language and those from the minoritized language and immigrant communities—benefit from the multiple language configurations within schools. Budach, focused on a German/Italian dual-language education program that benefits both language-minoritized and majority children, also delineates how multilingualism becomes legitimized as cultural capital for the dominant society and, as a result of its global recognition, increases in status and is positioned internationally beyond the nation-state as part of an overarching goal of peacekeeping and political economic integration. Simultaneously, she signals how this formidable movement serves to expand the rights of the autochthonous language minorities such as the Sorbs, the Danish, and the Fries within Germany, while still excluding those groups not considered European—the many large immigrant groups that have incorporated into German society as guest workers in search for improvement in their lives.

Within the United States, we have been experiencing the growth of dual-language education and language enrichment (heritage- and second-language) programs that include nontraditional populations who see the need for multilingualism within our society. These efforts need to be supported, and those who receive the services may become allies of the traditionally served student populations because they understand the value of bilingualism at the individual level. While the advocacy has been for the less privileged, as Bialystok (2001) proposes, most of the literature of bilingual education has been based on its implementation in middle-class educational settings. We have to acknowledge this as a reality and attempt to learn what is applicable within and across settings and populations. We also have to have policies that are more robust in the adaptation process as programs are implemented, so that they are more inclusive of diverse populations.

Modes of Bi/Multilingualism and Instructional Design

Bloch and Wildsmith-Cromarty call for schools to account for the rift between the oral and literate language in designing curricula and in defining multilingualism. They propose that the healing of the oral/literacy rift and an appropriate instructional design will occur by introducing the mother tongue and literacy in the mother tongue prior to and side by side with the gradual introduction of the English language. Bloch suggests that this also will honor a fundamental principle of learning—that is, going from the known to the unknown—in practice. Wildsmith-Cromarty advocates for differentiating goals while considering multilingual modes in instructional designs.

Wildsmith-Cromarty shows how people speak in their everyday lives might be different in a variety of settings. Wildsmith-Cromarty distinguishes between school types—rural, urban township, and urban suburban—to explore how each has different language-learning situations and thus different educational purposes that arise from them. She mentions explanations, empathy as seen in group identity, as well as tolerance of others, meaning, creating bridges from cultural to scientific understandings, and uncovering privilege through understanding hidden discourses as they relate to the different educational purposes of language use. The varied language uses and circumstances within different school types call for different forms of multilingualism—from language awareness, to the development of academic language in both the mother tongue and English, to developing positive self-images and more positive home language learning among African students. They call for more inclusive situations within education that reflect the reality of the multilingual's everyday existence. What this means is that while most of the instruction is designed as if the sole medium of instruction were English, the reality is that more than one language is used in systematic ways to create learning and understanding among pupils—whether in the form of code-switching or mixing of diverse home languages or of urban codes that are no one's home language.

Vančo, like Bloch and Wildsmith-Cromarty within the South African context, advocates for education that is minoritized-language-based. She suggests that Hungarian-language schools are significant to the embodiment of the Hungarians' identity and to maintaining its integrity. At the same time, she pushes for recognition of the hybridity and transcultural nature of the Hungarian population in Slovakia, pointing out that a portion of the population has shifted toward Slovakian language and culture, many Slovakian words have entered the Hungarian language as borrowings, Slovakian Hungarians are becoming distanced from the standard language of Hungary, and that the country has negotiated entry into the European Union. She utilizes the traditional dualism of additive-subtractive (Lambert, 1980) bilingual models to substantiate the need for strong models of Hungarian-language schooling and for extending these schools into institutions of higher learning. What we understand is that under the circumstances in which the Hungarian community finds itself, that is, in a context in which it has been silenced through conquest, there is a need for strong Hungarian-language schools that will permit the Hungarian community within a Slovakian state to renew itself. The reconstruction of the Hungarians, as proposed by Vančo, acknowledges the linguistic changes and variations of the language and the culture, and recognizes the historical past while forging into an imagined future that is inclusive of new survival modes that use multilingualism as a resource.

De Mejía, Tejada, and Colmenares argue that language policies that guide curriculum development may or may not be transformative, and that they may fall anywhere within the continuum of types of multilingualism. They believe that transformation will come from understanding the students' multilingualism as a resource for learning. Therefore, they propose expanding the notion of multilingualism as they try to locate its perceived value not in what teachers think about the language per se, but rather in how the teachers project "others" as well as their own theories of bi/multilingualism into the construction of bilingual curricula. The empowerment of bi/multilingual teachers comes from their participation in bilingual curriculum development as they apply, interpret, and create new perspectives in the process of understanding. The focus is on multilingualism as a resource for cognitive as well as linguistic development.

Budach also explores the need to reconceptualize multilingualism as a mode of learning in the actual curriculum design and goes beyond this to examine how students experience it in the classroom. She proposes that instructional designs need to take into account how multiple languages coexist in the process of learning and acting, as a set of social practices that are designed and negotiated within classrooms and their surroundings. She illustrates not just how classrooms can mirror, by design, those everyday situations in which two languages are needed, but how the actual classroom can become a way of working through a window (Sleeter, 2005) into some of the tensions of living multilingual lives and learning how to increase respect for others. She advocates for instructional designs that create cultures of cooperative learning where each individual is valued for what he or she is and how he or she can contribute to the accomplishment of joint tasks.

Neumann and Roth also reference multilingualism as reflective of how people use more than one language during their everyday affairs. They confirm that the different populations have different needs, and they identify the need for stronger language models for children with home languages other than German, as the classrooms with fewer native-language models did not do as well as those with a good mix of children. Furthermore, they call for linguistic heterogeneity in student grouping and team teaching, as students need to practice and pay attention to the contrast between languages, supporting the theoretical proposition that metalinguistic awareness is important when learning more than one language.

The contributors push on the need to see multilingualism not just as the addition of another language, but also as the use of more than one language in the course of a day. They also press us on the need to think more deeply about instruction and the goals of multilingualism in learning institutions. They consider the different relationships—the oral/literacy continuum, the premises associated with standards and norms, and the types of instructional designs where languages must be negotiated. They all speak to the need for the young to be in situations where they use language(s)—metalinguistics—to learn about languages as a way of understanding the content of what is taught. They speak to understanding the people who speak the different languages within their historical and present circumstances.

Within the United States, we believe that the interpretation of equity has led to standardization and to a call for surface sameness. This is an issue that goes beyond multilingualism while affecting how bi/multilingualism is implemented in many schools. Rather than seeing multiple languages as distinct linguistic resources that have distinguishable strengths, we have hardly moved beyond the translation of curricular material. The industry of diversity is yet to be mined for what it can offer humankind.

Democratization and Globalization

Li positions the phenomenon of multilingualism squarely within the context of globalization, as the world experiences the markets, world politics, development and use of high technology, and communication within the world of the English language. While doing so, he also positions Taiwan's renewal as part of the country's democratization process. He proposes that the democratization of Taiwan requires greater awareness of the need to preserve and develop local and aboriginal languages while it expands English within its national boundaries. He proposes the iZemia's harmonious yet social and linguistically diverse context not just because of the present movement of peoples, cultures, and languages, but also because of past histories of such encounters. Li signals how the language complexity of almost all nations in the world can be constructed and proposes that the issue of multilingualism is important not just in schools but in "social commentary and day-to-day conversation."

From Bloch to Li, the issue of expanding multilingualism goes beyond the goals of neoliberalism. It is not just a matter of acknowledging diversity but of an inclusive diversity that is grounded in social justice. The contributors highlight the need to acknowledge a more complex population. Today's multilingualism has to include the elite, dominant, expatriate, immigrant, language-minoritized, and indigenous populations. They are all part of the complex mosaic of the multilingual societies we live in.

To move forward means acknowledging and learning from the past and bringing that learning into our renewal of selves in the present as we project our imagined futures. Democracy means recognizing the Hakka as a language to be preserved and developed. It means recognizing that a mother tongue was used in apartheid South Africa as a way of blocking access to the world of power and that English is still symbolically and practically the key. It understands that if the parents of children in South Africa favor English as the language of power, it is because the issue of access to power needs to be revisited with the parents as they deconstruct and reconstruct their postapartheid world and recognize the value of mother tongue bilingual education. It is the reason for shifting from an either/or perspective to one in which multiple languages need to be embraced as we try to understand the different histories of participation with the different languages within different contexts.

While there are many populations that have migrated to Slovakia, the case Vančo focuses on is that of the Hungarians, who have faced the need to become multilingual due to nation-building histories and changes in boundary configurations. She brings in the historical legacies embodied in identity and statuses more traditionally associated with land. She suggests that going from a nation-state to a multiple-nation configuration such as the European Union highlights the relationships between democracy and the importance of minority rights, including language. Within this context, she envisions Hungarians having more language rights and more policies and practices addressing and ensuring those rights. She, like many of the other contributors, proposes a role for history as a resource for building a new understanding of multilingualism.

Neumann and Roth bring together two major demographic and political issues—increasing immigration and the growth of the European Union—as raising the need for iZemia's proposition of unity in multilingualism. Within this context, they examine the role and effectiveness of bilingual schooling in promoting multilingualism while raising the achievement bar for both immigrants and German young people, an issue of social justice.

Multilingualism, according to Barnard, is a moral imperative within a democratic society. He addresses the complexity of the multiple-language situations within New Zealand, from the indigenous to the recent immigrants. The moral imperative is embedded not only in a nation's past with respect to its relation to the indigenous population, but also in relation to the immigration needs arising from the world's economies and unequal distributions of goods. Yet Barnard also raises the need to take a look at the feasibility of multiple languages and proposes that the potential resolution lies in the connections between language and culture.

Within the United States, we have moved in the direction of serving immigrant populations—which we need to do—but in doing so we have let the heritage languages disappear and this lopsidedness has been detrimental to the view of bilingual education as a whole. We need to recover the view of multilingualism that is inclusive of the range of linguistic needs of the different populations and we need to push for cultural metaphors that will anchor the unity within diversity and democracy as one and the same.

Linking Languages and Cultures

While multilingualism is promoted within the construct of social justice and as moral necessity within an increasingly diverse linguistic and cultural world, Wildsmith-Cromarty and Barnard speak to the multiple linguistic needs of the different populations. They raise the issue of goals and propose that the different needs call for different manifestations of multilingualism. We could see some of this as we looked at Vančo's proposal for a strong minoritized-language schooling system, whereas presently this would not be possible within the South African situation. It could be an envisioned future only if the infrastructure associated with the development of creative African language writers were supported by the partnering with publishing houses that would bank on the motivation coming from the connections with the Pharaonic literacy traditions that gave birth to humanity's use of literacy as a daily practice.

We also could see how, within a country such as New Zealand, the multiple needs were associated with both historical legacies and present conditions. As Wildsmith-Cromarty proposed, not all the populations need to develop the same goals—some situations may call for the oral knowledge of more than one language, some for the knowledge of more than one literacy, and some for becoming aware of what multiple languages mean to others. As Barnard proposes, feasibility may mean that multilingualism is available for the different types of populations but may not be taken up by all. What may be even more necessary for the entire population is a coherent multilingual/multicultural philosophy for all children that takes critical stances that transform our world into a more desirable and feasible possibility. Barnard, within the context of New Zealand, finds the disruptive and incommensurable in past Maori metaphors and images—focused on cooperation, commitment, connectedness, and quality teaching of language—that might help us imagine a different future in which multilingualism is a resource for understanding one another as well as recreating ourselves anew as we understand it as a phenomenon. It is embracing iZemia's linguistic diversity as a way to unity.

The images and metaphors that the United States may use to promote the idea of diversity in unity may be different from or similar to those identified in this volume. This still requires more investigation and discussion. We feel that it is imperative to do such work collectively.

THREADS, CONSTRAINTS, AND OBSTACLES

As we move to closure, we believe a word of caution is in order. We need to acknowledge that a concept like *multilingualism for understanding* will have to overcome constraints and obstacles, and we returned to our contributors to find the threads here as well. The contributors point out numerous difficulties that they have encountered in promoting linguistic diversities in their societies; some echo in different parts of the world, while others are unique to the specific conditions in which they are implemented. We have categorized the difficulties, obstacles, and constraints into three areas: public and parental attitudes, policies and curriculum, and human and material resources.

Public and Parental Attitudes

One of the fundamental issues impacting the use of multiple languages for education is the general public and parental views toward languages and education; that is, that one language of instruction is better than multiple languages. The pervasive views and beliefs about linguistic diversity continue to be those of the Tower of Babel—that the use of multiple languages creates a problem because it leads to confusion (Ruiz, 1984). This view of linguistic diversity typically feeds on local biases and prejudices against the language(s) of minority groups, and we need to challenge these pervasive views. In addition, the overwhelmingly global push toward English supports the Tower of Babel argument as it promotes the dominance of one language over several while proposing its *lingua franca* role.

As many of our contributors propose, and we have argued above, a shift to a more inclusive embracing of multilingualism is a necessary alternative. While new democracies embrace the hope and openness of new laws and policies, in other countries commitments for the use of multiple languages for instruction are enshrined in law but are far from implementation, as adequate funding and human resources are lacking. Even while funding and efforts have been made in the direction of breathing life into threatened languages, the attitudes of their own speakers have been found to be critical and not supportive of encoding the languages. Within a multilingualism for understanding framework, we see the need for the new metaphors to be taken up by the public so that the different populations in contact can see and embrace fully a role for learning in more than one language, albeit in different ways.

Policies and Curriculum

Multilingualism alone may not be enough; the dynamics of symbolism and meanings within the different cultures need to be delineated in ways that are more transparent. Multiple languages in education need systematic and cohesive implementation, and, beyond this, the implementation needs to embody and respond to a cohesive philosophy. Multilingualism for understanding challenges not only the existing linguistic hierarchies but also the culturally and socially based hidden curricula and the philosophies that continue to privilege the few.

The hidden curriculum and the status of minority, immigrant, and expatriate communities also emerge in the debates around the role of languages as medium or subjects of instruction. English, as the language of the market economy, is at the same time a *lingua franca* in many multilingual countries. Thus, at times it is difficult to pinpoint English as one or the other. Multilingual policy and curriculum depend on the specific student populations, the country's desire to enter the world of modernity and globalization, the institutional mission, the parents' shrewdness in pushing to ensure social mobility locally and globally for their children, the efficiency of funding formulas, the existing materials and human resources, and the societal goal of justice for all.

In the new social order of globalization, the markets and new political arrangements like the European Union are triggers for multilingualism for understanding, as is evident in the range of language programs in European-language schools and the language awareness projects in France (Helot & Young, 2006). Some of the multilingual programmatic designs in schools bridge different social classes and are grounded in the belief that there are advantages in knowing more than one language. They bring together the interests of language-minority parents who want to support and develop social spaces for their children for the use of the heritage language beyond the home, and the parents of language-majority children, who want to prepare their children for the multilingual world of the future.

Human and Material Resources

The transference of resources from the more powerful to the less powerful is not the focus of advocacy within this volume, but we do advocate for a more equitable distribution in which we all have access to the resources to meet our basic educational and linguistic needs. Promoting ways in which all language groups have a voice, not at the expense of others, but in acknowledgment and support of one another, is what we would like our imagined future to hold for the world. We started with a premise that knowing the "other" is a way of knowing the "self." Our proposal, we believe, is a proposal for human preservation in a new, ever-changing, and shrinking world.

Some of the issues fundamental to making multilingualism for understanding a reality in educational institutions are found in the arena of human and material resources. Developing instructional materials, such as putting into print oral literacy traditions and standardizing languages—including varieties of local languages and varieties of global languages, like English—is a must. Equally important is the creation of new materials that reflect the legacies of those who have remained voiceless for too long and those new voices that are arising. Only mutually beneficial agreements with publishing houses will make a difference. Furthermore, the contributors make a strong call for a shift in the conceptualizations of the relationship between languages and the language used for subject matter instruction. New materials cannot just be translations of what is, but need to reflect new ways of treating school curriculum.

An issue that resonates widely around the world, and in the contributors' chapters specifically, is that of teacher preparation and the role teachers play in nurturing the development of knowledge and thinking in multiple languages. The challenges in teacher education include shifting the view of teachers to undertake new roles, such as facilitators and co-constructors of knowledge, creators and theorizers in curriculum development, and reflective practitioners. Besides, we need to assist teachers in finding their voices and in creating their worlds in relationship to the worlds of the children. While helping teachers to understand why helping the children find their place and their voice is meaningful, we need to make sure they understand that this directly calls on the use of all the languages the children have at their disposal. The teachers need to feel a level of competence in the languages they teach and the ability to use those languages for the linguistic and social purposes established by the pedagogical programs. Teachers need to work through both their linguistic and content insecurities as part of the process of co-constructing knowledge with one another and with their students.

Many, if not all, of the authors call for shifting metaphors. The call, collectively speaking, is for a transformation from subtractive bi/multilingualism in education to one that goes beyond being additive to being a flexible, all-embracing philosophy of multilingualism for understanding. It is a call for the possibility of multiple ways of promoting and enhancing educational language responses and imagined futures. The call is for learners and their communities to serve as active rather than passive recipients of the curriculum and for their languages to be used as mediums of instruction, ranging from language awareness to strong minority- and second-language learning models for all students. It calls for teachers to assist students to break away from their parochial past to embrace the blurriness of our relationships to one another and to the world—in identity, in discourse, and/or in worldviews—as they imagine new futures for themselves and others.

CONCLUSION

The four new understandings—the definition of multilingualism, the modes of multilingual learning and instructional designs, the relationship between democracy and multilingualism, and the linkage between language and culture—illustrate the need to continuously examine assumptions made within a field. For these are important in determining who is included or excluded, the future envisioned within a conceptualization, and the potential for imagined futures toward which we can act in the present. In this volume, we chose to take up iZemia's story as a metaphor of unity in language diversity, and we propose the concept of multilingualism for understanding as a new way of speaking of the variety of ways two or more languages can be used in instruction and in schools within our glocalized worlds. We do not see the debates on multilingualism as either/or situations. We feel there are ample ways in which we develop multilingualism through schooling. We ought to have policies that would provide us with the freedom to choose the best solutions for the specific situations faced by children and their families as they become not just bilingual, but multilingual. Moreover, we see multilingualism as a way of understanding how we relate to the world as, by knowing more than one language, we come to understand ourselves and others in new ways. Those understandings are important for a future world where greater inclusion of diverse populations and greater tolerance and understanding of multiple language and cultural situations may be a feasible reality.

By choosing to dream in new metaphors of linguistic unity and abundance of opportunities with the goal of creating a systemic view of multilingualism for understanding, we take all the excellent examples of language experiences in this volume, isolated as they are, as evidence of multilingualism as beneficial for all. We are not presenting this as a panacea or utopia, but as our portrait of what *is* possible. We acknowledge that such a systemic and coherent vision of an imagined multilingual world, based on iZemia's story as a metaphor, is far from reality and will require a few decades of coordinated work.

REFERENCES

Banks, J. A. (2003). Introduction: Democratic citizenship education in multicultural societies. In J. A. Banks (Ed.), *Diversity and citizenship education* (pp. 3–15). San Francisco: Jossey-Bass/Wiley.

Bialystok, E. (2001). *Bilingualism in development: Language, literacy, and cognition*. Cambridge: Cambridge University Press.

Block, D. (2007). Bilingualism: Four assumptions and four responses. *Innovation in Language Learning and Teaching, 1*(1), 66–82.

Cenoz, J., & Genesee, F. (1998). Psycholinguistic perspectives on multilingualism and multilingual education. In J. Cenoz & F. Genesee (Eds.), *Beyond bilingualism: Multilingualism and multilingual education* (pp. 16–32). Clevedon: Multilingual Matters.

Cook, V. (1995). Multicompetence and the learning of many languages. *Language, Culture & Curriculum, 8*, 93–98.

Cummins, J. (2001). Instructional conditions for trilingual development. *International Journal of Bilingual Education and Bilingualism, 4*(2), 61–75.

Dascal, M. (1999). Chapter 8: An alternative view. Retrieved February 1, 2006, from http://www.tau.ac.il/humanities/philos/dascal/papers/8.htm

Encino, P. (2007). Reframing history in sociocultural theories: Toward an expansive vision. In C. Lewis, P. Encino, & E. B. Moje (Eds.), *Reframing sociocultural research on literacy: Identity, agency, and power* (pp. 49–74). Mahwah, NJ: Erlbaum.

García, O., Skutnabb-Kangas, T., & Torres-Guzmán, M. E. (Eds.). (2006). *Imagining multilingual schools: Languages in education and glocalization*. Clevedon: Multilingual Matters.

Grosjean, F. (1982). *Life with two languages: An introduction to bilingualism*. Cambridge, MA: Harvard University Press.

Helot, C., & Young, A. (2006). Imagining multilingual education in France: A language and cultural awareness project at primary level. In O. García, T. Skutnabb-Kangas, & M. E. Torres-Guzmán (Eds.), *Imagining multilingual schools: Languages in education and glocalization* (pp. 69–90). Clevedon: Multilingual Matters.

Hornberger, N. H. (2004). The continua of biliteracy and the bilingual educator: Educational linguistics in practice. *Bilingual Education and Bilingualism, 7*(2&3), 155–171.

Ladson-Billings, G. (1995). Toward a theory of culturally relevant pedagogy. *American Education Research Journal, 35*, 465–491.

Lambert, W. E. (1980). The social psychology of language: A perspective for the

1980s. In H. Giles, W. P. Robinson, & P. M. Smith (Eds.), *Language: Social psychological perspectives* (pp. 415–424). Oxford: Pergamon.

Lo Bianco, J. (2002). National language policy. Retrieved on June 11, 2008, from http://www.multiculturalaustralia.edu.au/library/media/Audio/id/420

Nieto, S. (2002). *Language, culture and teaching: Critical perspectives for a new century.* Mahwah, NJ: Erlbaum.

Ricento, T. (2000). Historical and theoretical perspectives in language policy and planning. *Journal of Sociolinguistics, 4*(2), 196–213.

Ruiz, R. (1984). Orientations in language planning. *The Journal for the National Association for Bilingual Education, 8*(2), 15–34.

Sleeter, C. E. (2005). *Un-standardizing curriculum: Multicultural teaching in the standards-based curriculum.* New York: Teachers College Press.

Valdes, G. (1997). Dual-language immersion programs: A cautionary note concerning the education of language-minority students. *Harvard Education Review, 67*(3), 391–429.

Wiggins, G., & McTighe, J. (2006). *Understanding by design.* Upper Saddle River, NJ: Pearson Education.

About the Editors and Contributors

Roger Barnard is a senior lecturer at the University of Waikato, where he has been teaching in a range of graduate and undergraduate programs in applied linguistics since 1995. Before taking up his present post, he worked in Europe and the Middle East as a teacher, teacher trainer, and English language adviser to Ministries of Education. His research has focused on: (1) second-language learning and, in particular, the acculturation of immigrant and international students, (2) issues relating to the introduction of second-language teaching in the primary sector, (3) the professional development of teachers, and (4) language-in-education policy and planning. Recently he has accepted visiting professorships/fellowships in Japan, New York, and Hanoi. He currently is researching aspects of language teacher cognition and beliefs. Among his recent publications is *Bilingual Children's Language and Literacy Development* (2003), which he coedited with Ted Glynn.

Carole Bloch is coordinator of the Early Literacy Unit of the Project for the Study of Alternative Education in South Africa (PRAESA) and central coordinator of Stories Across Africa (StAAf). The Early Literacy Unit, which includes teacher education, research, and materials development, is concerned with transforming the way early literacy and biliteracy are taught/learned in multilingual settings. StAAf, which has regional coordinators in each of the regions of Africa, is developing common anthologies of stories for children to read in their own languages as part of its work to help develop African languages in print, promote reading and writing habits among diverse African communities, and foster a sense of unity among African children.

Gabriele Budach is a lecturer in French linguistics in the department of modern languages at the University of Southampton, UK. She completed her Ph.D. in French adult literacy in Ontario, Canada, in 2002 and currently is conducting an ethnographic qualitative study on German–Italian bilingual schooling in a primary school in inner-city Frankfurt. Her recent publications address issues of language minorities, linguistic diversity in educational settings, and language and identity in the context of (trans-)nationalism.

Sol Colmenares holds a postgraduate diploma in bilingual education from Universidad del Valle, Cali, Colombia. She is the author of various school textbooks in the area of Spanish and English. Her main professional interests are concerned with discourse analysis, processes of empowerment, and bilingual education. She is coauthor of *Empowerment* (2006) published by Universidad del Valle.

Joel Gómez is an associate professor of educational leadership and interim associate dean for research at the Graduate School of Education and Human Development at George Washington University. Professor Gómez's interests span widely into the areas of comparative and international education; diversity, multilingualism, and multiculturalism; and policy, leadership, and teacher education. Professor Gomez has edited numerous monographs, articles, and online sites as executive director of the former National Clearinghouse of Bilingual Education at GWU.

Chen-ching Li is a prolific writer, with 16 books, and more than 300 articles published in English and Chinese in academic journals, magazines, and prestigious newspapers. He has held university posts as dean of the College of Humanities and Social Sciences; professor of English at Shih Hsin University; professor of translation and interpretation at the National Taiwan University; director of the National Taiwan University's Mandarin Training Center; adjunct professor at the Graduate Institute of Translation and Interpretation, National Taiwan Normal University; and adjunct professor in the Department of Asian and East European Languages and Cultures at the University of Maryland, College Park. Li has served in various governmental posts, such as Ministry of Education coordinator in San Francisco, California, and Washington, DC, for the educational and academic exchange programs between American and Chinese (Taiwan) scholars and institutions of higher learning, and Director General of the Bureau of International Cultural and Educational Relations, Ministry of Education. He was elected international coordinator of the APEC Education Network (formerly APEC Education Forum) from 1998 to 2002 and to many other posts.

Anne-Marie de Mejía has a Ph.D. in linguistics in the area of bilingual education (Lancaster University, UK) and an M.A in applied English linguistics (Birmingham University). She currently is working at el Centro de Investigación y Formación en Educación (CIFE) at Universidad de los Andes, Bogotá. She worked in the Linguistics Department of the School of Language Sciences at Universidad del Valle, Cali, Colombia, where she was director of postgraduate programs and coordinator of the Bilingualism Research Group, and was a visiting lecturer at the University of Wales at Aberystwyth. Her research interests include bilingual classroom interaction, the construction of bilingual curricula and processes of empowerment, and bilingual teacher development. She authored *Power, Prestige and Bilingualism* (2002) and *Empowerment/Empoderamiento y Procesos de Construcción Curricular Bilingüe* (2006), and edited *Bilingual Education in South America* (2005). She also has published academic articles in the area of bilingual classroom processes and bilingual curriculum development.

Ursula Neumann is a professor at the Institute for International Comparative and Intercultural Education at Hamburg University. She researches and teaches multicultural education with a focus on socialization and education processes in Turkish migrant families, support of immigrant minority children and youth, reactions of the German education system to immigration, and scientific steering of a model project for bilingual education in primary schools in Hamburg.

Tope Omoniyi is a professor of sociolinguistics in the School of Arts at Roehampton University, London. His research interests straddle issues in language and identity, language in education, and language policy and planning in Europe and Africa. His scholarly articles have appeared in *TESOL Quarterly, International Journal of the Sociology of Language, Text, AILA Review, Language Policy,* and *International Journal of World Englishes.* He is the author of the monograph *The Sociolinguistics of Borderlands: Two Nations, One People* (2004) and editor and coeditor of several volumes of essays, including *Contending with Globalisation in World Englishes* (coedited with Mukul Saxena and forthcoming).

Hans-Joachim Roth is a professor of humanities with a focus on multicultural education at the University of Cologne, Germany. He studied pedagogy, German and Scandinavian language and literature, and philosophy. Recent research projects have focused particularly on questions of bilingual education for language minorities and the development of bilingualism in the context of education and schooling.

Harvey Tejada is currently a professor at the Universidad del Valle, Cali, Colombia, and has 25 years of university teaching experience. Professor Tejada has written coauthored research and reviewed articles. His research interest is in bilingual education, particularly in teacher empowerment and curriculum design. He is also involved in the area of reading and writing for academic purposes in both English and Spanish.

María E. Torres-Guzmán, a professor of bilingual/bicultural education in the Department of International and Transcultural Studies at Teachers College, Columbia University, has taught and conducted research in the states of Michigan, Texas, California, and New York. She also has done so in various parts of the world, including Puerto Rico, Spain, and New Zealand. Her research focuses on the Spanish-speaking populations within the United States but extends beyond that, as she is interested in how classrooms are *linguocultural* spaces of freedom, where cultures meet, interact, and realize themselves through language. She is interested in how teachers think about the spaces of freedom within the context of strong forms of bilingual education. She has published extensively.

Ildikó Vančo holds a Ph.D in psycholinguistics, and is an associate professor in the Hungarian Language and Literature Department at the Konstantin the Philosopher University in Nitra, Slovak Republic. Her research interests include bilingualism, second-language acquisition, perception, and text comprehension. The focus of her work is on the system of education of the Hungarian ethnic group in Slovakia, especially at the tertiary level. She is the author of *Perception and Text Comprehension of Hungarian-Slovak Bilingual Children* (2007).

Rosemary Wildsmith-Cromarty is a professor of applied language studies and head of the School of Language, Literature & Linguistics at the University of KwaZulu–Natal. Her research interests include multilingualism, language acquisition, cross-linguistic transfer across languages, the teaching of noncognate languages with a particular focus on the African languages, and the translation of academic discourse across languages. She is a member of the Provincial Language Committee for KwaZulu–Natal, South Africa, and chairs the Language-in-Education Technical Committee, which is a subcommittee of the English National Language Body in South Africa.

Index